EUL VERLAG

KIELER SCHRIFTEN FÜR OSTRECHT

Herausgegeben von Prof. Dr. Alexander Trunk, Kiel, und Prof. Dr. Dr. h. c. Mark M. Boguslawskij, Kiel/Moskau

Band 3
Alexander Trunk (Hrsg.)
Die Transformation dinglicher Rechte an Immobilien in Russland und anderen Staaten Mittel- und Osteuropas
Lohmar – Köln 2010 • 196 S. • € 49,- (D) • ISBN 978-3-89936-926-7

Band 4
Friedrich-Carl Freiherr v. Gersdorff
Die Registerpublizität im deutschen und im russischen Unternehmensrecht
Lohmar – Köln 2011 • 228 S. • € 55,- (D) • ISBN 978-3-8441-0067-9

Band 5
Sibila Tasheva
Die Stellung des Gesellschafters in der bulgarischen GmbH – Ein Rechtsvergleich mit dem deutschen Recht
Lohmar – Köln 2013 • 200 S. • € 49,- (D) • ISBN 978-3-8441-0220-8

Band 6
Adrian Rusu
Rumänisches Insolvenzrecht
Lohmar – Köln 2013 • 280 S. • € 58,- (D) • ISBN 978-3-8441-0283-3

Band 7
Alexander Trunk und Susanne Rieckhof (Hrsg.)
Schneller, höher, weiter! – Aktuelle Themen des Sportrechts im östlichen Europa
Lohmar – Köln 2014 • 184 S. • € 48,- (D) • ISBN 978-3-8441-0352-6

Band 8
Alexander Trunk, Nazar Panych and Susanne Rieckhof (eds.)
Legal Aspects of the EU Association Agreements with Georgia, Moldova and Ukraine in the Context of the EU Eastern Partnership Initiative
Lohmar – Köln 2017 • 188 S. • € 54,- (D) • ISBN 978-3-8441-0509-4

JOSEF EUL VERLAG

Reihe: Kieler Schriften für Ostrecht · Band 8

Herausgegeben von Prof. Dr. Alexander Trunk, Kiel, und
Prof. Dr. Dr. h. c. Mark M. Boguslawskij, Kiel/Moskau

Prof. Dr. Alexander Trunk
Dr. Nazar Panych, LL.M.
Dr. Susanne Rieckhof
(editors)

Legal Aspects of the EU Association Agreements with Georgia, Moldova and Ukraine in the Context of the EU Eastern Partnership Initiative

EUL VERLAG

Bibliografische Information der Deutschen Nationalbibliothek

Die Deutsche Nationalbibliothek verzeichnet diese Publikation in der Deutschen Nationalbibliografie; detaillierte bibliografische Daten sind im Internet über <http://dnb.d-nb.de> abrufbar.

ISBN 978-3-8441-0509-4
1. Auflage Juni 2017

JOSEF EUL VERLAG GmbH
Brandsberg 6
53797 Lohmar
Tel.: 0 22 05 / 90 10 6-80
Fax: 0 22 05 / 90 10 6-88
E-Mail: info@eul-verlag.de
https://www.eul-verlag.de

Bei der Herstellung unserer Bücher möchten wir die Umwelt schonen. Dieses Buch ist daher auf säurefreiem, 100% chlorfrei gebleichtem, alterungsbeständigem Papier nach DIN 6738 gedruckt.

Foreword

Hardly have any EU Association Agreements (AAs) attracted more public interest and dispute than the three agreements, which the European Union concluded in 2014 with Georgia, Moldova and Ukraine[1]. In the case of Ukraine, the conclusion of the Association Agreement with the EU was the triggering factor for the bitter Ukrainian conflict, which has led to a political revolution in Ukraine, the secession of the Crimea and its ensuing annexation by (or accession to)[2] the Russian Federation and the still ongoing bloody conflict in Eastern Ukraine. While the political dimensions of the three Association Agreements (with particular focus on the Agreement with Ukraine) have been widely discussed, the circumstance that they are legal documents, which need to be read und understood, is often neglected. Practically non-existent is, at the present time, a comparative legal analysis of these Agreements, despite the fact that they share many commonalities and at the same time differ in significant details.

The present volume is probably the first comparative publication on this highly political subject from a legal perspective. The book is the result of a three months student and PhD candidates research project, which was carried through in 2014/2015 at the University of Kiel with a grant by the Germany Academic Exchange Service in a program funded by the Foreign Ministry of Germany. The scholarship grantees – most of the contributors to this book – were students and PhD candidates from the three association countries – Georgia, Moldova and Ukraine. All of them have in the meantime finished their studies or PhD theses and many of them now work in responsible positions in ministries or other parts of the public administration of their countries or in academia. For many of them this is their first publication in "the West" and the first time they had to do serious comparative research, all the more in a subject matter often completely new to them. This background has to be taken into account. The very important topic of competition law within the Agreements has been dealt with in an additional contribution by an associate professor (lecturer) of Kiev Taras Shevchenko National University, Dr. Kseniya Smyrnova. We are highly grateful to Ms. Smrynova for contributing this article.

1 The present public dispute in the EU with regard to TTIP and its "smaller brother" CETA shows some comparable elements, but has not sparked the kind of bitter international conflict, which was caused by the Association Agreements with Georgia, Moldova and Ukraine. Technically, the three Association Agreements include many provisions similar to CETA and TTIP, they even go beyond CETA and TTIP in political terms, but they do not include extensive provisions on investment dispute resolution, one of the main bones of contention of CETA/TTIP.

2 The terms "annexation" or "accession" by themselves express a certain legal interpretation of the 2014 developments in Crimea and are in dispute between Russia and the West (and Ukraine), cf. Rechtliche Aspekte der Eingliederung der Halbinsel Krim in die Russische Föderation, Kieler Ostrechts-Notizen 2/2014 – 1/2015 (passim).

The present book is certainly not a comparative encyclopedia of the three Association Agreements, and it cannot deny the student background of many of its authors. However, it may be seen as a pilot project for coordinated comparative legal research on a subject and a region, which is usually approached on a bilateral EU – partner country basis, while it would make much more sense to use a comparative, region or topic based approach.

The academic style of the contributions reflects the national backgrounds of the contributors and has been kept for reasons of authenticity. For highly appreciated editorial work in reviewing contributions and helping prepare them for publication the editors would like to cordially thank Ms. Lena Döpper, Mr. Kim Kube, Mr. Moritz Cunow and Mr. Christian Ertel, student assistants at the Institute of East European Law of Kiel University. Last but not least we would also like to express our gratitude to the Germany Academic Exchange Service for supporting the research project including this publication.

Kiel, im September 2016

Prof. Dr. Alexander Trunk
Dr. Nazar Panych, LL.M.
Dr. Susanne Rieckhof

Content

Alexander Trunk:
Introduction 1

A. General Aspects

Felicia Badalova:
Comparison of the EU Association Agreements with Georgia, Moldova and Ukraine – An Overview 4

Ala Otgon:
Comparison of the Association Agreement EU-Moldova with other EU Association Agreements 12

Tetiana Iliushyna:
Comparison of the EU-Ukraine Association Agreement with other EU Association Agreements, in particular with Turkey 21

Mykhailo Smeshko:
The Present Inner Conflict Situation in Georgia (Abkhazia, South Ossetia), Moldova (Transnistria) and Ukraine (Crimea, Eastern Ukraine) in the Context of the three Association Agreements 37

Oleksandr Shevchuk:
Legal Aspects of the Effects of the Association Agreements of the Three Countries to their Relations with Russia 42

Vadym Karnaukh:
Approximation of Law as a General Topic of the Three Association Agreements in Comparison with the PCAs 50

B. Trade and Investment Aspects: the DCFTAs within the Three Association Agreements

Marta Zakharko:
The DCFTAs in the Context of the Association Agreements of the Three Countries: Overview, Basic principles, Comparison 66

Anastasiia Romanchenko:
The Deep and Comprehensive Free Trade Area Parts of the Association Agreements with Georgia, Moldova and Ukraine: a Comparison of the Provisions on Technical Barriers and National Legislation 75

Kseniya Smyrnova:
Issues of Competition Law in the EU-Ukraine, EU-Moldova and EU-Georgia Association Agreements: Comparative Aspects 81

Anastasiia Rogozina:
Investment Protection in the Framework of the Three EU Association Agreements: Substantive Issues 86

C. Economic and Sectoral Cooperation within the Three Associations Agreements - Overview and Examples

Alexander Trunk:
Introduction 102

Ana Tokhadze:
Enhancement of Corporate Social Responsibility – An Analysis from the Perspective of Economic and Sectoral Cooperation under the Three Association Agreements 104

Olena Serpukhovitina:
Cooperation in the Framework of the Three Association Agreements: Intellectual Property Law - Geographical Indications and Liability of Intermediary Service Providers 112

Solomon Menabdishvili:
How Georgia has Fulfilled its Obligations Assumed under Article 204 of the Association Agreement 123

D. Cooperation in the Area of Justice, Freedom and Security in the Three Association Agreements and Related Issues

Ludmila Negritu:
Cooperation in the Area of Justice, Freedom and Security in the Three Association Agreements in the Overview: Comparison between the AAs and with EU law 136

Salome Kavtaradze:
Elements of Freedom of Movement of Persons in the Three Association Agreements 143

E. Dispute Settlement under the three Association Agreements

Yulia Khomyn:
Settlement of Trade Disputes under the Three Association Agreements 156

Anastasiia Bessonova:
Investment Dispute Settlement between the EU and Ukraine in the Light of the Adoption of the Association Agreement 170

Biographical notes 177

Alexander Trunk

Introduction

The three Association Agreements between the European Union and its member States, on the one hand, and Georgia, Moldova and Ukraine, one the other[3], were signed on the same day – 27 June 2014[4] – and are all based from the EU's perspective on the same legal basis in EU law (Art.217 TFEU)[5] and are politically anchored in the EU's Eastern Partnership Initiative. Nevertheless, they differ significantly in size and contents. The basic structure of these agreements is comparable, differing from other association agreements which the EU has concluded. They all consist of a – already very detailed - basic agreement[6] with numerous extremely detailed annexes[7]. Looking more into detail, one can see that the Ukrainian agreement is particularly detailed, while the agreements with Georgia and Moldova are more similar to each other and at the same time somewhat less demanding than the Agreement with Ukraine. In order to correctly interpret these agreements one can and should read them in conjunction, drawing conclusions from accordances or differences between them. While there are many parallels in the political background of these Agreements (all three countries have a long-term political hope to become members of the EU)[8], the treaty negotiations between the EU and the three countries were conducted separately, and the political and economic situation (as well as their historic development) of each of these countries is specific. The Association Agreements therefor have to function in or with the three countries in partly different surroundings. Another line of comparison can be drawn to the (formally still existing) Partnership and Cooperation Agreements, which the EU concluded in the 1990s with the three countries. Although the new Association Agreements are far more detailed

---

3 Association Agreement between the European Union and the European Atomic Energy Community and their Member States, of the one part, and Georgia, of the other part, of 27.6.2014, OJEU 30.8.2014 L 261, 4; Association Agreement between the European Union and the European Atomic Energy Community and its Member States, of the one part, and the Republic of Moldova, [of 27.6.2014] OJEU 30.8.2014 L 260, 4; Association Agreement between the European Union [and the European Atomic Energy Community] and its Member States, of the one part, and Ukraine, of the other part, of 21.3,2014 [and 27.6.2014], OJEU 29.5.2014 L 161, 3.

4 The Agreement with Ukraine was signed in two steps: the „political" parts of the Agreement were signed on the „economic" parts (DCFTA parts) were signed together with the other two AAs on 27.6.2014, see https://en.wikipedia.org/wiki/Ukraine-European_Union_Association_Agreement#Signing.

5 Form the EU perspective, they are mixed agreements as the legislative competence for the matters dealt with in the Agreements lies partly with the EU, partly with EU member States. For this reason, Contracting Parties on the EU side are both the EU and its Member States.

6 AA with Georgia: 432 Articles, AA with Moldova, 465 Articles, AA with Ukraine: 486 Articles.

7 Total length of the agreements including annexes: AA with Georgia 740 pages, AA with Moldova 735 pages, AA with Ukraine 2135 pages.

8 This brings the AAs with the three countries into a similar context as the so-called Europe Agreements, which the EU concluded in the 1990s with countries of Central Eastern Europe (Czechoslovakia, Poland, Hungary etc.), which some years later became members of the EU. Another parallel is with the Stabilization and Association Agreements, which the EU concluded since 2000 with countries of the Western Balkans.

than the preceding PCAs, they resemble the PCAs in many aspects, in particular in fields, which were already covered by the PCAs and have been retaken and transferred, though with amendments, into the Association Agreement. Finally, for interpretation of the Association Agreements one can sometimes take a look at the provisions of the WTO (which are sort of a basis for the DCFTA provisions in the Association Agreements) and even of the Treaty on the Functioning of the European Union, which contains similar provisions to some parts of the Association Agreements and was the "mental" basis of the EU's negotiators in their negotiations with the three countries. However, none of these parallels leads automatically to certain interpretative results. Differences between the Agreements of the TFEU may be deliberate, and even textual accordances may nevertheless allow different interpretations of the Agreements, if there are other more decisive arguments than the text of the Agreements. In any case, when the Agreements are interpreted one should not neglect the comparative dimension, and – probably – more often than not the Agreements can be interpreted uniformly. To study this interrelationship between the three Agreements more concretely and find out, in which areas their differences are significant and where the accordances overweigh is the purpose of the book and the professional duty of lawyers, who will have to apply and interpret these Agreements in the future.

Since the end of the research project, which is the basis of this publication, a number of new developments have occurred. The most important is the ratification of the Agreements with Georgia and Moldova by all parties, which has led to the entry into force of these Agreements on 1 July 2016. With regard to the EU-Ukraine Agreement the situation is more complicated. After the negative result of a people's referendum on the EU-Ukraine AA in the Netherlands on 6 April 2016, the Dutch Government did not see itself in a position to deposit its ratification documents. The consequence is that the phase of a provisional application of the Ukrainian AA, which was decided by the Council of the EU for all AAs for the time until their full entry into force, is still continuing. Provisional application of the AA includes many, but not all provisions of the AA[9]. Another complicating factor is, of course, the continuing economic and political conflict between the EU and Russia because of the Euromaidan revolution in Ukraine and its repercussions on the Crimea and the Donbass area. As long as this conflict is not resolved the practical functioning of the EU-Ukraine AA will remain complicated. Nevertheless, all three AAs are applied – fully or at least partly – already today and need to be interpreted both by academics and legal practitioner.

9 In detail, see http://eur-lex.europa.eu/legal-content/EN/TXT/HTML/?uri=CELEX:22014X1031(01)&from=DE.

A. General Aspects

Felicia Badalova

Comparison of the EU Association Agreements with Georgia, Moldova and Ukraine – An Overview

Future membership in the European Union (EU) is a key foreign policy objective both for Georgia, Moldova and Ukraine[10]. All three countries consider this a logical step as they have always been an inseparable part of Europe in terms of culture and history. European integration is considered by Ukraine, Moldova and Georgia to be a project that would bring many more advantages than harm. Officially, relations between EU on the one hand, and Georgia, Moldova, Ukraine on the other hand started with the Partnership and Cooperation Agreements (PCAs) of the 1990s. More recently, the European Union has adopted action plans for each country (Moldova, Georgia, Ukraine), in order to make the European Neighborhood Policy (ENP)[11] work and to foster the bilateral relations and to take into account new conditions of cooperation, particularly in the context of the 2004 EU enlargement. The fact that the relations between the EU, on the one hand, and Georgia, Moldova and Ukraine, on the other, are growing deeper is now additionally proven by the signature and even provisional application of the Association Agreements.[12] The Association Agreements were signed by the EU with the three countries on the same day, on 27 June 2014, but Georgia's, Moldova's and Ukraine's capacity of cooperation and integration are different. On that account, the comparative overview of the EU Association Agreements with Georgia, Moldova and Ukraine has to take into consideration the previous steps that have led to the Association Agreements, the forgoing instruments continuing to be a vital supplement of the Association Agreements.

I. Steps to the signature of the EU Association Agreements with Georgia, Moldova and Ukraine

As already mentioned above, officially the relations between the EU on the one hand, and Georgia, Moldova, Ukraine on the other hand started with the PCAs. But the situation of Georgia and Ukraine is a somewhat different from the situation of Moldova regarding the beginning of the relationship with the EU. The relationship between Georgia and Ukraine, on the one hand and the EU, on the other hand were established in 1991-1992. For example, relations between Ukraine

---

10 European Commission, EU Cooperation for a Successful Eastern Partnership, 2012, page. 2, http://ec.europa.eu/europeaid/sites/devco/files/eastern_partnership_flyer_final_en.pdf.

11 The ENP remained distinct from the enlargement processes and did not provide for any possibility of the EU membership. Instead of this, EU aimed to develop a ring of friends, with whom the EU could enjoy close peaceful and cooperative relations. http://eeas.europa.eu/enp/index_en.htm.

12 http://eeas.europa.eu/top_stories/2014/270614_association_agreement_en.htm.

and the European Union were first established in December 1991, when the Minister of Foreign Affairs of the Netherlands, holding the presidency of the EU at that time, officially recognized the independence of Ukraine on behalf of the European Union[13].Relations between the European Union and Georgia started in 1991-1992, just after Georgia regained its sovereignty in the wake of the brake-up of the Soviet Union[14].So, for these two countries, the relations with European Union started before signing the Partnership and Cooperation Agreement. For Moldova, relations with the EU were launched on 28 November 1994, when the Partnership and Cooperation Agreement was signed entering into force on 1 July 1998[15]. Georgia signed with the EU the Partnership and Cooperation Agreement on 22 April 1996, which entered into force on 1 July 1999. The legal basis of the Ukraine-EU relations was laid down by the Partnership and Cooperation Agreement of 14 June 1994, which came into force on 1 March 1998. Until the time when the Partnership and Cooperation Agreement was signed, there was something specific for the relations of EU and Georgia, in comparison with Moldova and Ukraine: Since 1995, Georgia has benefited from the EU's Generalized System of Preferences (GSP)[16]. In 2005, it became a beneficiary of the new System of Preferences Special Incentive Arrangement for Sustainable Development and Good Governance (GSP+).

In order to foster the bilateral relations and to take into account new conditions of cooperation, particularly in the context of the 2004 EU enlargement, Ukraine and the EU worked out and approved at the Cooperation Council meeting on 21 February 2005 the Ukraine-EU Action Plan. On 14 November 2006, the EU-Georgia ENP Action Plan was adopted. The EU-Moldova Action Plan was signed on 22 February 2005. Starting with the signature of the action plans, the relations of the three countries with the EU continued in a distinct way.

1. The reason and the background of the relationship between the European Union and CIS member states

Beginning with the historical point of view, Georgia, Moldova and Ukraine are post-Soviet States. The dissolution of the USSR in December 1991 coincided with the foundation of the Commonwealth of Independent States (CIS) on 21 December 1991.[17] The fact that Georgia and

---

13 http://ukraine-eu.mfa.gov.ua/en/ukraine-eu/relations.

14 http://www.mfa.gov.ge/index.php?lang_id=ENG&sec_id=462.

15 http://www.eumission.mfa.md/rm-eu-relations/.

16 International Journal of Social, Education, Economics and Management Engineering Vol:7, No:10, 2013 (World Academy of Science, Engineering and Technology), page 1418, http://waset.org/publications/17029/the-european-union-s-generalized-system-of-preferences-gsp-and-the-prospect-of-a-unified-database.

17 See Protocol to the Agreement establishing the CIS (21 December 1991); http://www.cvce.eu/en/obj/protocol_to_the_agreement_establishing_the_commonwealth_of_independent_states_alma_ata_21_december_1991-en-3c5af941-61e4-4810-83ee-27bc499c15e3.html.

Ukraine were CIS states until recently[18] and Moldova still continues to be a member state of the CIS, leads to the question of the background of relations between the EU and the three countries. It may be first be noted that there were always different views between the member states of the CIS concerning the purpose of this organization, in particular whether the CIS should one day become an effective confederation.[19] The second reason is the EU's enlargement to Eastern Europe, which has changed the geopolitical landscape of the European continent. This has encouraged the Union to intensify its policy towards countries that are either its new immediate neighbors or which affect its vital interests.[20] Thirdly, economically, the European Union is interested in Georgia, Ukraine and Moldova as future members of the EU because these countries might be on this basis become new marketplaces for European goods, while at the same time the three states see in a process towards EU membership an instrument to develop their specific sectoral interests, for example enjoy the benefits of the common free market, increase the rule of law, etc.

As a result, the interest in European integration exists on both sides: in each of the three States and the European Union, and this is not excluded by the Soviet past of the three countries, as everything starts with an idea and the wish to become a member state of EU one day is supported by the clear majority of the population in all of these three counties.[21]

2. A comparative view of the PCAs of Georgia, Moldova and Ukraine

When back in 1994-1996, the Partnership and Cooperation Agreements between the European Communities and their member states, and Georgia, Moldova, Ukraine on the other side, were signed, it was a big step forward for the "young" states in the all-European space.

Ukraine was the first country that signed the PCA with the EU and the last one was Georgia. For Georgia and Ukraine, in comparison with Moldova, relations with the EU started before the PCA signature. The only difference between these two countries is that Georgia was not a CIS member state in 1991-1992, when the informal relations with EU started.

18 Georgia left the CIS in 2009 after the Georgian-Russian conflict of 2008, and Ukraine has left the CIS in 2014 in view of the present conflict with Russia.

19 Kembayev, The Compatibility between Regional Integration Processes in the Post-Soviet Area and within the European Neighborhood Policy, Osteuropa Recht 2013, p.370.

20 Menkiszak, Kononczuk, Kaczmarski, CIS Countries' Interests vis-à-vis the European Union and Its Eastern Policy, № 365/2008, Warsaw: Case, page 7.

21 E.g. in Moldova, around 39 percent of citizens have acknowledged that they are rather uninformed about the European integration process, while 23 percent said they are very poorly informed about the process. An equally 'illuminating' finding is that 39 percent of the population believes that politicians are those who will gain the most from European integration, while only 12 percent ascertained that citizens have the most to benefit and 32 percent said that citizens and politicians will equally benefit from European integration. In spite of these computations, the direction of the whole country continue to support the idea of EU integration and it is proved by different reforms. Alison Mutler, ValeriuProchniţchi, Ion Osoianu, European Aspirations and Human Development of the Republic of Moldova, Chişinău: "Nova-Imprim", 2012, page. 15.

Between the PCAs of the three countries there are more similarities than distinctions. Amongst differences, the following may be mentioned: from the point of view of the size in articles, the EU's PCA with Ukraine is the broadest, it contains 109 articles[22], the PCA with Moldova contains 106 articles[23] and the PCA with Georgia has one article less[24]. As to general principles, the PCA with Ukraine includes some norms that cannot be discovered in the other two PCAs, e.g. Art. 3 of the Agreement provides that for a good development of relations between Ukraine and EU, the wish of Ukraine to maintain cooperative relations with other independent states should be taken into account. The Georgian PCA, in comparison with the other two PCAs, does not have any article about the possibility of making amendments to any part of the Agreement in view of the situation arising from Georgia's accession to GATT. The PCAs of Moldova and Ukraine hold those norms that are based on the principle of mutual consent. From the point of view of trade in goods, the PCA with Moldova contains a specific norm, due to which article 11(3) will not be applied during a transitional period expiring on the date of the Republic of Moldova acceding to the GATT or on 31 December 1998. A similar norm exists in the PCA with Georgia. Another difference exists between the PCAs with Moldova and Georgia on one side and the PCA with Ukraine, on the other. The first two PCAs provide the import of goods into the community and the Republic of Moldova under free quantitative restrictions, the Ukrainian PCA also contains such a norm, but also grants an exemption for the other party from import charges and duties on goods admitted temporarily.

Even if one can find differences between the PCAs, this is not the most important aspect as it does not reveal the real problem. The real problem regarding the three mentioned PCAs is connected with one of their similarities. In judicial literature there is an opinion according to which the PCAs in fact generated a major handicap: they did not provide a clear and well-defined goal for the relations between the three countries and the EU in terms of the States' gradual integration into the European family[25]. In a certain way I do agree with this opinion because the PCA potential has not been fully used. This problem is accompanied by another one that consists in the lack of the political will among the three states authorities for the implementation of the PCA, which resulted in insufficient legislative work at the early stages of the PCA implementation, as well as

22 Partnership and Cooperation Agreement between the European Communities and their Member States, and Ukraine, signed on 14 June, 1994, entered into force on 1 March, 1998.

23 Partnership and Cooperation Agreement between the European Communities and their Member States, and Moldova, signed on 28 November, 1994, entered into force on 1 July, 1998.

24 Partnership and Cooperation Agreement between the European Communities and their Member States, and Georgia, signed on 22 August, 1996, entered into force on 1 March, 1998.

25 Victor Chirila New Opportunities for Moldova, IPG 3/2011, page 1; http://library.fes.de/pdf-files/ipg/2011-3/10_chirila.pdf.

poor implementation of the legislation adopted[26]. This was confirmed also by the adoption of a political document called individual Action Plan, which was drawn up between the EU on one side and Georgia, the Republic of Moldova, Ukraine on the other hand, the purpose of which was to accelerate the political, economic, and social reforms in the country in exchange for deepening its relations with the EU.

II. Comparison between the EU Association Agreements with Georgia, Moldova and Ukraine

The new EU Association Agreements with Georgia, Moldova and Ukraine have set up a new generation of agreements as they envisage significant effective mechanisms of an approximation with the EU. The EU uses the idea of 'privileged relations' to describe the formula for its relations (only) with Ukraine. From this results the main difference between the three Association Agreements: the Agreement with Ukraine is in some fields is deeper than the other AAs. One can prove this in simple numbers: the AA with Ukraine contains 486 articles, the AA with Moldova - 465, the AA with Georgia - 432.

For Georgia and Moldova important provisions regarding conflict prevention, crisis management and regional stability are to be implemented[27]. For Ukraine there is a provision on regional application (consistent with the non-recognition policy of the illegal annexation of Crimea) included in the Final Act to the Agreement.

1. A comparative view of justice, freedom and security through the instrumentality of EU Association Agreements with Georgia, Moldova and Ukraine

The respective titles of the Association Agreements mention issues like rule of law; protection of personal data; cooperation on migration, asylum and border management; movement of persons and readmission; fight against organized crime and corruption; illicit drugs; money laundering and terrorism financing; cooperation in the fight against terrorism; legal cooperation. The AA of Ukraine in comparison with the other two AAs, contains two more norms regarding treatment of workers (art. 17) and mobility of workers (art. 18)[28]. It should be mentioned, however, that there are no differences between the AAs in this respect, which could influence the essence of the norm. All the three AAs are based on the idea of promoting the rule of law, the right to a fair trial, cooperation of the law institutes and respect for human rights.

---

26 http://parlament.org.ua/index.php?action=magazine&id=9&ar_id=682&iar_id=623&as=2.
27 Marek Menkiszak, op. cit. (fn. 10), page 33.
28 Association Agreement between the European Union and the European Atomic Energy Community and their Member States, of the one part, and Ukraine, of the other part, signed on 27th of June, 2014.

In conjunction with the protection of personal data, it is worth mentioning that the AAs of Ukraine and Moldova, in comparison with the AA of Georgia contain a specification that consists in the transfer of personal data between the parties that will take place if such transfer is necessary for the implementation, by the competent authorities of the parties.

The EU AA with Ukraine accentuates the basic principles of migration: fundamental principle of solidarity, mutual trust, joint responsibility and partnership. The Agreement with Ukraine also provides the fact that inclusion of migration should be concerned in the national strategies.

So, the most important difference is that the EU Association Agreement with Ukraine contains some new articles regarding the treatment of workers and the mobility of workers. But it is not sufficient to reveal the difference, more important is to understand why this difference exists. It could be assumed that this difference exists because for Ukraine the importance of the introduction of a visa free travel regime for the citizens of Ukraine is established in due course, provided that the conditions for well-managed and secure mobility are in place and had to be recognized in the AA[29]. For Moldova there is no necessity of such norms because the Commission proposed on 27 November 2013 to allow visa-free travel to the Schengen area for Moldovan citizens holding a biometric passport. This proposal builds on the successful implementation by the Republic of Moldova of all the benchmarks set in its Visa Liberalization Action Plan[30]. But in comparison with Ukraine that has issued its third Progress Report, Georgia has issued only the second Progress Report, so why does the EU Association Agreement with Georgia not contain norms regarding the mobility of workers? Probably this is due to the political situation in Ukraine[31]. The political and social surroundings in Georgia being favorable for EU integration, this might lead to a faster visa liberalization with Georgia than with Ukraine.

2. A comparative view of trade and trade-related matters through the instrumentality of EU Association Agreement with Georgia, Moldova and Ukraine

Trade is one of the most important area of cooperation between the European Union and Georgia, Moldova and Ukraine. The Association Agreements will offer a framework for modernizing their trade relations and for developing their economies to their signatories. Opening the markets through the progressive removal of customs tariffs and quotas, and harmonizing laws, norms and regulations in various trade-related sectors will make this possible. As well as contributing to stability and the promotion of democratic values in the EU's neighborhood, the AAs will benefit

[29] http://eeas.europa.eu/images/top_stories/140912_eu-ukraine-associatin-agreement-quick_guide.pdf.
[30] http://ec.europa.eu/dgs/home-affairs/what-we-do/policies/international-affairs/eastern-partnership/visa-liberalisation-moldova-ukraine-and-georgia/index_en.htm.
[31] http://en.wikipedia.org/wiki/Ukraine%E2%80%93European_Union_relations.

EU businesses by opening up new markets and providing for a more secure business environment when investing in these three countries.

Among differences that exist in this field between the three EU Association Agreements, the following may be noted: The AA with Georgia doesn't contain the term of 10 years for establishing a free trade area. The AA with Ukraine contains Art. 29, that is a specific norm, due to which Ukraine will eliminate customs duties on imports of worn clothing and other worn articles. The Georgian AA contains a list of products which can be imported into the Union free of customs duties. The AA with Moldova contains a specific norm that provides that during the third year after the entry into force of the AA, the Parties shall assess the situation taking account of the pattern of trade in agricultural products. In the Ukrainian AA there is no special article concerning an anti-circumvention mechanism[32].

Thus, it could be concluded that regarding this branch, there are specific norms for each of the three countries and this is due to different levels of establishing the relations between the EU and Georgia, Moldova and Ukraine. More than this the differences are based on the specifics of individual goods that could form the object of international trade.

III. A forecast of further relations with the EU

Summing up, it should be mentioned that although the support of the European partners is an important element in promoting the European course of the three countries and to create a positive image of the mentioned states within the European Community, it must be taken into account that European integration is a continuous reform process domestically, it is not only a vector of foreign policy, but most of all, a vector of domestic state policy. Taking into account the steps that each of the three countries has made to sign the Association Agreement, the Republic of Moldova holds the position of a leader among the partner countries taking into account the progress registered in negotiating the Association Agreement and DCFTA, as well as the Action Plan on visa liberalization.

The greatest problem for all of the three states mentioned, is that their fulfillment of the EU membership criteria is a very slow process, often restricted to declarations and propaganda[33]. In spite of this, it should be revealed that the EU AAs of the three countries in comparison with their PCAs, establish concrete time for different reforms achieving. So we cannot forecast precisely the

32 http://eprints.ucl.ac.uk/3879/1/3879.pdf.
33 Menkiszak, op. cit. (fn. 10), page 9.

further development of relations with EU, as this depends on how fast and effectively our countries will make reforms taking into account the time established in the Association Agreements.

Ala Otgon

Comparison of the Association Agreement EU-Moldova with other EU Association Agreements

The purpose of this contribution is to gain a better understanding for the three Association Agreements by comparing one of them – the Agreement with Moldova – with some other EU association agreements, mainly the one with Turkey.

From the begining of negotiations between the EU and Moldova the parties decided that the EU Association Agreement (AA) with the Republic of Moldova should be based on an innovative and ambitious approach and that it should include intensive economic cooperation in the form of a „Deep and Comprehensive Free Trade Area" (DCFTA part of the Agreement). The agreement reflects the strategic importance of EU-Moldovan relations, providing for political and economic integration. The EU-Moldova Association Agreement contains binding provisions, regulatory rules and cooperative arrangements, which are defined more broadly than in the traditional agreements. Moreover, it is comprehensive and covers all sectors of interest. Special attention is given to the implementation and enforcement of AA provisions, including by stipulating clear deadlines and establishing an institutional and administrative framework, thus creating the necessary conditions for an effective implementation. The AA is the legal basis for the future developing of EU-Moldova relations. Although it does not provide for an express encouragement of a future EU membership of Moldova, it does not limit any possible developments in this direction, deepening the level of integration of the Republic of Moldova in the European community space within the meaning of Art. 49 of the EU Treaty34. Cooperation for the purpose of integration shall take place by gradual harmonization with the acquis communautaire and, where relevant, with international standards.

I. General aspects of major EU Association Agreements which are relevant to the relations with Moldova

1. The EU Association Agreement with the Republic of Moldova

On 27 June 2014, the Republic of Moldova signed the European Union Association Agreement[35], which will be the basic document for Moldova-EU cooperation relations in the coming years. The agreement is part of a new generation of Association Agreements, with a comprehensive,

[34] Art. 49 of the Treaty of Lisbon of13.12.2007.

[35] Association Agreement between the European Union and the European Atomic Energy Community and their Member States and the Republic of Moldova, L 260/4, OJEU 30.8.2014, V.9.

ambitious and innovative content. Negotiations on the AA were completed in June 2013, after 15 rounds of negotiations, including 7 rounds separately for the DCFTA. After initialling the Summit Eastern Partnership in Vilnius, which took place on 29 November 2013, there were taken a number of technical, additional steps necessary for preparing the AA signature, including the DCFTA, in 2014.

The EU-Moldova Association Agreement includes, first, a Preamble which is the introduction of the Agreement, specifying its purpose and objectives. Then follow seven titles: General Principles; Political Cooperation and Policy Foreign and Security; Justice, Freedom and Security; Sector and Economic Cooperation; Trade and issues related to Trade (DCFTA); Financial cooperation including clauses Anti-Fraud and Institutional, General and Final Provisions. The basic text of the agreement is, thirdly, complemented by Annexes, which include specific references to EU legislation following to be taken of Moldova, with precise deadlines for implementation, and four Protocols.

The EU Moldova Association Agreement is an ambitious treaty, establishinng a concrete way to enhance the dynamics of EU-Moldovan relations. It focuses on supporting key reforms, on the development of the economy, on governance and on cooperation in sectors such as energy, transport, environment, industry and the development of small and medium enterprises, social protection, equal rights, consumer protection, education, research and innovation, cultural cooperation, etc. It is devoloping an enhanced cooperation in terms of foreign policy and security, focusing on regional issues, non-proliferation and disarmament, conflict prevention and crisis management. The DCFTA, which exceeds the classical arrangements related to free trade, requires not only mutually opening markets for most goods and services, but implies a gradual harmonization of norms and EU standards for trade and trade-related sectors.[36]

2. EU Stabilisation and Association Agreements

Another group of association agreements, which the EU has concluded with Eastern European countries, who also have an interest in later becoming members of the EU, are the Stabilization and Association agreements (SAA) between the EU and countries of the Western Balkan region. They are of interest for EU-Moldovan also because of the fact, that the Western Balkan region is not very far away from the Western Black Sea region where Moldova is situated. The SAAs are part of the EU Stabilization and Association Process (SAP) and European Neighborhood Poli-

36 Guide Association Agreement between Moldova and the European Union, This publication has been produced with the support of the project "Strengthening Institutional Capacity of the Ministry of Foreign Affairs European "implemented and co-financed by the United Nations Development Programme (UNDP)., 2014, p.5.

cy (ENP). SAAs are a new, third generation of European agreements offered exclusively to the Western Balkan countries, in the framework of the Stabilization and Association Process[37].

The SAAs are structured as follows: First comes a general provision on the aims of the agreement (Art. 1). Then follow Title I - General principles, Title II - Political Dialogue, Title III – Regional cooperation, Title IV –Free movement of goods, Title V – Movement of workers establishment, supply of services, current payment and movement of capital, Title VI –Approximation of law, law enforcement and competition rules, Title VII – Justice, Freedom and Security, Title VIII – Cooperation policies, Title IX – Financial cooperation, Title XX – Institutional, general and final provisions, Annexes and Protocols.

The SAAs are mainly based on the EU's *acquis communautaire* and are predicated on its promulgation in the cooperating states' legislation. The depth of the policy harmonization expected by SAAs is less than for EU member states; some policy areas in the acquis may not be covered by a given SAA[38]. The main elements of the SAA are: promoting the free movement of goods; creating efficient institutions; developing a market economy; reducing crime and corruption; promoting higher education reforms; developing democracy, human rights and independent media and improving the region's transport infrastructure. Stabilisation and Association Agreements concluded with the Balkan countries require that the duty free importation into the EU market involves: all industrial products; all processed agricultural products; agricultural products except beef, fish products, wines.

3. Euro-Mediterranean Association Agreements

A further group of EU association agrements are the agreements of the EU with countries in the Mediterrean area, which are a part of the Euro-Mediterranean partnership between the European Union and the countries of the Southern Mediterranean that was created in 1995 under the name of the Barcelona process and renamed Union for the Mediterranean in 2008.[39] Under this framework, the Association Agreements have been adopted by the EU, the Member States and the Mediterranean country partners. These bilateral agreements replace the first generation of agreements, i.e. the cooperation agreements of the 1970s.[40] The Euro-Mediterranean Association Agreements reflect the general principles governing the new Euro-Mediterranean relationship,

---

37 See http://ec.europa.eu/enlargement/policy/glossary/terms/sap_en.htm.

38 http://en.wikipedia.org/wiki/Stabilisation_and_Association_Process.

39 http://eeas.europa.eu/euromed/index_en.htm.

40 http://europa.eu/legislation_summaries/external_relations/relations_with_third_countries/Mediterranean_partner_countries/r14104_ro.htm.

although they each contain characteristics specific to the relations between the EU and each Mediterranean country.

The Euro-Mediterranean AAs are built-up in the following way: a general provision on the aims of the agreement (Art. 1), Title I - Political Dialogue, Title II – Free movement of goods, Title III – Right of establishment and supply of services, Title IV – Capital movements, payments, public procurement, competition and intellectual property, Title V – Scientific and technological cooperation, Title VI – Economic cooperation, Title VII – Cooperation on cultural matters, information and communication, Title VIII – Social matters, Title IX – Institutional, general and final provisions, Annexes and Protocols.

In contrast with the new AAs between the EU and Georgia, Moldova and Ukraine as well as with the SAAs, the Mediterranean partner countries do not have the political intention to become members of the EU, but they – and the EU – are interested in all other kinds of good cooperation. The Euro-Mediterranean Agreements have therefore, a more limited purpose than the AAs with Georgia, Moldova and Ukraine and the SAAs, but they also provide an appropriate framework for a political dialogue; to promote the harmonious development of economic relations between the EU and Israel and to encourage regional cooperation with a view to the consolidation of peaceful coexistence and economic and political stability.

The key objective of the EU-Mediterranean trade partnership is the creation of a deep Euro-Mediterranean Free Trade Area, which aims at removing barriers from trade and investment between both the EU and the Southern Mediterranean countries and between the Southern Mediterranean countries themselves. The scope of these agreements is essentially limited to trade in goods and a number of bilateral negotiations is on-going or being prepared in order to deepen the Association Agreements. These ongoing or future negotiations are related to further liberalization of trade in agriculture, to a liberalization of trade in services, to an accreditation and acceptance of industrial products and regulatory convergence.[41]

4. EU Association Agreement with Turkey (Ankara Agreement) of 1963

One of the oldest association agreements of the EU is the so-called Ankara Agreement, which was signed by the European Economic Community and Turkey on 12 September 1963 and took effect on 1 December 1964[42]. The Ankara Agreement still constitutes the main legal basis of the Association between Turkey and the EU. The Ankara Agreement is a relatively short document,

41 http://ec.europa.eu/trade/policy/countries-and-regions/regions/euro-mediterranean-partnership/.
42 http://ec.europa.eu/enlargement/pdf/turkey/association_agreement_1964_en.pdf.

its main text consists of only 33 Articles. The Agreement includes a Preamble, Title I – Principles, Title II – Implementation of the transitional stage, Title III – General and final provisions and Protocols.

The Ankara Agreement envisages three stages for the integration of Turkey and the EU, namely a preparatory stage, a transitional stage and a final stage. The completion of the Customs Union was planned at the end of the transitional stage. With the finalization of the preparatory stage as foreseen in the Agreement, provisions of the transitional stage and the obligations of the parties were determined in the Additional Protocol signed on 13 November 1970 and put into effect in 1973.[43] Although the Ankara Agreement envisaged the free circulation not only of goods, but also of natural persons, services and capital between the parties, it excluded Turkey from the EEC decision-making mechanisms and precluded Turkey from the recourse to the ECJ for dispute settlement. The Customs Union that was to be established between the parties went much further than the abolition of tariff and quantitative barriers to trade between the parties and the application of a Common External Tariff to imports from third countries, and envisaged a harmonization with EEC policies in virtually every field relating to the internal market. An important feature of the Ankara Agreement that it give the Council of Association the power to pass binding decisions, which may even have direct effect for citizens.

Despite the rather limited content of the Ankara Agreement, the EU and Turkey have, starting from the basis of this agreement, over the years developed a very close cooperation in many fields, and when Turkey declared its wish to later become a member of the European Union, the EU granted Turkey in 1999 candidate status and opened accession negotiations in 2005.[44]

II. Comparison between the EU Association Agreement with Moldova and other EU Association Agreements

1. Common elements

The SAAs are similar in principle to the so-called Europe Agreements concluded with Central and Eastern European countries in the 1990s and to the Association Agreement with Turkey of 1963. But they have different elements in comparison with the new Association Agreements with Moldova, Ukraine and Georgia. All of these AAs are bilateral agreements and provide for specific arrangements with each partner State. The association agreements share a similar structure, each AA is divided into a Preamble, Titles, consists of Chapters, (divided into articles), Annexes,

---

43 http://www.mfa.gov.tr/relations-between-turkey-and-the-european-union.en.mfa.
44 See http://ec.europa.eu/enlargement/candidate-countries/turkey/eu_turkey_relations_en.htm.

Protocols and Joint declarations. Both types of agreements intend to promote the following: a regular dialogue on political and security matters in order to promote a mutual understanding, cooperation and joint initiatives; economic, trade and financial cooperation in particular aimed at gradual trade liberalization, a sustainable development of the region and of investment; a social and cultural cooperation and on educational matters, in particular through intercultural dialogue, migration control, developing qualifications, promoting labor, law and gender equality.

The SAAs, like the AA with Moldova, are a tool that provides the formal mechanisms and agreed 'benchmarks' that allows the EU to work with all these countries to bring it closer to EU standards. Since the signing of the SAAs, institutions of the signatory countries have been obliged to ensure that their existing laws and future legislation are gradually made compatible with the EU acquis and are also obliged to ensure that all existing and future legislation is fully implemented. The most important element that makes all these agreements have something in common is that they have similar aims, objectives and that they are based on the same values and principles like: common values, namely democracy, respect for human rights and fundamental freedoms as well as the rule of law, a market economy and a sustainable development.

The association agreements with the Mediterranean countries provide for the gradual establishment of a Mediterranean free trade area in accordance with the rules of the World Trade Organization (WTO). This free trade area shall be established after a transitional period of twelve years following the entry into force of the agreements. However, a free trade between the EU and Israel already exists[45]. Similarly, the Association Agreement with Moldova includes a Deep and Comprehensive Free Trade Area that will further strengthen political, economic and trade relations between the EU and the Republic of Moldova.

Under each association agreement institutional structures are set up. An Association Council, organized at ministerial level, takes decisions and makes recommendations so that fixed objectives can be attained, while an Association Committee manages the agreement and settles differences regarding its application and interpretation. In the case of the EU-Moldovan Agreement the highest level within the treaty framework will be the EU-Moldovan Association Council, which may meet in various formats. It is important to note that the EU-Moldovan Association Council may under Art. 436 of the Agreement pass binding decisions based on the consensus of both parties.

---

[45] http://europa.eu/legislation_summaries/external_relations/relations_with_third_countries/mediterranean_partner_countries/r14104_ro.htm.

2. Differences

As we saw before, the SAAs have their own specifics depending on the geographic location, the level of development and the main aims that all these countries try to accomplish. It is important to mention that the only differences which make all these agreements particular depend on the way of evolution of each member state. The basic difference between the two types of mentioned agreements is to be found in the content of the "evolution clause" in the SAAs and in the emphasis on regional cooperation in Western Balkans. Another difference is reflected in the regional cooperation, where a signatory country commits itself to signing bilateral agreements with other countries of the region and EU candidate countries. The SAAs provide a framework for a political dialogue and strengthen regional cooperation, they promote the expansion of markets and economic relations among the parties and establish the basis for technical and financial support.

In the previous section, the existence of provisions in the AAs on a free trade area were mentioned. This is a feature all EU AAs have in common, but the DCFTA provisions in the EU-Moldova AA go significantly further than classical forms of economic integration, offering not only improved trade and investment opportunities but also assistance in trade-related reforms with the aim to contribute to economic recovery and growth and to better integration of the Moldovan economy with the world markets. Each SAA contains a set of approximation clauses. But, in difference from the EU's Europe Agreements with Central and Eastern European countries, in every single SAA the wording of the approximation provisions is different and also differs from the AA with Moldova. This reflects the developments in the Stabilization and Association Process with a particular country. The differences can be seen in the prescribed time framework as well as in the general scope of approximation works. The Euro-Mediterranean agreements cover trade in goods and are complemented with a number of additional ongoing negotiations and preparations for future negotiations: to open up additional agricultural trade, to liberalize trade in services and investment, to negotiate agreements on accreditation and acceptance of industrial products, to establish deep and comprehensive free trade areas.

3. Looking more closely at the Ankara Agreement

The main common element between the EU-Moldova AA and the Ankara Agreement consists in that that they both promote a prerequisite for membership and that they strengthen relationships with the EU. Technically, however, both agreements do not have a lot in common as they were signed in different periods of time and have different objectives. This may be somewhat different for the Additional Protocols, which they were signed to supplement the Association Agreement and to make the collaborative relationship with the EU tighter. In addition to providing for a common external tariff for the covered products, the EU-Turkey Customs Union foresees that Turkey has to align to the *acquis communautaire* in several essential internal market areas, notably with regard to industrial standards. Another important aspect is about the administrative and judicial capacity to implement the acquis communautaire. This topic is regulated in a very detailed manner in the AA with Moldova, but not in the Ankara Agreement. However, the issue has come-up in the EU accession process since 1995.

In conclusion, it can be mentioned that there are common aspects only based on the general principles of cooperation, of integration in the EU and about the implementation of a free trade area. If the differences of these agreements are pointed out, it can be easily said that there are a lot of aspects provided in a different manner. Starting with the structure, it can be observed that the AA with Moldova is a more developed one, that it has provisions on a lot of different aspects and consists of a larger implementation phase duringthe whole agreement. In the Ankara Agreement three titles can be observed, based on principles, on the implementation of the transitional stage and on general and final provisions. Something differentcan be stated for the AA with Moldova, which contains 7 titles - general principles; political cooperation and policy foreign and security; justice, freedom and security; sectoral and economic cooperation; trade and issues related to Trade (DCFTA); financial cooperation including clauses anti-fraud and institutional, general and final provisions.

III. Conclusion

As to the comparison of the EU-Moldova AA with other EU Association Agreements, it can be concluded that the AA with Moldova takes part in a new generation of European agreements. All of them have different as well as common elements, but in general, the implementation of all of them is different. This appears so because all these countries have different objectives, needs and proposals. All of them have different levels of development, different ressources, more or less progressive reforms to continue.

The EU-Moldova Association Agreement goes significantly further than classical forms of economic integration, offering not only improved trade and investment opportunities but also assistance in trade-related reforms with the aim to contribute to economic recovery and growth and to a better integration of the Moldovan economy into the world markets. Independent economic research suggests that Moldova's participation in the DCFTA will boost its exports to the EU to

16%, and its imports from the EU to 8%. The DCFTA as a whole is expected to boost the GDP to 5.4% annually, if the reforms are completed[46].

According to expert estimates, the benefits for the region Transnistria that will occur as a result of the DCFTA's implementation are an increase of 3.6% of the local GDP and a refusal to benefits from this arrangement would reduce the region's GDP to 5.2%. An increase of the GDP of 3.6% in the long term will happen due to the fact that the region will be able to maintain exports to the EU and, in addition, to extend them, given that the DCFTA includes a number of new liberalized branches, including the agribusiness[47]. The Association Agreement is a concrete way to take advantage of the positive dynamics in EU-Moldova relations. It focuses on the support for core reforms, economic recovery, governance, sector cooperation and brings about a far reaching liberalization of Moldova's trade with the EU.

46 Memo/14/430, European Commission, The EU's Association Agreements with Georgia, the Republic of Moldova and Ukraine, Brussels, 23 June 2014, p.4.

47 Guide Association Agreement between Moldova and the European Union, This publication has been produced with the support of the project "Strengthening Institutional Capacity of the Ministry of Foreign Affairs European "implemented and co-financed by the United Nations Development Programme (UNDP). The contents of this publication are the responsibility Ministry of Foreign Affairs and Integration and do not necessarily reflect official position of UNDP, 2014, p.21.

Tetiana Iliushyna

Comparison of the EU-Ukraine Association Agreement with other EU Association Agreements, in particular with Turkey

For Ukrainians, the inclusion of Ukraine into the integrated European community is a great excitement and is recognized as a common strategic goal for this country. More broadly, we can talk about this process as one of the important components of the Ukrainian national idea in general, as a logical way and the process at the same time means self-affirmation of Ukraine as an independent state.It is important to understand that the realization of this goal will facilitate the formation of a stable and strong Europe and European security and does not hinder the development of equal and dynamic relations with other countries.The process of European integration has a special and very important place among Ukraine's priorities in international relations. Integration does not only mean partnership and mutually beneficial cooperation. it can not be interpreted only as one of the areas of foreign policy of the state, but it also provides significant internal transformation in accordance with accepted standards of community integration.

The following contribution will try to analyze the EU-Ukrainian Association Agreement from a comparative perspective, not comparing it with the AAs with Georgia and Moldova, but with some other EU association agreements, in particular the one with Turkey. Comparison with the EU-Turkey agreement is of interest for different reasons. Not only is Turkey also a Black Sea country, and there are many economic contacts between Ukraine and Turkey, but the EU-Turkey Agreement, which dates already from 1963, can also be studied as an example how an Association Agreement can be used as an instrument for an later EU accession strategy.

The prospects for a European integration of Ukraine and Turkey should be assessed on the basis of understanding what the European Union is today. The EU is a union that has reached the so-far highest level of integration in history, it shows significant development potential and has become a natural embodiment of the European idea. Today, unfortunately, the EU is in crisis, primarily due to tensions between the inviolable principle of national sovereignty and the idea of supranational integration. But nevertheless, the European Union has been and still remains an attractive and, generally, stable form of interstate cooperation, which is the primary motivation of the wish of other countries to join the EU.

In this article the historical background of the conclusion of association agreements by the EU, the historical genesis of the development of relations between the parties, features of signing and ratification of some of such agreements, in particular the EU Agreements with Ukraine and Turkey, are analyzed. The article also highlights the main differences in these processes, comparing the levels of the development of Turkey and Ukraine at the moment of signing their Agreements with the EU. The actuality of this research lies in the fact that for both these countries joining the EU is a foreign policy priority, exactly as the EU provides for this enlargement on its agenda. Important factors influencing the EU enlargement process are, of course, the political situation, the development of internal political and economic relations within the EU and the international situation. Assessing the prospects for a EU integration of Ukraine and Turkey, it may be noted that the EU's relations with the aspirants can be compared to a dynamic system which is balanced, taking into account the output pulse on both sides. European integration of these countries is a product of the interaction of the aforementioned processes within the EU and within these countries. Of course, the European Union on the one hand, and Ukraine and Turkey, on the other, assess the possible effects of integration in the light of an analysis of costs and effectiveness, and it does not always clearly look like a «win-win» outcome to both. Differences concerning the construction and development of the relations between Turkey, Ukraine and the EU appear primarily in the historic features of the signing and the ratification of the Association Agreements. This determines different principles and objectives of the Agreements, their basic structure and content.

I. Historical background

1. EU – Turkey

The history of relations between Turkey and the EU reaches back to the initial stages of the European Community.In July 1959, shortly after the creation of the EEC in 1958, Turkey made its first application to join. The EEC's response to Turkey's application in 1959 was a suggestion to establish an association until Turkey's circumstances permitted its accession. The ensuing negotiations resulted in the signature of the Agreement Creating An Association Between The Republic of Turkey and the European Economic Community (the «Ankara Agreement») on 12 September 1963. This agreement, which entered into force on 1 December 1964, aimed at securing Turkey's full membership in the EEC through thetri-phase establishment of a customs union which would serve as an instrument to bring about an integration between the EEC and Turkey. The Ankara Agreement envisaged the progressive establishment of a Customs Union which would bring the parties closer together in economic and trade matters. In the meantime, the EEC would offer financial assistance to Turkey. Under the First Financial Protocol which covered the period from 1963to 1970, the EEC provided Turkey with loans worth 175 million ECU. The trade concessions which the EEC granted to Turkey under the form of tariff quotas however proved not to be as effective as expected. Yet, the EEC's share in Turkish imports rose from 29%

in 1963 to 42% in 1972. Although the Ankara Agreement envisaged the free circulation not only of goods, but of natural persons, services and capital between the Parties, it excluded Turkey from the EEC decision-making mechanisms and precluded Turkey from recourse to the ECJ for dispute settlement[48]. The Additional Protocol of 13 November 1970 set out in a detailed fashion how the Customs Union would be established. It provided that the EEC would abolish tariff and quantitative barriers to its imports from Turkey (with some exceptions including fabrics) upon the entry into force of the Protocol, whereas Turkey would do the same in accordance with a timetable containing two calendars set for 12 and 22 years, and called for the harmonization of Turkish legislation with that of the EU in economic matters. Furthermore, the Additional Protocol envisaged the free circulation of natural persons between the parties in the next 12 to 22 years[49].

On 24 January 1980 Turkey shifted its economic policy from an autarchic import-substitution model and opened its economy to the operation of market forces. Following this development in the economic area and the multiparty elections in 1983, the relations between Turkey and the Community, which had come to a virtual freeze following the military intervention of 12 September 1980 in Turkey, began returning to normality. In the light of these positive developments, Turkey applied for full membership in 1987, on the basis of the EEC Treaty's article 237 which gave any European country the right to do so. Turkey's request for accession, not filed under the relevant provisions of the Ankara Agreement, but those of the Treaty of Rome, underwent the normal procedures. The Council forwarded Turkey's application to the Commission for the preparation of an Opinion. This has reconfirmed Turkey's eligibility, given that a similar application by Morocco was turned down by the Council on the grounds that Morocco is not a European country. The Commission's Opinion was completed on 18 December 1989 and endorsed by the Council on 5 February 1990. It basically underlined Turkey's eligibility for membership, but yet deferred an in-depth analysis of Turkey's application until the emergence of a more favorable environment. It also mentioned that Turkey's accession was prevented equally by the EC's own situation on the eve of the Single Market's completion which prevented the consideration of further enlargements. It went on to underline the need for a comprehensive cooperation program aiming at facilitating the integration of the two sides and added that, as envisaged[50], the Customs Union should be completed in 1995. Since then, active negotiations on cooperation were re-

48 Turkey and EU. Embassy of the Republic of Turkey, Washington, D.C, accessible athttps://web.archive.org/web/20070927211417/http://www.turkishembassy.org/index.php?option=com_content&task=view&id=57&Itemid=235[Accessed 10/12/14].

49 Salomon Ruysdeal, Vedat Yücel, New Trends in Turkish Foreign Affairs: Bridges and Boundaries (2002)Lincoln, pp. 52-53.

50 History of Turkey – EU relations. Official website of Republic of Turkey Ministry for EU Affairs. Available from: http://www.abgs.gov.tr/?p=111&l=2. [Accessed 10/12/14].

sumed, given the opportunity to begin the development of a mechanism to improve the integration process.Under these circumstances, Turkey chose to complete the envisaged Customs Union with the Community. Talks began in 1994 and were finalized on 6 March 1995 at the Turkey-EU Association Council, the highest ranking organ of the association and composed of the Foreign Ministers of Turkey and the EU Member States. On that day the Association Council adopted its decision 1/95 on the completion of the Customs Union between Turkey and the EU in industrial and processed agricultural goods by 31 December 1995. At the same meeting, another resolution on accompanying measures was adopted and the EU made a declaration on a financial cooperation with Turkey as a part of the customs union «package». With the entry into force of the Customs Union, Turkey abolished all duties and equivalent charges on imports of industrial goods from the EU[51]. A new round of negotiations started on3 October 2005 in Luxembourg, and Turkey has consequently changed its status from "candidate" to "accession" country.

2. EU – Ukraine

While cooperation between Turkey and the EU has acquired a structured comprehensive character over a long time, the same does not, unfortunately, pertain to the cooperation of Ukraine and the EU. After getting its independence, Ukraine also recognized integration with the EU as one of the main foreign policy objectives. But due to some factors, progress in this area was lower than expected and hoped-for. This is related to numerous manifestations of negative character in the field of politics, economy, social security, international relations, etc. in Ukraine, which are inevitable on the way of the young state. The slow pace of reforms in all spheres of the Ukrainian society, as the Ukrainian ruling elites largely kept-on to the declared policy of the Soviet model, the permanent economic crisis – these are just some major problems encountered by Ukraine on its "European" way. Thus, the path itself and the negotiation, development and signing of the Association Agreement in 2014 and its– still not completed by all sides - ratification were rather long and complicated.During the years from 2007to 2012 twenty-one rounds of negotiations for the preparation of the Association Agreement between Ukraine and the EU were held within three working groups: 1) political dialogue, foreign and security policy; 2) justice, freedom and security; 3) economic, sectoral issues and human development. Moreover, a total of 18 rounds of negotiations on a free trade were conducted, after the start of the negotiations, thefourth corresponding working group was established.As reflected in the Joint Declaration on the Association Agreement between Ukraine and the EU approved at the Ukraine-EU Summit in Paris on 9 September 2008, the Association Agreements should:update the common institutional framework

---

51 Turkey – EU history. Official website of the Economic Development Foundation (Turkey). Available from: http://oldweb.ikv.org.tr/icerik_en.asp?konu=tarihce&baslik=History [Accessed 11/12/14].

between Ukraine and the EU;promote relations in all areas;strengthen political association and economic integration based on mutual rights and obligations.[52] The parties also stated that creating a deep and comprehensive free trade area with a large-scale regulatory approximation of Ukraine to the EU standards would contribute to the gradual integration of Ukraine into the EU market.The name of the agreement - "Association Agreement" was previously agreed by the Foreign Ministers of the European Union on 22 July 2008 in Brussels at a meeting of the European Union[53]. On 30 March 2012 senior officials of Ukraine and the European Union initialed the texts of an Association Agreement between the EU and Ukraine (but as of November 2012 the 27 EU governments and the European Parliament had yet to sign the accord), and also the Deep and Comprehensive Free trade Agreement (DCFTA) as an integral part of the package in Brussels.Further, the XVI Summit was held on 25 February 2013. During this summit Ukraine committed itself to solve the existing problems. On the signing of the Association Agreement, the most optimistic forecasts came together at the end of 2013, but it depended on the domestic political processes and on the effectiveness of the execution of the terms and conditions of the EU-Ukraine Association Agenda. The main requirement was the release of political convicts, such as Yulia Tymoshenko and Yuriy Lutsenko. However, concerning Yulia Tymoshenko, this was not fulfilled. At the Eastern Partnership Summit on28/29 November 2013 then president Yanukovych rather unexpectedly did not sign the agreement which caused violent negative reactions of Ukraine‘s population, causing the emergence of the 2013/2014 Ukrainian revolution – the Euromaidan. Actions in support of the Ukrainian population also began in many EU countries. Mass protests led to the removal of President Viktor Yanukovychand of Prime Minister Mykola Azarov from leadership.

On 21 March 2014 the political part (sections on political cooperation, security issues and the fight against terrorism) of the Association Agreement between Ukraine and the EU was signed in Brussels. On the Ukrainian side the Association Agreement was signed by the new Prime Minister of Ukraine, Arseniy Yatsenyuk, EU´s signature was done by then President of the Council of the EU Herman Van Rompuy, then President of the European Commission José Manuel Barroso and the heads of all EU member states. The so-called economic part of the Association Agreement, which envisages creating a free trade area and related issues such as market access, trade in energy, cooperation in agriculture, transport, industry, space, scientific research, tourism, entre-

---

52 Спільні заяви Самітів Україна – ЕС/Spilni zayavi Samitiv Ukraiina – ES (Joint declarations of the Summits Ukraine-EU), accessible athttp://www.kmu.gov.ua/control/publish/article?art_id=234609702 [Accessed 10/12/14].

53 Reitman, A.EU-Ukraine summit 'unlikely' this year, November 2012, accessible at http://euobserver.com/foreign/118094 [Accessed 15/12/14].

preneurship, intellectual property protection, dispute settlement procedure and taxation issues was signed by both sides on 27 June 2014.

The Association Agreement will contribute to the deepening of relations between the two sides and will strengthen the political and economic integration with the EU. However, this is only the beginning of a difficult work. The Ukrainian authorities have to execute contractual requirements, especially in the area of adaptation of Ukrainian legislation to EU legislation and its implementation into national law, and this process is a dynamic complex work on reforming many areas of life. The advanced process of adaptation of Ukrainian legislation to the acquis communautaire (which started already several years ago on the basis of the existing Partnership and Cooperation Agreement of 1994 and was intensified after the Orange Revolution of 2004/2005) through the process of making changes and amendments of legislative acts and developing new acts requires an integrated approach. The meaning of acquis communautaire refers not only to normative legal acts of the EU (regulations, directives, decisions, resolutions, etc.), but includes also the general principles of EU law, decisions of the European Court of Justice, strategies, actions and common positions within the common foreign and security policy[54]. Thus, the dynamic process of the adaptation of national legislation to the acquis communautaire cannot restrict the definition of specific areas of adaptation and certain legislative acts of the EU. Two very important components of this process are the implementation and enforcement of approximated legislation. Without these components adaptation of law is purely formal and leads to inefficiencies of the process.[55]

II. The structure and content of the two Association Agreements

Association Agreements are for the EU the most advanced type of international agreements, which the EU has concluded with third countries - countries with which the EU is ready to develop strong long-term alliances based on mutual trust and respect for common values[56]. It may be mentioned that the association agreements which were concluded by European Economic Community with certain Mediterranean countries in the 1960s (Cyprus and Malta) determined the terms of the relationship of these countries and the Union for the so-called preparatory stage of their accession to the EU. Although the content and the text of these agreements were and are sometimes very similar,each agreement is unique and establishes specific questions of associa-

54 Stone, European Integration and Supranational Governance (1998), pp. 299–300.

55 Olinik, EU Association Agreements with third countries: the Polish experience. Ukrainian national idea: Realities and Prospects for Development (in Ukrainian), vol. 26, pp. 133-140.

56 Information on the EU-Ukraine Association Agreement, accessible at: http://eeas.europa.eu/top_stories/2012/140912_ukraine_en.htm [Accessed 11/12/14].

tions considering features and the duration of specific bilateral relations with the European Union, priorities and areas of mutual interest.

1. EU-Turkey Agreement of 1963

The EU-Turkey Agreement of 1963 (Ankara Agreement) relates to the category of international treaties of the EU, which were concluded between Member States of the European Economic Community, the European Economic Community and Turkey. The agreement contains a preamble, 3 chapters and 33 articles. The first chapter is «Principles» (it includes the purpose of the agreement and its basic principles, stages of the cooperation between Turkey and the EU, their duration, their content and the objectives and circumstances of their execution). The second chapter «Implementation of the transitional stage» provides the establishment of the principle of non-discrimination on grounds of nationality, it envisaged the progressive establishment of a Customs Union which would bring the parties closer together in economic and trade matters, it regulates the possibility of bilateral cooperation in agriculture and the other provisions provided by the Treaty establishing the European Economic Community. The third chapter «General and final provisions»provides for the creation of an institutional system for the administrative management of bilateral issues, it describes the procedure of the authorities establishment, their competence and powers to consider the disputes. The Association between the EEC and Turkey did not gain any substantial form until 1970, when the EC and Turkey signed an Additional Protocol (the «1970 Protocol») that has largely governed their relations since. The Additional Protocol and Decisions of the Association Council are part of EEC law. The European Court of Justice has decided that these give specific rights to Turkish nationals and businesses which the EEC Member States are required to respect by EEC law.[57]

The Additional Protocol provides for the regulation of economic issues such like the expiry of the ECSC treaty and ECSC products, aspects of cooperation in the field of agriculture (adjustment of tariff quotas for agricultural products), some transitional provisions (proof of status under the provisions on free circulation for industrial products). For today a whole array of decisions of the Turkey–European Union Association Council relating is developed as well. It concerns such areas as agriculture and fisheries (products of agriculture and fisheries; agricultural cooperation and

57 Judgment of the Court (Sixth Chamber) of 26 November 1998. - Mehmet Birden v Stadtgemeinde Bremen.- EEC-Turkey Association Agreement - Freedom of movement for workers - Article 6(1) of Decision No 1/80 of the Association Council - Scope - Turkish national with a fixed-term employment contract under a programme financed by the public authorities and designed to assist the integration of persons dependent on social assistance into the labour market. - Case C-1/97. Available from: http://eur-lex.europa.eu/legal-content/EN/TXT/HTML/ELX_SESSIONID=JNvLJvsZdlVRpHNMhLv2ktcSnLQytLV7pGs1NmtLMcWLdLBgv12y!1908644068?isOldUri=true&uri=CELEX:61997CJ0001 [Accessed 11/12/14].

rural development; processed agricultural products;veterinary and plant-health issues;legislation applicable to trade), the internal market and competition (free movement of goods, including standardization, certification, conformity; assessment and market surveillance; intellectual and industrial property rights; public procurement, data protection and civil law; company law, accounting and e-commerce; consumer protection; competition and state aid; services, including financial services (banking, insurance, investment) and postal services; the movement of workers, except the coordination of social security; the right of establishment and provision of service; Turkish participation in Community programs), trade, industry and ECSC products (trade issues; ECSC products; investment promotion; small and medium-sized enterprises and Turkish participation in the Community; SME programs; industrial policy and cooperation, tourism), economics and monetary issues, capital movements and statistics economic and monetary issues; current payments and movements of capital, including investment protection; a reform of the financial sector; statistical cooperation), transport, environment and energy (including trans-European networks), customs, taxation, drug trafficking and money laundering etc.

2. EU-Ukraine AA of 2014

In view of its recent development the EU-Ukrainian AA is, understandably enough, much more elaborated than the Ankara Agreement. The structure of the EU-Ukrainian Association Agreement, which embraces more than 2000 printed pages, consists of the following parts[58]:

a) The main text of the agreement starts with a preamble, general objectives and principles.

b) It then continues with a title on a political dialogue, containing provisions devoted to the development and the strengthening of the political dialogue in various fields, which, in particular, should contribute to the gradual convergence of Ukraine with the EU's foreign and security policy;

c) Then follows a title on justice, freedom and security, which outline the issues of justice, law enforcement, migration management, ensuring the rule of law, protection of personal data, strengthening the judicial system, improving its efficiency, guaranteeing its independence and impartiality:

58 For a detailed analysis of the EU-Ukrainian AA see the recent publication by van der Loo, The EU-Ukraine Association Agreement and Deep and Comprehensive Free Trade Area, A New Legal Instrument for EU Integration Without Membership (2016), passim.

d) Thereafter comes a title on economic and sectoral cooperation (appropriate measures of reform in areas such as taxation, transportation, environment, industrial policy and entrepreneurship, tourism, audiovisual policy, space research, health, culture, education etc.);

e) A special title is devote to the topic of energy, which introduces a harmonized legal regime for operation of the industry's enterprises on the territory of Ukraine and the EU;

f) Economically very important is then the title on trade and trade-related matters ("Deep and Comprehensive Free Trade Area"), which provides for a liberalization of trade in both goods and services, a liberalization of the flow of capital and to some extent – the labor force flow;

g) Finally, the main text of the agreement concludes with a title on general, institutional and final provisions. This title introduces new formats and levels of cooperation between Ukraine and the EU after the entry into force of the Agreement, furthermore the introduction of a mechanism for monitoring and dispute resolution.

In addition, the Association Agreement comprises 43 Annexes and 3 Protocols. The Annexes and Protocols to this Agreement form an integral part of the AA.

3. Comparison

Generally speaking, it can be said that the different structure of the two Association Agreements is due to their specific development. The association between Turkey and the EU is not only based on the primary and basic Association Agreement, but is also regulated by a vast array of legal documents like The Additional Protocol of 1970, agreements on cooperation between the parties and numerous decisions of the Association Council.[59] This list is consistently growing with new documents which are signed in consequence of the on-going accession negotiations between Turkey and the EU. The initial agreement (Ankara Agreement) regulates the most important and priority areas which correspond to the state development trends of that time - increasing the economic potential of the expense of international trade. Then, only issues of economic cooperation, the movement of services, of capital and labor in the international market were affected. In the following years already there started a bilateral cooperation in a wider range of areas as a consequence of the development of social relations in general, in which there was a mutual benefit of the joint projects and a great desire of Turkey to join the EU as a full member. The EU-

59 Ukraine-European Union Association Agreement (2015) Ukraine–European_Union_Association_Agreement. [Online] Available from: http://en.wikipedia.org/wiki/Ukraine–European_Union_Association_Agreement [Accessed 19/12/14].

Ukrainian Association Agreement is structurally more expanded, it involves a wider range of areas in which cooperation will be carried out. It details the issues of the procedural implementation of the aims, it provides an opportunity to revise the Agreement in the event of successful execution of its objectives and provides an opportunity to formalize more ambitious plans of the parties (especially the prospect of full membership).It should be noted that none of the Agreements establishes a strict hierarchy of goals, but the procedure for negotiating and increased public attention indicates the priority of objectives in the economic cooperation. In addition, this is evidenced by the character and the content of the Ankara Agreement.

III. General objectives and principles

Considering Article 2 of the Ankara Agreement, it appears that the aim of this Agreement is to promote the continuous and balanced strengthening of trade and economic relations between the parties, while taking full account of the need to ensure an accelerated development of the Turkish economy and to improve the level of employment and living conditions of the Turkish people. Title I of the Ankara Agreement called Principles does not contain a list of principles that should be the legal basis, the framework for a cooperation. The Ankara Agreement established stipulated far-reaching rights for Turkish nationals. Unfortunately, most of these rights are still not operational even after more than 50 years of association. The principle of non-discrimination, a basic principle of EU law, also forms a fundamental principle of the Turkey-EU association law. Turkish nationals cannot be evaluated as any third country nationals in the EU. EU institutions, particularly the European Court of Justice and the European Commission should take action to secure the rights of Turkish nationals in accordance with EU law embodying EU-Turkey association law.[60]

Article 1 of the EU-Ukrainian AA establishes six main aims of the joint cooperation in four dimensions: 1) Values: a gradual rapprochement between the parties based on shared values and close and privileged relations, as well as an increased participation of Ukraine in EU policies, programs, and agencies; 2) Politics and security: an enhanced political dialogue on all issues of mutual interest for the parties and a maintenance of regional and international peace and stability based on principles of the UN and the OSCE; 3) Economic: the establishment of enhanced economic and trade relations leading to a deep and comprehensive FTA, as well as a completion of Ukraine's transformation into a functioning market economy, especially through the harmoniza-

60 The principle of non-discrimination in the European Union and rights of Turkish nationals, program of a conference, held on 8October 2013, in Istanbul, accessible at http://oldweb.ikv.org.tr/icerik_en.asp?konu =haberler&id=577&baslik=PRINCIPLE_OF_NON-DISCRIMINATION_IN_THE_EUROPEAN_UNION_AND_RIGHTS_OF_TURKISH_NATIONALS [Accessed 12/12/14].

tion of the Ukrainian legislation with EU legislation; 4) Legal: strengthening cooperation in the fields of justice, freedom and security to enhance the rule of law and respect for human rights and fundamental freedoms.Furthermore, it should be noted that the agreement provides the establishment of conditions for an increasingly close cooperation in other areas of mutual interest, so that the parties are ready to set new goals.

The general principles by which the parties of Association Agreements are governed are regulated in a more detailed manner in the EU-Ukrainian Association Agreement. Articles 1 and 2 of the EU-Ukrainian AA provide that the parties are required to follow the principles defined in particular in the Helsinki Final Act of 1975 of the Conference on Security and Cooperation in Europe and the Charter of Paris for a New Europe of 1990, and other relevant human rights instruments, among them the UN Universal Declaration of Human Rights and the European Convention on Human Rights and Fundamental Freedoms. Article 2 of the Agreement sets out the system of general principles which seem to be organized by their significance and the degree to which they are legally binding: 1) "form the basis of internal and external policies of the parties, and are essential elements of the Agreement": respect for democratic principles, human rights and fundamental freedoms, and respect for the rule of law; 2) "also constitute essential elements of the Agreement": promoting respect for the principles of sovereignty and territorial integrity, inviolability of borders and independence, and combating proliferation of weapons of mass destruction, related materials, and means of their delivery; 3) the "relations of the parties rely" on the principles of free market economy; 4) "central to enhancing relations between the parties" are: the rule of law, good governance, counteracting corruption, counteracting various forms of trans-national organized crime and terrorism, a support for sustainable development, effective multilateralism.[61]

Thus the EU-Ukrainian Association Agreement in the view of its modernity is more detailed and regulates fundamental principles not only of cooperation but also of the activities of associated member state as a whole more extensively. This Agreement contains a reference to the main documents of the European Union, while in the Ankara Agreement a reference to main principles is absent, references to them are,however, contained in special agreements on specific issues of cooperation. It can be assumed that the reason for this is the explicitly economic nature of the Ankara Agreement in which economic rights and freedoms of the citizens of Turkey and the EU are the priority.

---

61 Sushko, EU-Ukraine Association Agreement: Guideline for reforms. Kyiv (2012) [Konrad Adenauer Stiftung].

IV. Stages of Association

It should be noted that each of the two Association Agreements contains a certain stage of cooperation with the EU, each of these stages has its duration and purpose at the end of which a certain result is achieved. Article 2 of the Ankara Agreement provides for three main stages of economic cooperation. The Association shall comprise: 1) a preparatory stage; 2) a transitional stage; 3) a final stage. During the preparatory stage Turkey should, with the Community's aid, strengthen its economy to enable it to fulfill the obligations which would devolve upon it during the transitional and final stages. The detailed rules for this preparatory stage, in particular those for the aid from the Community, are set out in the Provisional Protocol and in the Financial Protocol to this Agreement. The preparatory stage was to last five years, unless it should be extended in accordance with the conditions laid down in the Provisional Protocol. During the transitional stage the Contracting Parties should, on the basis of mutual and balanced obligations: progressively establish a customs union between Turkey and the Community; align the economic policies of Turkey and the Community more closely in order to ensure the proper functioning of the Association and the progress of the joint measures which this requires. This stage was to last no more than twelve years, subject to such exceptions as many are made by a mutual agreement. The exceptions were not to impede the final establishment of the customs union within a reasonable period. The final stage was to be based on the customs union and should entail a closer coordination of the economic policies of the contracting parties. In order to attain the objectives set by the Ankara Agreement during the transitional stage the customs union should be established. Also, the parties should take all the economic means of deepening a bilateral cooperation in the field of agriculture. The contracting parties also agreed to be guided by the Treaty establishing the Community for the purpose of progressively securing freedom of movement for workers, for the purpose of abolishing restrictions on freedom of establishment and for the purpose of abolishing restrictions on freedom to provide services between them. Monitoring the implementation of each stage was to be exercised by The Council of Association, which on the basis of an annual analysis of indicators of national economic sector, makes conclusions about the adequacy of the implementation of each period's goals. It had to decide about the possibility of moving to the next stage.

Article 25 (Title IV – trade and trade-related matters) of the EU-Ukrainian Association Agreement establishes a transition period whose duration shall not exceed 10 years from the date of entry into force of the Association Agreement. During this period, a free trade zone should be established between the EU and Ukraine, it will gradually decrease the base rate of customs duties. Each party shall reduce or cancel the duty on goods in accordance with established schedules, and for Ukraine the transition period will last up to 10 years, while the change in the tariff schedule of the EU will take place immediately after the entry into force of the Agreement. The gradual removal of export duties will stimulate the exports of these goods and at the same time would increase internal prices. Due to the lengthy transition period, producers have the ability to adapt to changes.

Summing-up, all these steps are designed primarily to issues of economic cooperation, trade and business. They do not cover all areas of cooperation, which in our opinion, makes a reference to the basic, the main purpose of each Association Agreement. It is important to note that Article 28 of the Ankara Agreement states that as soon as the operation of this Agreement has advanced far enough to justify envisaging a full acceptance of the obligations arising out of the Treaty establishing the Community by Turkey, the Contracting Parties shall examine the possibility of the accession of Turkey to the Community. However, as noticed, the deadlines of each stage have passed, between the EU and Turkey fairly strong and stable economic relations are established, the number of import-export operations grows, but the question of full membership is still open.

V. Free movement of workers

A legal reference to the rights for workers to freedom of movement could be found even before the foundation of the European Economic Community, in Article 69 of the Treaty establishing the European Coal and Steel Community (ECSC) and Article 96 of the Treaty on the European Atomic Energy Community (EURATOM) (mentioning free movement of workers in the nuclear energy sector). The free movement of persons was mostly formulated in the context of workers and perceived to be one of the key elements in the way towards a common market. It was then so vital to ensure the free movement of labor, one of the factors of production, in order to achieve a well-functioning market among the member states. In other words, the initiative for a free movement of workers was mainly motivated by economic purposes. In fact, it is argued that such freedom was seen as a prerequisite for the realization of an economic goal.

In EU-Turkey relations, the basic references on this issue are the Ankara Agreement, the Additional Protocol (1970) and the Association Council Decisions No 2/76, 1/80 and 3/80 concluded between the EU and Turkey. Article 12 of the Association Agreement and Article 36 of the Additional Protocol envisage that the free movement of workers should be provided gradually between Turkey and the EU member states. Articles 6 to 18 of the Association Council Decision No 1/80 introduce provisions on the employment and the free movement of workers.[62] The first decision

[62] National Programme for the Adoption of the Acquis(2010), accessible at http://ec.europa.eu/enlargement/

concerning the right of free movement of Turkish workers was taken by the Council in 2/76, which was temporarily concluded in 1976 for four years. Decision no 1/80 of the Association Council of 19 September 1980 on the development of the Association has repealed the Decision no 2/76. Under Article 6(1) of the Association Council Decision 1/80, Turkish nationals legally employed in an EEC Member State for certain periods gain the rights to remain or to switch their employment in that state:

- a Turkish national legally employed by the same employer for one year has the right to permission from the Member State to remain in that employment;
- a Turkish national legally employed for three years in a particular area of work has the right to permission from the Member State to take an employment with any employer in that area;
- a Turkish national legally employed for four years has the right to permission from the Member State to take an employment with any employer[63].

There are also some casesof the European Court of Justice on free movement of Turkish workers within the Community, such as Meryem Demirel v.Stadt Schwäbisch Gmünd (C-12/86), S.Z. Sevince v Staatssecretaris van Justitie», Ömer Nazli, Caglar Nazli and Melike Nazli v Stadt Nürnberg (C-340/97), Süleyman Eker v. Land Baden-Württemberg (C-386/95)and others. Most of the cases provide for the settlement of disputes concerning the rights of families of Turkish workers.[64] The ECJ case law has illuminated the rights and their limits of those Turkish workers and their family members, which can be classified briefly: 1) four years of legal employment confers access to the labor market and implies a residence right connected with free access to employment; 2) non-discrimination on grounds of nationality subject to priority given to EU citizens regarding recruitment under certain circumstances; 3) equal treatment concerning the working conditions and earnings; 4) extension of work and residence permits after one year of legal work; 5) the right to take up an employment and education for Turkish workers' children only in the Member State where the Turkish workers are legally employed; 6) in the event of losing their

pdf/turkey/npaa_ full_en.pdf [Accessed 14/12/14].

63 Judgment of the Court (Sixth Chamber) of 26 November 1998. - Mehmet Birden v Stadtgemeinde Bremen. - EEC-Turkey Association Agreement - Freedom of movement for workers - Article 6(1) of Decision No 1/80 of the Association Council - Scope - Turkish national with a fixed-term employment contract under a programme financed by the public authorities and designed to assist the integration of persons dependent on social assistance into the labour market. - Case C-1/97. Available from: http://eur-lex.europa.eu/legal-content/EN/TXT/HTML/?isOldUri=true &uri=CELEX:61997CJ0001 [Accessed 10/12/14].

64 Yonah, Brenner, Tutuncuoglu, Krause,Turkey: Terrorism, Civil Rights, and the European Union, New York (2008).

worker status, Turkish workers are no longer considered within the province of the Agreement and the Association Council decisions.[65]

In the EU-Ukraine relationship, legal issues regulating the freedom of movement of workers and opening up the European labor market for Ukrainians were, first, affected by the 1994 Agreement on Partnership and Cooperation (PCA) between Ukraine and the EU. The PCA contains two chapters, which address working conditions and conditions affecting the establishment and the operation of companies. The principle of non-discrimination on nationality applies only to citizens of Ukraine legally employed in the EU. Unlike agreements with the candidate countries, the right of access to the labor market does not apply to family members of the employee who legally live in the EU. Now, Article 18 (in Title III – justice, freedom and security) of the EU-Ukrainian AA establishes in principle the mobility of workers. In does so taking into account the labor market situation in the Member States, subject to the legislation and in compliance with the rules in force in the Member States and the EU in the area of mobility of workers, stating more in detail that the existing facilities of an access to employment for Ukrainian workers accorded by Member States under bilateral agreements should be preserved and if possible improved; and other Member States shall examine the possibility of concluding similar agreements. Thus, all the provisions established by the pre-existing PCA of 1994 will remain in force. The freedom of movement can be used by workers, their family members, as well as by persons who are not engaged in economic activities (students, etc.). Workers can stay on the territory of the other party in order to find work up to six months. During this period, they may be excluded from the social security system of the host country. Information about their locations may also be required by the workers. Workers who have found work get a residence permit for five years with an option to extend it. The residence permit gives a number of important rights to the employee which include: equal rights to those of citizens of the European Union with respect to working conditions, salaries and dismissal from work; access to training necessary to perform the work stipulated by the permission; a recognition of diplomas, certificates and other qualification certificates issued by the authorized institutions; social security inclusive health insurance; access to social housing, etc. However, Member States may restrict the employee's right to the enjoyment of social housing. For those who work on their own, the residence permit is issued for up to five years with a possible extension for a similar period. Member States may restrict the permission on the grounds of public policy, public security or public health. A refusal of a permit or an extension thereof will

[65] Gürcün E. (2007) The Legal Situation of the Turkish Community in the EU after the Long-term Resident Directive: The end of the Matter?, accessible at http://www.gurcun.av.tr/makaleler/The_Legal_Situation_of_the_Turkish_Community_in_the_EU_after_the_Long-term_Resident_Directive_The_end_of_the_Matter.pdf [Accessed 14/12/14].

be motivated and notified to the applicant. Parties to the agreement have pledged to coordinate the social security system in respect of nationals of the other side.

In general, the system of movement of workers in the context of relations between Turkey and the EU is more mature and perfect, as it used to be for a long time and is based on a number of programs for cooperation between the two sides in this area. On the other hand, it should be noted that the legal regulation of the EU-Ukrainian AA concerning the mobility of workers is more contemporary, but rather brief. Yet there is no array of laws developed that would regulate this issue in full measure. For the moment, in practice, there are gaps in this regulation, such as the lack of a uniform system of printing passports and passport data protection.

VI. General conclusion

The EU-Ukrainian Association Agreement is in the view of its modernity more detailed than the Ankara Agreement and regulates the fundamental principles not only of cooperation but also of the activities of associated member state as a whole more extensively. The EU-Ukraine Agreement contains a reference to the main documents of the European Union, while in the Ankara Agreement the reference to such main principles is absent, references to them are however contained in special agreements on specific issues of cooperation. It can be assumed that the reason for this is the more limited economic nature of the Ankara Agreement, in which economic rights and freedoms of the citizens of Turkey and the EU are prior.

Mykhailo Smeshko

The Present Inner Conflict Situation in Georgia (Abkhazia, South Ossetia), Moldova (Transnistria) and Ukraine (Crimea, Eastern Ukraine) in the Context of the three Association Agreements

I. Introduction

Association agreements are treaties between the EU and non-EU countries, which create a framework for closer cooperation. The areas of cooperation in the Associataion Agreements between the EU and Georgia, Moldova and Ukraine do not limit themselves to economic relations, but include the development of political relations. This is important to understand what an association agreement may offer in the context of the territorial conflicts in Moldova, Georgia and Ukraine, in order to solve these issues. The relevance of the topic stems from the fact that although the territorial conflicts in Georgia and Moldova (Transnistria, South Ossetia and Abkhazia) are currently inactive, there is an urgent need for solving a number of issues concerning the possible conflict settlement in Eastern Ukraine, which despite the Minsk agreements continue to gain momentum[66], as well as the illegal annexation of the Crimea by the Russian Federation, which violates basic principles of international law.[67] In this contribution it will be tried to answer the question how the Association Agreements with Moldova, Georgia and Ukraine could possibly affect the resolution of conflicts in these countries.

II. The general mechanism of conflict regulation under the AAs in the context of territorial conflicts in Moldova, Ukraine and Georgia

All three Association Agreements (Ukraine, Moldova, Georgia) use the same mechanism for resolving territorial conflict situations. It is a mechanism of political dialogue. In all agreements, without exception, this mechanism is laid-down in the second chapters (titles)[68]. The key provisions, which are common for all AAs and are the basis of a political dialogue state, for example, the principle of respect of sovereignty and territorial integrity, the inviolability of borders and the respect for independence, as established in the UN Charter and the 1975 Helsinki Final Declaration of the Conference on Security and Cooperation in Europe. Also, commitments of the Contracting Parties to promote these principles in their bilateral and multilateral relations are included

66 Minsk agreements, see http://www.telegraph.co.uk/news/worldnews/europe/ukraine/11408266/Minsk-agreement-on-Ukraine-crisis-text-in-full.html.

67 UN Charta, chapter 2.

68 See, in particular, Art. 7 and 8 of the EU-Moldova AA, Art. 7 – 9 of the EU-Georgia AA and Art. 9 and 10 of the EU-Ukraine AA.

in these chapters. Despite the fact that all AAs adhere to the same principles in this regard, as to territorial conflicts one can find in the agreements some differences.

III. Moldova's and Georgia's Association Agreements and the conflicts in Transnistria, Abkhazia and South Ossetia

1. Conflict resolution

Article 8 of the EU-Moldova AA specifies the main direction of the settlement of the conflict in Transnistria. According to Art.8 para. 2 "the parties reiterate their commitment to a sustainable solution to the Transnistrian issue, in full respect of the sovereignty and territorial integrity of the Republic of Moldova as well as to facilitating jointly post-conflict rehabilitation. Pending its resolution and without prejudice to the established negotiating format, the Transnistrian issue will constitute one of the central subjects on the agenda of political dialogue and cooperation between the Parties, as well as in the dialogue and cooperation with other interested international actors." Thus, the Agreement pays special attention to the present conflict in Transnistria.

Similarly, the EU-Georgia Association Agreement addresses the present conflicts in Abkhazia, South Ossetia specifically, though not expressly mentioning the geographic terms. Article 9 of the Agreement ("Peaceful conflict resolution" states in paragraph 2 that „the Parties recognize the importance of the commitment of Georgia to reconciliation and its efforts to restore its territorial integrity in pursuit of a peaceful and lasting conflict resolution, of pursuing the full implementation of the Six-Point Agreement of 12 August 2008 and its subsequent implementing measures, of pursuing mutually supportive non- recognition and engagement policies, of supporting the Geneva International Discussions and of safe and dignified return of all internally displaced persons and refugees to their habitual places of residence in line with principles of international law; and of a meaningful international field involvement, including, as appropriate, that of the EU".

2. Application of the AAs to inner conflicts regions

Another dimension of this problem is the general question, whether the Agreements apply to parts of the territory of the associated countries, which are not under the control of the respective governments, e.g. in the case of "frozen conflicts" such as Abkhazia, South Ossetia and Transnistria. Generally, the EU-Georgia and EU-Moldova Association Agreements are applied "to the whole territory of [Moldova and Georgia]"[69], however, the provisions contain some specific remarks on the territorial application. It is stated that the application of the DCFTA in relation to those areas "over which the Government of [Moldova and Georgia] does not exercise effective control, shall

[69] See Art. 462 EU-Moldova AA and Art. 426 EU- Georgia AA.

commence once [Moldova and Georgia] ensures the full implementation and enforcement of this Agreement, or of [its DCFTA], respectively, on its entire territory".[70] It is also pointed out that the decision about the full implementation and enforcement of the DCFTA and the AA is ensured on the entire territory of Georgia and Moldova and should be adopted by the Association Council. This means that both parties have to agree [Georgia and Moldova and the EU] that the government can carry out effective control on these conflict territories to ensure the implementation of the AA.[71] If the parties believe that the implementation cannot be guaranteed in these areas, the use of the DCFTA can be suspended in those areas. These procedures do not only apply to trade in goods and tariff reduction but to the entire amount of the deep and comprehensive trade areas. Accordingly the EU-Moldova or the EU-Georgia Association Councils may only suspend all or apply the DCFTA generally and may not apply only part of the agreement.[72]

IV. The EU-Ukraine Association Agreement and the conflicts situations of Crimea and Eastern Ukraine

As the text of the EU-Ukraine Association Agreement had been already initialled before the Russian annexation of Crimea and the emergence of the conflict in Eastern Ukraine, there is no direct reference to the Crimean issue and Eastern Ukraine in the Association Agreement itself. Such references are, however, contained in the Final Act between Ukraine and the EU on the EU-Ukraine Association Agreement. Here the parties agree that the Agreement "shall apply to the entire territory of Ukraine as recognized under international law and shall engage in consultations with a view to determine the effects of the Agreement with regard to the illegally annexed territory of the Autonomous republic of Crimea and the City of Sevastopol in which the Ukrainian Government currently does not exercise effective control"[73].

At present Ukraine considers the Crimea as "a temporarily occupied territory" and takes the position that the Constitution of Ukraine and its legal system are applicable in the Crimea. This means that residents of the Crimea and Sevastopol holding Ukrainian passports may enjoy all benefits of the Association Agreement between the Ukraine and the EU. Despite the fact that the Crimea is recognized by the Ukraine and the EU as Ukrainian territory, the Russian Federation exercises complete control over this territory. So in reality the Ukrainian side cannot control the implementation of the Agreement in the Crimea and thus, as in the case of Moldova and Georgia, a suspen-

---

70 See Article 462 EU- Moldova AA and Article 426 EU-Georgia AA.

71 The Association Councils decide "by agreement".

72 Article 462 EU-Moldova AA, Article 426 EU-Georgia AA.

73 Final Act between the European Union and the European Atomic Energy Community and their Member States, of the one part, and Ukraine, of the other part, as regards the Association Agreement, 27 June 2014.

sion of the application of the AA to this area could be declared (arguably by the Association Council). Similar considerations would seem to apply to the separatist regions in Eastern Ukraine (Donbass), which are presently not under the control of the Ukrainian Government.

On the basis of its general competences under the EU Treaties the European Unionhas adopted and renewed several times since the year 2014 sanctions against Russian and several Ukrainian (Crimean and Donbass) entities and individuals because of the unlawful occupation of the Crimea or because of their responsibility for the conflict in Eastern Ukraine. Starting from 20 December 1994 investments in the Crimea and Sevastopol are illegal. Europeans and registered in EU companies cannot buy real estate or law firms in the Crimea, Crimean finance company or provide them with related services. In addition, EU tour operators are no longer able to offer tourist services in Crimea and Sevastopol. In particular, European cruise ships will no longer stop at the ports of the Crimean peninsula, except for emergency cases. In addition, it was forbidden to export certain goods and technology for Crimean companies or for use in the Crimea. The ban is applied to transport, telecommunications and energy sectors or prospecting, exploration and production of oil, gas and mineral resources. In general, the list consist of 200 items.[74]

It is currently very difficult to say how the Association Agreement will be applied to those areas of the Eastern Ukraine, which still remain in a war-like situation. That again raises the question of effective governmental control over Eastern Ukraine. If the conflict comes to a frozen stage, the EU will probably pass similar trade, economic and financial restrictions as in the Crimea situation. This would mean that all products from this region (Eastern Ukraine) would not be subject to the DCFTA, like in the case of the Crimea. An exception might concern products that will have received certifications from the Ukrainian authorities, in such cases these products may be imported into the EU.[75]

V. Conclusion

An Association Agreement is a political document that covers many areas. It directs the country to achieve the uniform standards that facilitate economic and political cooperation. Unfortunately it should be stated that the EU Association Agreements with Georgia, Moldova and Ukraine do not impose any effective mechanisms to resolve the mentioned conflicts (Crimea, Eastern Ukraine, Transnistria, Abkhazia, and South Ossetia). The only mechanism provided by the Asso-

[74] Information Note to EU business operating and/or investing in Crimea/Sevastopol, amending Regulation (EU) No 692/2014 concerning restrictive measures in response to the illegal annexation of Crimea and Sevastopol.

[75] Council of the European Union, 'EU prohibits imports of goods from Crimea and Sevastopol', Presse 346, 23 June 2014.

ciation Agreements is a political dialogue that can be carried out in any format on the request of the parties. Unfortunately in today's realities and state of international law in general, one can directly assert that such a mechanism is inefficient and lengthy. Political dialogue can inhale decades without a real result.

At the same time, the Association Agreements establish a very important moment of political cooperation and full recognition of territorial integrity and provide also for rules applicable to territories where effective control by the Governments of the associated countries is not achieved. By signing the Association Agreements the EU and its member countries recognize the affiliation of those disputed territories to the associated States. Such recognition hopefully will support a further possible resolution of conflict situations, having on one's side powerful allies. This can facilitate and speed-up a future resolution of these conflicts.

The Association Agreements themselves do not set sanctions for violations of the territorial integrity of the associated States. This issue is to be resolved by international law: "All Members shall refrain in their international relations from the threat or use of force against the territorial integrity or political independence of any state, or in any other manner inconsistent with the Purposes of the United Nations"[76] and "To maintain international peace and security, and to that end: to take effective collective measures for the prevention and removal of threats to the peace, and for the suppression of acts of aggression or other breaches of the peace, and to bring about by peaceful means, and in conformity with the principles of justice and international law, adjustment or settlement of international disputes or situations which might lead to a breach of the peace;"[77]. The resolution of such disputes remains at the discretion of the States.

Thus it can be stated that the Association Agreements touch the topic of inner conflicts situations in associated countries only to a very limited degree and do not offer a significant mechanism that could affect the resolution of such situations.

---

76 Art. 2 Charter of the United Nations.
77 Art. 1 Charter of the United Nations.

Oleksandr Shevchuk

Legal Aspects of the Effects of the Association Agreements of the Three Countries to their Relations with Russia

I. Introduction

A short time after Georgia, Moldova and Ukraine signed the Association Agreements (AA) with the EU, Russia imposed "punitive" sanctions against these three Eastern European states.[78] Officially, these measures were grounded on seemingly neutral allegations of non-conformity of certain imports with technical standards, but the correlation of these allegations with movements in Russia's geopolitical postures makes it apparent that the Russian technical agencies are following political recommendations. These sanctions have an immediate impact on trade flows, especially for agricultural-food products. In the case of Ukraine, Russia initiated trilateral talks between the EU, Ukraine and Russia, reaching a postponement of the 'provisional' application of a large part of the free trade provisions (DCFTA) of the Association Agreement until the end of 2015. When these talks finally failed, Russia unilaterally suspended CIS free trade preferences in its relationship with Ukraine. In addition the war of sanctions between the EU, the USA and many other countries including Ukraine on the one side, and Russia on the other, which arose out of the illegal annexation of the Crimea by Russia, has also significantly reduced trade between Ukraine and Russia.

The following contribution will analyze whether and to which degree the effects of the Association Agreements can be seen as damaging to Russia's economic interests and (co-) responsible for the sharp deterioration of the relations between Russia and these countries.

II. Integration processes: The Eurasian Customs Union (now Eurasian Economic Union) or Association Agreements with the EU

1. Eurasian Customs Union (now Eurasian Economic Union)

A customs union is a form of regional free trade area (FTA) that leads to a liberalization of trade exclusively among its members. Customs unions contain, on top of a FTA, a common external tariff and a common external trade policy. They are easier to administer than FTAs because there is no need to agree on rules of origin for traded products. Customs union members, however,

78 CEPS WORKING DOCUMENT: Russian's Punitive Trade Policy Measures towards Ukraine, Moldova and Georgia edited by Denis Cenusa, Michael Emerson, Tamara Kovziridse and Veronika Movchan №.400/September 2014.

cannot pursue their own tariff or trade policies with third parties. This limitation on national sovereignty is often difficult to accept and partly explains why customs unions are rather uncommon – as opposed to classic FTAs.[79]

On 6 October 2007 Russia, Belarus and Kazakhstan signed a treaty founding a Customs Union. The three countries established a Customs Union Commission as its constantly functioning regulatory body and continued negotiating and drafting agreements necessary for the functioning of the ECU over the whole period of 2008 and 2009. On the 1 January 2010, a common customs tariff[80] was launched and the Commission formally began its work. In July 2010, the existence of a common customs territory was declared and the Union's Customs Code entered into force. In July 2011, the elimination of internal physical border controls was announced[81]. Since that time the three member States have been increasing their ambitions. They intended to carry out the ECU project within a wider framework for advanced economic integration – a single economic space, followed by an economic union. They envisaged a common market of goods, capital and labour, and the operation of common macroeconomic, competition, financial and other regulation. In November 2011, in their Declaration on Eurasian Economic Integration, the heads of state of the three countries announced that the Single Economic Space would be launched as of 1 January 2012. They also established a new body, the Eurasian Economic Commission, which replaced the Customs Union Commission as of 1 July 2012, as the common coordinating institution to assure the achievement of the agreed intentions. The legal basis of the ECU and the Single Economic Space were planned to be fully in place within three years. Developments then culminated in the conclusion of a basic treaty creating a Eurasian Economic Union on 29 May 2014, which has entered into force on 1 January 2015.[82]

Until recently regional integration in the post-Soviet space was largely declarative. But the Eurasian Customs Union (ECU) and now the Eurasian Economic Union, the latest initiative, proves more competitive because of its better institutional framework, commitment to implementation and introduction of a system of rules harmonized with international norms and the WTO regime.

79 Dreyer/Popescu, The Eurasian Customs Union: The economics and the politics, p. 2, see also: http://www.iss.europa.eu/uploads/media/Brief_11_Eurasian_Union.pdf, 21.09.2016.

80 The common customs tariff of the Customs Union of the Republic of Belarus, Kazakhstan and Russian Federation (UCT of the CU) is a set of rates of import customs duties applied to goods imported into the common customs territory of the Customs Union from third countries, classified according to the unified Foreign Economic Activity Commodity Nomenclature of the Customs Union (FEACN of the CU). http://www.eurasian commission.org/en/act/ trade/catr/ett/Pages/default.aspx.

81 Dragneva/Wolczuk, Russia, the Eurasian Customs Union and the EU: Cooperation, Stagnation or Rivalry?, p. 4,
See also: https://www.chathamhouse.org/sites/files/chathamhouse/public/Research/Russia%20and%20Eurasia/0812bp_dragnevawolczuk.pdf, 21.09.2106

82 See http://eaeunion.org.

The Eurasian Economic Union (EAEU) is an attempt by Russia to create a competitor to the European Union and its Eastern Partnership project in the post-Soviet space, and it attracted international attention when Moscow started to pressure Georgia, Moldova and Ukraine to join the grouping and queer their pitch to sign Association Agreements with the EU. The EAEU is an instrument through which Russia increasingly engages in 'normative rivalry' with the EU in the so-called 'shared neighborhood'. This means that Russia relies not only on 'soft' power, energy conditionality and military strength, but also on an organizational instrument with a broader economic and political orientation. It could be discussed whether through the EAEU Russia attempts to make its own hunt to become a normative power as an actor whose prospect of its foreign policy role and behavior is bound to particular aims, values, principles, as well as forms of influence and instruments.[83]

2. Association Agreements

The Association Agreements proposed by the EU to Georgia, Moldova and Ukraine are pioneering documents: they were the first comprehensive agreements based on the results of a political association between the EU and any of the Eastern Partnership countries, and they are unprecedented in their breadth (number of areas covered) and depth (detail of commitments and timelines). The key elements of these AAs focus on support to realize reforms, economic recovery and growth, and governance and sector cooperation in areas such as energy, transport and environmental protection, industrial cooperation, social development and protection, equal rights, consumer protection, education, youth, and cultural cooperation. The Agreements also draw attention on values and principles: democracy and the rule of law, respect for human rights and fundamental freedoms, good governance, a market economy and sustainable development.[84] The EU clarified and reinforced its offer around three major pillars:

First, the "upgrading" of the existing bilateral treaty relations with an Association Agreement that should include a deep and comprehensive free trade area (DCFTA[85]) with each country. Secondly, a progressive visa liberalization in exchange for creating a secure environment; thirdly, deeper cooperation to enhance the energy security of the partners and the EU.[86] The creation of a DCFTA in the framework of an AA involves a profound influence on the regulatory framework

83 Diez, Constructing the Self and Changing Others: Reconsidering Normative Power Europe 33(3) Millennium Journal of International Studies (2005), p.613, 617.

84 http://eeas.europa.eu/delegations/ukraine/eu_ukraine/association_agreement/index_en.htm.

85 A Deep and Comprehensive Free Trade Area will go further than classic free trade areas, as it will open up markets, but also address competitiveness issues and the steps needed to meet EU standards and trade on EU markets.

86 European Commission: "Eastern Partnership", Communication to the Council and to the European Parliament, COM(2008), 823 final, 3 December 2008,4.

of the country associated with the EU in a wide range of areas. Among other things, EU regulations have to be implemented entirely – no selection is permitted. This is to ensure the credibility of commitment and prevent selective implementation based on self-serving interpretations of the country entering into an association agreement with the EU.[87] Flexing its "market power" strength, the EU demands the adoption of the economic acquis communautaire by third countries, which are granted accession to the single European market, to ensure the coherence of the internal market, reflecting the centrality of sector-specific, technical international rules to the EU as an international organization and foreign policy actor.[88] The EU's strategy demands adoption of reforms in a short period of time – five to eight years – while the positive influence of these changes may not be immediately visible. Therefore, as was the case during enlargement, the ENP/Eastern Partnership relies on 'deferred gratification' along the lines of reforms now, benefits later'.[89] Many aspects of the reforms promoted by the EU are highly technocratic and relate to a wide range of policies and institutions, such as intellectual property, regulation of state aids, migration legislation and phytosanitary standards, making it difficult to target and engage non-governmental organizations and a broader domestic audience. An EU Association Agreement can be briefly described as an instrument for the promotion of domestic reforms in its Eastern neighbours.[90]

III. Legal, political and economic effects of the AAs of Ukraine, Georgia, Moldova on their relations with Russia

1. Ukraine

On 27 June 2014, the European Union Heads of State and Government and the Ukrainian President Petro Poroshenko signed the EU-Ukraine Association Agreement in Brussels. The Verkhovna Rada and the European Parliament simultaneously ratified the Association Agreement on 16 September 2014[91].The economic effects of the Deep and Comprehensive Free Trade Area established by the AA will go further than classic free trade areas, as the DCFTA will open up

87 Eurasian Economic Integration: Law, Policy and Politics, edited by Rilka Dragneva and Kataryna Wolczuk, p.186.

88 Lavenex/Schimmelfennig 'EU Rules Beyond EU Borders' Theorizing External Governance in the European Politics 2009, 16 (6) Journal of European Public Policy 791; Damro, 'Market Power Europe' (2012) 19(5) European Public Policy, p. 682.

89 European Commission on 'Strengthening Neighborhood Policy: Time for a Rethink ', ELIAMEP Thesis, Hellenic Foundation for European and Foreign Policy, April 2009.

90 Eurasian Economic Integration: Law, Policy and Politics, edited by Rilka Dragneva and Kataryna Wolczuk, 186.

91 http://eeas.europa.eu/delegations/ukraine/eu_ukraine/association_agreement/index_en.htm.

markets, but also address competitiveness issues and the steps needed to meet the EU standards and trade on the EU markets.[92]

Russia sees this incoming orientation of the economies of Georgia, Moldova and Ukraine to Western markets a threat to its own position in these countries and has since been exceedingly active in rising a series of punitive trade sanctions against Ukraine (but also against the other two countries) as from the date of the signing of the AA/DCFTA with the EU. These measures were substantially increased at a time from April to August 2014, after the election on 27 May 2014 of President Poroshenko. Most punitive sanctions concern agri-food products, for which the Russian regulatory agency produced allegations of non-conformity with required standards. Though, also was stopped by Russia for several weeks the import from Ukraine of railcars on grounds of alleged technical defects. Moreover, gas supplies from Russia were entirely stopped in June 2014.

Some examples of Russian punitive measures against Ukraine:

- Ban on imports of Ukrainian confectionary producer Roshen (July 2013).
- Enhanced border control for imports from Ukraine (August 2013).
- Ban on imports of Ukrainian railcars (September-October 2013).
- Ban on imports from a large Ukrainian poultry producer (February 2014).
- Ban on imports of selected kinds of cheese from Ukraine (April 2014).
- Ban on imports of potatoes from Ukraine (June 2014).
- Stoppage of gas supplies to Ukraine (June 2014).

In July 2014 the Russian government published a draft regulation[93] concerning the possible cancellation of the tariff-free trade preferences, which exist between Russia and the Ukraine under the CIS Free Trade Agreement (CIS FTA). This would lead (and has indeed since a presidential decree of December 2015) to the introduction of most favored nation (MFN) duties for selected categories of Ukrainian exports. As alleged by some researchers, a full cancellation of the Ukrainian CIS FTA preferences by Russia could result in a $3 billion decrease in exports from Ukraine, which would amount to 17% of its total exports to Russia, and come out at approximately 1.7% of its GDP[94]. The probability that Russia would implement its threat to suspend the CIS Free Trade Agreement in its relations with Ukraine was for an interim phase reduced at a trilateral meeting in Brussels between representatives of the EU, Ukraine and Russia on 12 September

92 http://eeas.europa.eu/images/top_stories/140912_eu-ukraine-associatin-agreement-quick_guide.pdf.

93 http://regulation.gov.ru/project/17072.html?point=view_project&stage=3&stage_id=1094.

94 Ryzhenkov/Movchan/Giucci (2013), "Impact assessment of a possible change in Russia's trade regime vis-à-vis Ukraine", Policy Brief 04/2013, Institute for Economic Research and Policy Consulting, Kyiv (www.ier.com.ua/en/publications/policy_briefing_series/archive_2013/?pid=4549).

2014. At this meeting it was decided to postpone the 'provisionalimplementation' of large parts of the Association Agreement, including the DCFTA, until 1 January 2016. At the same time Russian media were prompted to declare that this was a great breakthrough for Russian interests. Admittedly the Russian government apparently felt that it had reached an opportunity to negotiate an agenda of substantial significance, and that in the intervening period new political circumstances might emerge that could realize opportunities to frustrate the whole Association Agreement including the DCFTA. However, this did not take place, and now Ukraine has started to live without CIS FTA preferences with Russia.Ukraine has an unique and a key geographical position, because of its history of relations between the fraternal peoples of Russia and Ukraine, which is full of uncertainties and dramatic moments. Zbigniew Brzezinski in "The Grand Chessboard" argues that Russia needs Ukraine to restore the status of the Eurasian empire: "Ukraine is a new and important space on the Eurasian chessboard, it is a geopolitical center, because its existence as an independent country helps to transform Russia. Without Ukraine, Russia ceases to be a Eurasian empire. Russia without Ukraine can still fight for imperial status, but then it would be mostly an Asian imperial state". "If Ukraine gets fully integrated into the European structures, this will put a final end to the geopolitical onslaught of Russia to the West", Brzezinski writes and adds: "The new world order under US hegemony created against Russia and the wreckage of Russia. Ukraine for us - it is an outpost of the West against the restoration of the Soviet Union“.[95]

More recently, Jan Tombinski European Union Ambassador to Ukraine declared: "I notice with sadness that Russia has been putting Ukraine under intense pressure over the past months, through disruptions to trade, revocation of contracts, illegal use of food safety measures and other means. And the EU has condemned such actions as strong as possible. We deplore Russian interference in Ukraine's sovereign right to decide for itself its own future economic and foreign policy. Let me be clear: none of the problems being caused by Russia have got anything to do with the impact of the Association Agreement and the Deep and Comprehensive Free Trade Agreement (DCFTA). There is nothing in the Association Agreement which changes any aspect of the trade and economic relationship between Ukraine and Russia, or between Ukraine and any other trade partner".[96]

2. Georgia

Russia began to impose trade restrictions on Georgian agricultural products already at the end of 2005. By the first half of 2006 there was a complete embargo on all Georgian agricultural prod-

95 http://izvestia.ru/news/561395.
96 http://eeas.europa.eu/delegations/ukraine/press_corner/all_news/news/2013/2013_11_28_1_en.htm.

ucts. Russia used allegations of sanitary and phytosanitary standards and health concerns and then introduced an apparently political embargo on all agricultural products, which lasted for more than six years. The Russian trade sanctions were its first reaction in a series to Georgia's public statements after the Rose Revolution to become a part of the EU's political and economic space and a member of NATO. However, the Russian embargo provided to a healthy trend of divergence in Georgian exports. In the years of the Russian embargo Georgia's total agricultural exports increased by 90%. Consequently before the embargo Georgia exported wine to 36 countries, by 2011 Georgian producers had entered 15 new markets, including China, Poland, Germany and Singapore. Georgia's agricultural sector also continued to remain attractive to foreign direct investment (FDI) despite the Russian embargo. All this happened in the context of the international economic and financial crisis of these years, and before the DCFTA with the EU was concluded.

Georgia did not retaliate by an accusation against Russia's punitive measures. Despite of raising tensions between the two countries and their 2008 war, which resulted in Russia's occupation of approximately 20% of Georgia, Georgia under no circumstances provided restrictions in trade or investment. Also, the Georgian government by no means applied to Russia to lift the trade embargo, even in the framework of its WTO accession negotiations with Russia. However the Rus

sian embargo is counter to WTO rules and the Georgian-Russian FTA, its full abolishment has not been achieved and trade is not yet back to normal.[97]

3. Moldova

From September 2013 to September 2014, Russia applied a range of trade limitations with Moldova. Most cases concernedagri-food products and were based on the results of allegations of non-conformity with Russian safety requirements. The first punitive measures in September 2013 were passed to dissuade Moldova from initialing the AA/DCFTA with the EU, which actually took place at the Vilnius summit in November 2013. Comparable measures followed in April and July 2014, for a short while before and after the signing of the AA/DCFTA on 27 June 2014.On 31 August 2014, Russia's punitive actions were expanded by suspending the tariff-free preferences between Russia and Moldova under the 2011 CIS Free Trade Agreement for 19 categories of mainly agri-food products. It is noteworthy that there were no technical justifications, but Russia obviously claimed recourse to a general provision in Annex no. 6 to the CIS FTA agreement that states conditions "damaging or threatening to damage" industries of the Russian-led customs

---

97 CEPS WORKING DOCUMENT: Russian's Punitive Trade Policy Measures towards Ukraine, Moldova and Georgia edited by Denis Cenusa, Michael Emerson, Tamara Kovziridse and Veronika Movchan №.400/September 2014.

union may be used to justifying scrapping the tariff preferences and to impose the MFN tariffs applied to WTO members.[98]

Some examples of Russia's punitive trade measures against Moldova between 2013 and 2014:

- Ban on imports of Moldovan wine (September 2013).
- Ban on imports of processed pork meat products (8 April 2014).
- Ban on imports of canned vegetables (July 2014).
- Ban on fruit imports (July 2014).
- Cancellation of trade preferences for imports of 19 categories of products (31 August 2014).[99]

IV. Conclusion

Russia's political measures in the case of Ukraine, Georgia and Moldova lead to the following overall evaluation: The punishment has been a series of trade restricting punitive actions under the title of non-tariff barriers such as health and safety regulations, up to and including revocation of free trade preferences. Non-tariff trade barriers have been used with cunning. It is not plausible that the technical conformity of products from these three countries should be balanced in correlation with Russian geopolitical postures. This reversal of technical standards is counter to WTO rules, which demand that any such trade limitations are provided by a transparent presentation to the trade partners of their scientific bases. Russia's actions have a material economic influence, decreasing trade flows with Russia and pushing the three AA/DCFTA States to make intensified marketing efforts in the EU and other world markets. This will probably lead to sustainable changes in trade structures, since the reputational negatives being accumulated by Russia as a trade partner will be lasting. The reorientation of trade flows in relation to the EU has to outdo the strict technical standards that apply. These standards are strict in an inherent technical sense, and are administered free of political interference. For these three countries, their political and economic goals in having good trade relations with both the EU and Russia are certainly clear and rational. The European Union would doubtlessly welcome if Ukraine, Georgia and Moldova had sustainable and propitious CIS Free Trade Agreements with Russia.[100]

98 CEPS WORKING DOCUMENT: Russian's Punitive Trade Policy Measures towards Ukraine, Moldova and Georgia edited by Denis Cenusa, Michael Emerson, Tamara Kovziridse and Veronika Movchan №.400/September 2014.

99 Expert Group, "Economic Reality", July 2014 (http://expert-grup.org/ro/biblioteca/item/999-re-iulie2014-47&category=7).

100 CEPS WORKING DOCUMENT: Russian's Punitive Trade Policy Measures towards Ukraine, Moldova and Georgia edited by Cenusa/Emerson/Kovziridse/Movchan №.400/September 2014.

Vadym Karnaukh

Approximation of Law as a General Topic of the Three Association Agreements in Comparison with the PCAs

I. Introduction

The East European Neighborhood Policy is an essential part of EU foreign policy, which is not only an instrument of strengthening of geopolitics aspirations of the EU, but also a way of creating a unique field for cooperation, especially in the legal dimension. The main aim of this paper is to compare the Partnership and Cooperation Agreements (PCAs) of Georgia, Moldova and Ukraine with the recently concluded Association Agreements (AAs) which undoubtedly represent the modern approach of EU legal policy. This comparative analysis is devoted to the topic of approximation of law. At the start, some general remarks about such theoretical concepts as harmonization, approximation, *acquis communautaire* will be made in order to have a background view about initial conceptions, which will afterwards be seen in the PCAs and the AAs. Attention is also paid to legal reality and possible challenges for approximation of law in Ukraine in connection with the AA.

II. Interactions between harmonization and legislative approximation

This section of the paper deals with the basic understanding of harmonization and approximation of law. It also reveals peculiarities of interrelation between these concepts in the external dimension of the EU legal policy.

1. Definition of harmonization

There are meanings of harmonization as the method of legal integration[101] and the process.[102]

[101] As S. Ju. Kashkin puts it: "Harmonization is softer method of legal integration that takes place on the basis of approximation of the internal law to a certain legislative model. It does not mean uniformity but is based on legislation approximation between different states". See S. Ju. Kashkin 'Strategy and mechanisms of legislation harmonization between Russia and the European Union as key components of their effective mutual development in the XXI century' Russian-European Centre for Economic Policy Moscov, 2005, 41 p. at p.10.

[102] For E J Lohse "harmonization is conscious process that has the aim to lead to the insertion of a concept into the national legal orders, which triggers a process of adaptation to form a European concept as uniform as required to serve the objectives of the European Union". See E J Lohse 'The Meaning of Harmonization in the Context of European Community Law — a Process in Need of Definition' in Mads Andenas and Camilla Baasch Andersen (eds), Theory and Practice of Harmonization (Edward Elgar Publishing, 2012), pp.282-314 at p.313.

2. Definition and function of approximation of law in the EU context

In the European Union, the concept of approximation of law means the process of harmonizing of national legislation with the EU law. The process of approximation includes methods and techniques for transposing the EU legislation into the national law, its incorporation into the national legal systems and the process of implementation.[103]It should be noted that the approximation ensures the working model of common market in the EU.[104]

3. Interdependence of harmonization and approximation in the EU context

The necessity of the initial object for the completeness of meaning of the concept of legislative approximation seems undoubted. In our case such object is the legal order of the EU or the "existing standards" within the legal order of the EU.[105] To our understanding, approximation of law as a legal process is the essential precondition of harmonisation as a legal result, which is embodied in harmonised law. One can also agree with the understanding that approximation of law is a part of harmonisation in a wide theoretical dimension.[106]

4. Use of terms describing approximation and harmonization in the PCAs and the AAs

In the PCAs one can find the term "approximation of existing and future legislation to that of the Community".[107] "Approximation of national legislation to EU law" is used in the AAs.[108] Besides, in the PCAs we can find such terms as "approximation of a system to that of the Community", "approximation of standards", "improvement of laws", "achieving compatibility".[109] In the AAs the use of different terms is also common.[110]

103 'Practical Guidelines for Legal Approximation of the Legislation of the Republic of Kosovo with the Legislation of the European Union' Republic of Kosovo, 2014, 82 p. at p. 37.

104 According to E J Lohse: "approximation of laws and the establishment of a common market are inextricably linked, since harmonised law is perceived as one of the main instruments to build a common market and differences in the legal orders are seen as obstacles to the free movement of production factors, the core element of the internal market" E J Lohse op. cit. (fn.2), p.289.

105 This wording is used by E J Lohse scrutinizing the objects and directions of the harmonization in the context of European Community Law. E J Lohse considers such standard as "the standard for harmonisation to which the domestic law is to be approximated"E J Lohse op. cit. (fn.2), p.307, 313.

106 See A. Matta, 'Differentiating the methods of acquis export – the case of the Eastern Neighbourhood and Russia', pp. 21-45 at p.27 in P. Van Elsuwege, R. Petrov (Eds.) Legislative Approximation and Application of EU Law in the Eastern Neighborhood of the European Union. Towards a Common Regulatory Space?,(Routledge, 2014) 268 p.

107 Art. 43 EU-Georgia PCA; Art. 50 EU-Moldova PCA; Art. 51 EU-Ukraine PCA.

108 Art. 417 EU-Georgia AA; Art. 448 EU-Moldova AA; Art. 474 EU-Ukraine AA.

109 For instance, see Art. 55, 57, 66, 67 EU-Georgia PCA.

110 For example, "achieving compatibility with the EU acquis" in Art. 114 EU-Ukraine AA or "gradually achieving conformity with the Union's technical regulations and standards in Art. 173 EU-Moldova AA.

III. The general concept of *acquis communautaire*

This section of the contribution will first provide the definition of *acquis communautaire*. Then, we will briefly look into its mission in the EU legal policy through the prism of dynamic functioning.

1. Definition of acquis communautaire

The Community acquis is the body of common rights and obligations which binds all the Member States together within the European Union. It is constantly evolving and comprises: the content, principles and political objectives of the Treaties; the legislation adopted in application of the treaties and the case law of the Court of Justice; the declarations and resolutions adopted by the Union; measures relating to the common foreign and security policy; measures relating to justice and home affairs; international agreements concluded by the Community and those concluded by the Member States between themselves in the field of the Union's activities.[111]

2. Acquis communautaire as a transformative engagement instrument

The importance of the acquis communautaire as an influential and transformative instrument of the legal policy of the EU is fairly justified.[112]

3. Acquis export

The export of the acquis involves the establishment and development of cooperation, dialogue and monitoring (strengthened in some cases by financial assistance and technical aid) on issues such as trade, competition, standards, transport, environment, justice and home affairs, human rights and democracy.[113] It has been proposed to distinguish the following means of exporting the dynamic acquis communautaire: a) homogeneity; b) binding and soft-harmonization commitments; c) approximation clauses; d) a mutual recognition regime.[114] There are also further approaches to the differentiation of methods of the acquis export.[115]

---

111 <europa.eu/scadplus/glossary/community_acquis_en.htm>, accessed 27 February 2015.

112 A. Magen distinguished 'internal order' acquis that represents the inherited patrimony of the Community and acts to preserve the unique genetic code of European integration; and a second, 'transformative engagement' (or 'governance export') personality, whose purpose is the outward projection of EU norms and the advancement of its interests abroad. See Amichai Magen 'Transformative Engagement Through Law: The Acquis Communautaire as an Instrument of EU External Influence in European Journal of Law Reform Volume 9 Number 3, 2007, pp.361-393, at p.392.

113 A. Matta op. cit. (fn.6), p.34.

114 R. Petrov 'Exporting the Acquis Communautaireinto the Legal Systems of Third Countries' in European Foreign Affairs Review 13, 2008. pp. 33-52, at p.37.

115 A.Matta names such methods of acquis export to neighbouring countries: (binding) harmonization (aimed at countries in the context of accession); homogeneity and/or mutual recognition; approximation/compatibility; and the new approach of approximation/convergence (aimed at integration without accession with the Eastern

IV. Approximation of law in the PCAs

The main purpose of this section of the paper is to evaluate the PCAs mechanism of approximation of law as a complex object with some stable characteristics. It tries to explain also the role of PCAs in the context of the EU legal policy.

1. PCAs as the instrument of the EU legal policy

The EU-Ukraine PCA, which was signed in 1994, entered into force in March 1998.[116] The EU-Georgia PCA was concluded in 1996 and entered into force in 1999.[117] The EU-Moldova PCA was signed on 28 November 1994, entering into force on 1 July 1998.[118] The meaning of the PCAs as instruments that set both the legal framework for the cooperation between the EU and partner countries and the basis for voluntary harmonization has been noted.[119] The PCAs were sometimes classified as "entry-level agreements"[120] that do not provide for membership of the EU, but rather set up further mutual co-operation between the Parties. It was also emphasized that the legal sense of the PCAs was cooperation under significant control of the EU with a view to "keeping the distance".[121] To our understanding, the significance of the PCAs could also be understood in wider scope. On the one hand, these instruments reflect the expansion of the EU with simultaneous enlargement of the global market in a liberal economic institutional space supported by the WTO, the IMF and the World Bank. On the other hand, they serve as an instrument of strengthening the political influence of the EU itself as a supranational subject of power by providing opportunities for developing countries to enter the afore-cited world economy model. From our point of view, the same statement is fair for the AAs.

Partnership countries, and to a lesser extent Russia and perhaps the rest of the Euro-Mediterranean Partnership countries) A. Matta op. cit. (fn.6), p. 44.

116 <eu-un.europa.eu/articles/es/article_3345_es.htm>, accessed 27 February 2015.

117 <unece.org/fileadmin/DAM/env/epr/experts/Georgia/Policymaking/ENP/EU_Georgia_country%20report_2005.pdf>, accessed 27 February 2015.

118 <en.wikipedia.org/wiki/Moldova–European_Union_relations#Agreements>, accessed 27 February 2015.

119 V. Muravyov 'Legal approximation: evidence from Ukraine',The European Neighbourhood Policy: A Framework for Modernization? Workshop organized by Profs. Marise Cremona and WojciechSadurski in European University Institute 1-2 December, 2006 8 p., at p.1-2.

120 R. Petrov 'The Partnership and Cooperation Agreements with the Newly Independent States' in A. Ott and K. Inglis (eds), European Enlargement Handbook(Asser Press, the Hague 2002) pp. 175–194, at p.177.

121 As R. Petrov puts it: "the PCAs served their purpose as reliable legal instruments in sustaining long-term relations with the PCA countries, while holding them at a controllable distance from closer access to the EC Internal Market". See R. Petrov 'The New EU-Ukraine Enhanced Agreement Versus the EU-Ukraine Partnership and Cooperation Agreement : Transitional Path or Final Destination?' in F. Maiani, R. Petrov, E. Mouliarova (eds) EUI Working Papers MWP. - 2009. - No. 10: European Integration without EU Membership: Models, Experiences, Perspectives p. 39-45, at p. 43.

2. The structure of the mechanism of approximation of law in the PCAs

In what follows the approximation of law in the PCAs is analyzed in more detail in order to illustrate the level of complexity of the set of provisions related to approximation of law.

a) General approximation clause

The PCAs contain general clauses (provisions) on the approximation of law which are literally identical.[122] It is not difficult to observe that the PCAs general approximation clauses are more about encouraging states to start the process of approximation than containing solid legal commitments. The ambiguity of the approximation pattern in the PCAs has been noted.[123] The areas where approximation of law should extend to are named in the general provisions.[124]

b) Specific provisions on the approximation of law

There are specific provisions in the PCAs, which generally contain non-binding rules and relate to various areas. The specific provisions should be seen as incorporated in the mechanism of approximation of law although they rarely refer literally to approximation of law itself.[125] Very few of these provisions include binding rules and have time frames for fulfillment.[126] Thus, almost all these specific provisions do not create a complex mechanism of their implementation in national law systems.

c) Cooperation between parties

Here we will try to cover probable ways of cooperation between Contracting Parties in the field of legislative approximation.

122 See Art. 43 EU-Georgia PCA; Art. 50 EU-Moldova PCA; Art. 51 EU-Ukraine PCA. For example, Art. 50 EU-Moldova PCA says that: "The Parties recognize that an important condition for strengthening the economic links between the Republic of Moldova and the Community is the approximation ofthe Republic of Moldova and the Community is the approximation ofthe Republic of Moldova's existing and future legislation to that of the Community. The Republic of Moldova shall endeavor to ensure that its legislation will be gradually made compatible with that of the Community".

123 According to R. Petrov, "the PCAs' approximation clause is neither directly linked to the evolutionary clause, nor is it considered as the agreement's objective". See Roman Petrov, "How Far to Endeavour? Recent Developments in the Adaptation of Ukrainian Legislation to EU Laws", 8(1) European Foreign Affairs Review (2003), 17 p., at p.7.

124 They are: customs law, company law, banking law, company accounts and taxes, intellectual property, protection of workers at the workplace, financial services, rules on competition, public procurement, protection of health and life of humans, animals and plants, the environment, consumer protection, indirect taxation, technical rules and standards, nuclear laws and regulations, transport.

125 For example, we can consider consumer protection in Art. 75 EU-Ukraine PCA which says that: "the Parties will enter into close co-operation aimed at achieving compatibility between their systems of consumer protection".

126 For instance, Art. 49-2 EU- Moldova PCA which namely says that: "by the end of the fifth year after entry into force of the Agreement, the Republic of Moldova shall accede to the multilateral conventions on intellectual, industrial and commercial property rights referred to in Paragraph 1 of Annex III to which Member States of the Community are parties or which are de facto applied by Member States according to the relevant provisions contained in these conventions.".

aa) Monitoring of approximation

There are provisions in the PCAs solely providing for the establishment of a Cooperation Council with general competences, which shall supervise the implementation of the Agreement, examine any major issues arising within the framework of the Agreement and any other bilateral or international issues of mutual interest for the purpose of attaining the objectives of the PCA, make appropriate recommendations, by agreement between the two Parties, may decide to set up any other special committee or body that can assist it in carrying out its duties and shall determine the composition and duties of such committees or bodies and how they shall function.[127] Having this in mind, we can conclude that the monitoring of approximation is not directly defined nor detailed, but only hypothetically implied.

bb) Financial assistance

There is the institute of financial assistance which, though, is not directly linked with the approximation of law, but which implies such a purpose.[128] Financial assistance is presented in the form of grants which are given for setting up indicative programs reflecting established priorities to be agreed between the two Contracting Parties; covered within the framework of TACIS.[129]

cc) Technical assistance

This kind of cooperation between parties deals directly with the approximation of law.[130]

V. Approximation of law in the AAs

In this section of the paper the mechanism of approximation of law in the AAs will be scrutinized in order to compare it with the PCAs one and to prove its differences. The position of AAs in the context of EU legal policy is also addressed.

1. Association Agreements as instrument of the EU legal policy

The EU-Ukraine AA was signed in two steps on 21 March 2014 and 27 June 2014.[131] So far, the agreement has been ratified by the EU, Ukraine and 27 (of 28)EU member countries.[132] Due to a

127 See Art. 85,88 EU- Ukraine PCA, Art. 82,85 EU-Moldova PCA, Art. 81,84 EU-Georgia PCA.

128 See Art. 81-84 EU-Ukraine PCA, Art. 78-82 EU-Moldova PCA, Art. 77-80 EU-Georgia PCA.

129 Technical Assistance to the Commonwealth of Independent States. See <en.wikipedia.org/wiki/Technical_Aid_to_the_Commonwealth_of_Independent_States>, accessed 27 February 2015.

130 See Art. 43-44 EU-Georgia PCA, Art. 50-3 EU-Moldova PCA, Art. 51 EU- Ukraine PCA. In particular, Art. 50-3 EU-Moldova PCA states that: "The Community shall provide the Republic of Moldova with technical assistance as appropriate for the implementation of these measures which may include i.e.: the exchange of experts; the provision of early information especially on relevant legislation; organization of seminars; training activities; aid for translation of Community legislation in the relevant sectors.

131 The political provisions of the AA were signed on March, 21 2014 and Titles III, IV, V and VI, related Annexes and Protocols were signed on June, 27 2014. See <en.wikipedia.org/wiki/Ukraine–European_Union_Association_Agreement>, accessed 27 February 2015.

negative popular referendum against the AA in the Netherlands on 6 April 2016 the Dutch Government was not yet able to deposit the ratification documents, and the full entry into force of the EU-Ukraine AA is therefore still pending. However, the AA – including its provisions on approximation of law - is applied provisorily on the basis of two decisions of the Council of the EU of 17 March 2014 and 1 November 2014.[133] The EU-Georgia AA and the EU-Moldova AAs were signed on 27 June 2014 and have entered into force on 1 July 2016.[134] The AAs are considered to be agreements based on a 'privileged link' between an associate country and the EC.[135] The comprehensiveness, complexity and conditionality were noted as the three specific features of the EU-Ukraine AA as the innovative legal instrument. The comprehensiveness means covering an extremely wide range of fields where relations between a state and the EU exist. The complexity is related to the setting of a DCFTA with countries through complicated mechanisms of legal approximation. The conditionality refers to the preamble to the agreement which explicitly states that "political association and economic integration of Ukraine within the European Union will depend on progress in the implementation of the current agreement as well as Ukraine's track record in ensuring respect for common values, and progress in achieving convergence with the EU in political, economic and legal areas".[136]From our point of view, this set of features is fairly applicable in regard to the EU-Georgia AA and EU-Moldova AA.

2. The structure of the mechanism of approximation of law in the AAs

Below the approximation of law is being explored in more detail in order to illustrate the peculiarities of the mechanism of approximation of law in contrast to the PCAs.

a) General approximation clause

The AAs like the PCAs contain general clauses on the approximation of law which, however, are more complex and can be described as three levels. On the first level a general clause is placed among the objectives of the AAs.[137] It should also be noted here that the approximation of legisla-

---

132 <consilium.europa.eu/en/documents-publications/agreements-conventions/agreement/?aid=2014045>, accessed 6 September 2016. In a referendum in the Netherlands on 6 April 2016 the majority of voters voted against ratification of the AA. The Dutch Government has therefore not yet deposited the ratification documents; the time of final entering into force of the AA is therefore still open.

133 See http://eur-lex.europa.eu/legal-content/EN/TXT/HTML/?uri=CELEX:22014X1031(01)&from=DE#ntr1-L_2014311EN.01000101-E0001.

134 <en.wikipedia.org/wiki/Georgia–European_Union_relations> and <en.wikipedia.org/wiki/Moldova European_ Union_ Association_ Agreement>, accessed 6 September 2016.accessed 6September 2016.

135 R. Petrovop. cit. (fn. 20), p.178.

136 Guillaume Van der Loo, Peter Van Elsuwege and Roman Petrov, The EU-Ukraine Association Agreement: Assessment of an Innovative Legal Instrument EUI Working Paper LAW 2014/09 28 p., at p.2-3.

137 See Art. 1(d) EU-Ukraine AA; Art. 1 (g) EU-Georgia AA; Art. 1 (f) EU-Moldova AA For example, Art. 1 (g) EU-Georgia AA states that: "the aim of the association is, *inter alia*, to support the efforts of Georgia to develop its economic potential through international cooperation, including through the approximation of its legislation to that of the EU".

tion is considered among the objectives of the Agreement in contradistinction to the PCA's approach. On the second and more prominent level we can discover a general clause among the institutional, general and final provisions of the AAs.[138] The difference in comparison of the general provisions on approximation of law of the three AAs should be noticed on this level. Art. 474 of the EU-Ukraine AA sets the rule of gradual approximation.[139] The provisions of the EU-Georgia AA and the EU-Moldova AA set the rule of dynamic approximation in addition to the rule of gradual approximation.[140] On the third level a general approximation clause is related to technical regulations, standards, and conformity assessment where the countries are not only committed to ensure conformity of national legislation with relevant EU *acquis* but also to 'follow the principles and practices' laid down in the EU *acquis*.[141]

b) Standard approximation clauses

The AAs contain standard approximation clauses which cover different areas (sectors) where an approximation of law is necessary.[142] It is notable that in some areas standard approximation clauses are absent.[143] Having considered all this, we can observe that the number of sectors where an approximation of law is necessary is much wider than in the PCAs. Besides, the level of legal

138 See Art. 474 EU-Ukraine AA; Art. 417-418 EU-Georgia AA; Art. 448-449 EU-Moldova AA.

139 *Inter alia*, it namely says that: "In line with the objectives of this Agreement as set out in Article 1, Ukraine will carry out gradual approximation of its legislation to EU law as referred to in Annexes I to XLIV to this Agreement, based on commitments identified in Titles IV, V and VI of this Agreement, and according to the provisions of those Annexes".

140 For example, Art. 449 EU-Moldova AA says that: "In line with the goal of gradual approximation by the Republic of Moldova to EU law, and in particular as regards the commitments identified in Titles III, IV, V and VI of this Agreement, and according to the provisions of the Annexes, the Association Council shall periodically revise and update those Annexes, including to take into account the evolution of EU law as defined in this Agreement.

141 See Art. 56 EU-Ukraine AA; Art. 173 EU-Moldova AA; Art. 47 EU-Georgia AA.

142 See consumer protection (Art. 347 EU-Georgia AA, Art. 40 EU-Moldova AA, Art. 417 EU-Ukraine AA); customs legislation (Art. 75 EU-Georgia AA, Art. 201 EU-Moldova AA, Art. 84 EU-Ukraine AA); sanitary and phytosanitary and animal welfare legislation (Art. 55 EU-Georgia AA, Art. 181 EU-Moldova AA, Art. 64 EU-Ukraine AA); public procurement(Art. 146 EU-Georgia AA, Art. 273 EU-Moldova AA, Art. 153 EU-Ukraine AA); taxation (Art. 285 EU-Georgia AA, Art. 57 EU-Moldova AA, Art. 353 EU-Ukraine AA); statistics (Art. 286 EU-Georgia AA, Art. 46 EU-Moldova AA, Art. 358 EU-Ukraine AA); transport (Art. 296 EU-Georgia AA, Art. 85 EU-Moldova AA, Art. 368 EU-Ukraine AA); environment (Art. 306 EU-Georgia AA, Art. 91 EU-Moldova AA, Art. 363 EU-Ukraine AA); customs legislation (Art. 75 EU-Georgia AA, Art. 201 EU-Moldova AA, Art. 84 EU-Ukraine AA); company law, accounting, and auditing and corporate governance (Art. 319 EU-Georgia AA, Art. 30 EU-Moldova AA, Art. 387 EU-Ukraine AA); agriculture and rural development (Art. 70 EU-Moldova AA, Art. 403 EU-Ukraine AA); employment, social policy and equal opportunities (Art. 354 EU-Georgia AA, Art. 37 EU-Moldova AA, Art. 424 EU-Ukraine AA); public health (Art. 357 EU-Georgia AA, Art. 116 EU-Moldova AA, Art. 428 EU-Ukraine AA); information society (Art. 327 EU-Georgia AA, Art. 102 EU-Moldova AA, Art. 394 EU-Ukraine AA); postal and courier services (Art. 103 EU-Georgia AA, Art. 230 EU-Moldova AA, Art. 114 EU-Ukraine AA); electronic communication services (Art. 110 EU-Georgia AA, Art. 240 EU-Moldova AA, Art. 124 EU-Ukraine AA); financial services (Art. 323 EU-Georgia AA, Art. 249 EU-Moldova AA, Art. 385 EU-Ukraine AA); transport services (Art. 126 EU Georgia AA, Art. 253 EU-Moldova AA, Art. 138 EU-Ukraine AA.

143 For example, approximation clause in the area of agriculture and rural development is absent in EU-Georgia AA. In our opinion, it's because of economic potential of Georgia in this sector which seems to be not developed enough for the need of formulating appropriate approximation clause.

specification is greatly higher. In the AAs the general clause with standard approximation clauses making reference to the essential Annex of the AA design the complicated legal mechanism of approximation of law.[144] The great majority of the AAs standard approximation clauses in comparison to the PCAs provisions contain binding rules with timetables of their fulfillment in detailed lists of the EU sectoral acquis in appropriate Annexes to the AA where necessary. Although, the terminology for underlining bindingness may differ.[145] As it turned out, this is mainly due to the fact that "different DCFTA chapters were negotiated by different negotiating teams of DG Trade or other Commission DGs, each using their own legal vocabulary to define these approximation obligations".[146] There are also standard approximation clauses which consist of non-binding rules.[147]

c) Cooperation between parties

Here, we make attempt to systematize forms of cooperation in the field of legislative approximation. We deliberately exclude dispute settlement from consideration in this section as it does not fit the general line of our research and demands separate in-depth study.

aa) Monitoring mechanism of approximation of law

The monitoring mechanism can be analyzed on the basis of splitting it into various provisions which should be logically united. We try to illustrate this statement below.

i) General provisions which set the mechanism

Each AA contains general provisions which launch the monitoring mechanism of approximation of law.[148]

---

144 On the example of public procurement see Art. 153 of EU-Ukraine AA which says: "Ukraine shall ensure that its existing and future legislation on public procurement will be gradually made compatible with the EU public procurement *acquis*. Legislative approximation shall be carried out in consecutive phases as set out in Annex XXI-A and Annexes XXI-B to XXI-E, XXI-G, XXI-H, and XXI-J to this Agreement." In Annex XXI-A we can find, *inter alia,* indicative time schedule for approximation and implementation of basic elements of Directive 2004/18/EC on the coordination of procedures for the award of public works contracts, public supply contracts and public service contracts. It is fixed as 3 years after the entry into force of the Agreement.

145 For example, Art. 56 EU-Ukraine AA says: "Ukraine shall take the necessary measures in order to gradually achieve conformity with EU technical regulations…";Art. 64 EU-Ukraine AA states: "Ukraine shall approximate its sanitary and phytosanitary and animal welfare legislation".

146 Guillaume Van der Loo, Peter Van Elsuwege and Roman Petrovop. cit. (fn.36), p.18.

147 For example, Art. 286 of EU-Georgia AA says: "the national statistical system should respect the UN Fundamental Principles of Official Statistics, taking into account the EU acquis in statistics, including the European Statistics Code of Practice, in order to align the national statistical system with the European norms and standards".

148 See Art. 475 EU- Ukraine AA, Art. 450-453 EU-Moldova AA, 419-420 EU-Georgia AA. For example, Art. 475 EU- Ukraine AA states: "continuous appraisal of progress in implementing and enforcing measures covered by the AA; assessments by the EU of the approximation of Georgian law to EU law as defined in the AA, including aspects of implementation and enforcement; on-the-spot missions, with the participation of EU insti-

ii) Specific provisions on monitoring the process of approximation in trade-related areas

These provisions are substantively similar to the general afore-cited provisions.[149]

iii) Institutional and monitoring mechanism in trade and trade-related matters

This mechanism is launched in all three AAs.[150] It should be emphasized that all three provisions envisage similar approaches to define the legal instruments within this mechanism. Substantively all three complexes are mainly related to the communication between the parties on the trade issues in the way of designation a contact point and The Trade and Sustainable Development Sub-Committee for further coordination in overseeing the implementation of the Agreement in trade area. Undoubtedly, such model of cooperation also inevitably presumes the optional opportunity of monitoring the process of approximation of trade and trade-related laws.

bb) Information exchange

In particular, the information exchange in trade and trade-related matters may cover information about the process of approximation of law.[151] Appropriate provisions include the commitment of the Contracting Parties to provide information and respond to questions pertaining to any measure of general application or any proposal to adopt or to amend any measure of general application that the requesting Party considers might affect the operation of Title V (Trade and Trade-related Matters) of this Agreement, regardless of whether the requesting Party has been previously notified of that measure.

cc) Technical assistance

For example, technical assistance in trade and trade-related matters may include information about the process of approximation of law. Such assistance could be given by the Group (Panel) of Experts which are selected by the Parties under special procedures.[152]

dd) Financial assistance

Financial assistance may also cover the costs of the approximation of law.[153] The proposed approaches are similar but not literally.[154]

---

tutions, bodies and agencies, non- governmental bodies, supervisory authorities, independent experts and others as needed; the discussion the result of monitoring in all relevant bodies".

149 For example, Art. 407-410 EU-Moldova AA.

150 See Art. 300 EU-Ukraine AA, Art. 376 EU-Moldova AA, Art. 240 EU-Georgia AA.

151 See Art. 222 EU-Georgia AA, Art. 284 EU-Ukraine AA, Art. 358, 411 EU-Moldova AA.

152 See Art. 301 EU-Ukraine AA, Art. 379 EU-Moldova AA, Art. 243 EU-Georgia AA.

153 See Art. 453-459 EU-Ukraine AA, Art. 383-389 EU-Georgia AA, Art. 413-419 EU-Moldova AA.

154 In case of Georgia and Moldova the European Investment Bank (EIB), European Bank for Reconstruction and Development (EBRD) and other international financial institutions are defined, whereas in case of Ukraine vague wording "relevant EU funding mechanisms and instruments" is used.

VI. The reality and possible challenges for the approximation of law in Ukraine in connection with the AA

The first part of this section of the paper is devoted to the current legal and institutional framework for approximation of law in Ukraine. The contradictions and flaws of the institutional framework are addressed. The second part of this section deals with recent achievements and possible challenges in legislative approximation.

1. Legal framework for approximation

The current legal bases for approximation of law in Ukraine are The Strategy of Integration of Ukraine into the EU (Strategy of Integration)[155]; The Concept of Adaptation of Ukrainian Laws to the Legislation of the EU (Concept of Adaptation) 1999 which fixed the stage-by-stage approach to the approximation process[156]; the Programme of Integration to the EU (Programme of Integration)[157]; the National Programme for Approximation of Ukrainian Legislation to Legislation of the European Union[158]; the Resolution of the Cabinet of Ministers 'Some issues of Adaptation of Ukrainian legislation to that of the European Union', 15 October 2004, 1365/2004; the Action Plan for the implementation of the Association Agreement between Ukraine, on the one hand, and the European Union, the European Atomic Energy Community and their Member States, on the other hand, in the years 2014-2017[159], which launch the system of assignment of competences and time limits for the implementation of the various chapters of the AA.

2. Institutional framework for approximation

The Ukrainian institutional framework for the approximation to EU law can hardly be recognized as stable. In order to better understand this statement, we will illustrate it with some facts. The bodies which were established in the recent past to contribute to the European integration strategy of Ukraine did not succeed. The National Council for the adaptation of Ukrainian legislation to EU laws was eliminated in 2006.[160] The State Council on issues of European and Euro-Atlantic

155 Edict (Ukaz) of the President of Ukraine 'On approval of the Strategy of Integration of Ukraine to the European Union', 11 June 1998, 615/98.

156 Decree of the Cabinet of Ministers of Ukraine, 'Concept of Adaptation of the Legislation of Ukraine to the Legislation of the EU', 16 August 1999, 1496.

157 'Programme of Integration to the European Union', approved by the Edict of the President of Ukraine, 14 September 2000, 1072/2000.

158 Law of the Verkhovna Radaof Ukraine 'About the All State Programme of Adaptation of Ukrainian legislation to that of the EU', 18 March 2004, 1629-IV.

159 Order of the Cabinet of Ministers 'the Action Plan for the implementation of the Association Agreement between Ukraine, on the one hand, and the European Union, the European Atomic Energy Community and their Member States, on the other hand, in the years 2014-2017', 17 September 2014, 847.

160 <zakon4.rada.gov.ua/laws/show/340/2006>, accessed 28 February 2015.

integration was eliminated in 2010.[161] However, in June 2014 there was a proposal to renew the State Council and to establish the program of public information on European and Euro-Atlantic integration of Ukraine[162] which still remains without response. The Coordination Council for the adaptation of Ukrainian legislation to EU laws is the other prominent body in the approximation process.[163] Unfortunately, there is no information from the Coordination Council since 2012 nor any evidence of its activity. Especially the very last report of the Coordination Council and the last Adaptation plan were drafted in 2012.[164] The establishing of a new governmental body known as the Government Office on European integration does not clarify intricacies so far as this body visibly duplicates some parts of competences of the Coordination Council. In particular, the Government Office on European Integration organizes informing the public on European integration, monitors the performance and assessment of tasks in the field of European integration, participates in drafting legal acts for European Integration.[165] Moreover, there are some uncertainties with other authorities. The Department of Adaptation of Legislation at the Ministry of Justice of Ukraine (Department of Adaptation) was eliminated in 2011.[166] The Department of Adaptation was empowered, *inter alia*, to conduct compliance reviews between draft laws and the *acquis communautaire*; to carry out the monitoring of legislation of Ukraine, which projects were drafted in accordance with the *acquiscommunautaire*; to make recommendation on bringing the legislation of Ukraine in compliance with the acquis communautaire and suggestions on improvements of legislation; to organize the implementation of the Ukrainian translation of the EU *acquis communautaire*.[167] The weakness of the Parliamentary Committee for Issues of European Integration was illustrated as well.[168] It is revealing that the official web-page of the Parliamentary Committee makes reference to the Department of Adaptation of Legislation at the Ministry of Justice of Ukraine, which we have mentioned before as the eliminated authority.[169] Besides all

---

161 <zakon4.rada.gov.ua/laws/show/495/2010>, accessed 28 February 2015.

162 Minutes of meeting Parliamentary Committee for Issues of European Integration, 18.06.2014. See <comeuroint.rada.gov.ua/komevroint/control/uk/doccatalog/list?currDir=58607>, accessed 28 February 2015.

163 It was established and endowed with broad competence by the Resolution of the Cabinet of Ministers 'Some issues of Adaptation of Ukrainian legislation to that of the European Union' ,15 October 2004, 1365/2004. In particular, Coordination Council power to draft annual Adaptation Plans, coordinate the process of legislative approximation within the executive, to issue semi-binding decisions and to monitor the speed of the integration process.

164 <kmu.gov.ua/control/uk/publish/article%3fart_id=247677489&cat_id=247677375>, accessed 28 February 2015.

165 See the Resolution of the Cabinet of Ministers about Government Office on European integration August, 13 2014; 346.

166 <zakon4.rada.gov.ua/laws/show/346-2011-п>, accessed 28 February 2015.

167 <zakon4.rada.gov.ua/laws/show/1742-2004-п>, accessed 28 February 2015.

168 See Roman Petrov 'Legislative approximation and application of EU law in Ukraine' in P. Van Elsuwege, R. Petrov (Eds.) Legislative Approximation and Application of EU Law in the Eastern Neighborhood of the European Union. Towards a Common Regulatory Space?,(Routledge, 2014), pp. 137-159; at p. 147.

169 <http://comeuroint.rada.gov.ua/komevroint/control/uk/publish/article?art_id=48745&cat_id=45628>, accessed 28 February 2015.

this, it should be noticed that the present system of cooperation in the field of approximation of law[170] is built on four levels.[171]

3. Recent achievements and possible challenges in legal approximation

Below we illustrate both positive recent accomplishments of Ukrainian authorities and negative probabilities, which may become serious obstacles for Ukraine in the process of approximation.

a) Recent achievements in legal approximation

Undoubtedly, both the enactment of the Action Plan for the implementation of the Association Agreement and the availability of the Report on the implementation of the EU-Ukraine AA in September, 2014- January, 2015 to the public are promising signs for the further development of approximation.[172] The Implementation plans also should be positively evaluated.[173]The implementation plans are aimed at ensuring detailed planning, proper preparation for the implementation and comprehensive monitoring of implementing the relevant EU legal acts. This preparation is carried out in accordance with a developed unified methodology, taking into account the relevant experience of the EU Member States, candidate countries and peculiar characteristics of the governance system in Ukraine. In general, it is planned to approve implementation plans for about 180 EU legislation acts in the spheres determined by the Agreement for the period of 2014-2017. As of February 5, 2015 10 resolutions of the Cabinet of Ministers on approving 53 implementation plans of 60 EU legislation acts were taken. Starting from January 2015 a new edition of the Law of Ukraine "On Standardization" was enacted. The law provides for bringing the national system of standardization in conformity with the European model. A new version of the Law of Ukraine "On Metrology and Metrological Activity" has been adopted. The Law is aimed at harmonizing legislative acts with acts of the International Organization of Legal Metrology, the European Cooperation in Legal Metrology (WELMEC) and acts of the EU. A Law of Ukraine “On Technical Regulations and Conformity Assessment” has been adopted, which establishes

170 Which is legitimately considered to be functioning system.

171 First level is represented by Ministries, Deputy Ministers on European Integration, relevant Deputy Heads of central government authorities who monitor implementation of the Associated Agreement and relevant action plans. Second level is represented by Government Office on European integration and the Secretariat of the Association Council and Committee which, in particular, prepare expert appraisals for draft legal acts and regulations drafted by ministries and central government authorities. Third level is represented by Government Committee on European Integration, which addresses the issues of the EU-Ukraine Association Committee and implementation of the Agreement. The forth level is related *to* special meetings of the Cabinet of Ministers of Ukraine, devoted to the issues of the EU-Ukraine Association Council and implementation of the Agreement. See <kmu.gov.ua/kmu/control/uk/publish/article?art_id=247749544&cat_id=247749488>, accessed 28 February 2015.

172 See <kmu.gov.ua/kmu/control/uk/publish/article?art_id=247749544&cat_id=247749488>, accessed 28 February 2015.

173 See <kmu.gov.ua/kmu/control/uk/publish/article?art_id=247842640&cat_id=247749488>, accessed 28 February 2015.

common legal and organizational principles for the development, adoption and application of technical regulations and conformity assessment procedures according to the European requirements and provisions of the WTO Agreement on technical barriers to trade, cancellation of the centralized registration of certificates of conformity in the State certification system.[174]

b) Possible challenges in legal approximation

There are many challenges for Ukraine which cover the legal area and the institutional framework. Political, organizational and technical challenges also should not be forgotten. We will only generally list some challenges. In our opinion, they are: the choice of appropriate approximation techniques which should depend on the type of *acquis communautaire*; the need to respect domestic national law traditions which could not be destructed immediately; the chaotic and sporadic development of the law system which does not have time to respond in an holistic manner to the challenges of globalization; the tremendous dynamic of the broad *acquis communautaire*; the lack of qualified specialists in the areas related to the process of approximation; the 'frozen state' of some authorities which were originally created to take an active part in the process of approximation[175]; imbalanced relations between the legislative and the executive power in the field of legislative approximation; the Crimea question and the war in Donbass; the unusual for Ukrainian authorities need to follow the practice of EU institutions in different sectors; the inevitability of fragmentary and disorderly implementation of the *acquis communautaire* without effective and stable institutional mechanism; the necessity of economic and social reforms which are prerequisites for legislative approximation; the lack of consensus in society about the future of Ukraine; the low level of quality of translation of the *acquis communautaire* in Ukrainian; the lack of public information about the process of approximation; rational doubts about the feasibility of approximation of law in the strategic context of a world system transition period with unclear future of the elements of this system.

VII. Conclusion

This paper mainly aimed at a comparative analysis of the PCAs and the AAs of three countries (Georgia, Ukraine, Moldova) in the field of legislative approximation and at a description of the experience and challenges for Ukraine in that field. Thus, our concluding remarks could be also divided into two groups. Regarding comparative research, we have made the following observations. The general and specific provisions on approximation of law in the PCAs are similar be-

---

174 See the Report on implementation of the EU-Ukraine AA in September, 2014- January, 2015 which is available on <kmu.gov.ua/kmu/control/uk/publish/article?art_id=247749544&cat_id=247749488>, accessed 28 February 2015.

175 For example, Parliamentary Committee for Issues of European Integration.

cause the PCA is a model agreement, which only creates prerequisites and sets a basic level for future development of the legal institute of approximation of law. The PCAs' general approximation clauses are more about encouraging states to start the process of approximation than containing solid legal commitments. There are specific provisions on approximation in the PCAs which generally contain non-binding rules and relate to various areas. The AAs' general clauses on approximation of law are multilevel and more complex. The number of sectors where approximation of law is necessary is much wider in the AAs than in the PCAs. In the AAs the general clause together with standard approximation clauses making reference to the essential Annex of the AA design a complicated legal mechanism of approximation of law. The great majority of the AAs' standard approximation clauses in comparison to the PCAs provisions contain binding rules with timetables of their fulfillment. The quality of the monitoring mechanism on approximation of law in the AAs also visibly distinguishes their provisions from the PCA provisions. Regarding the Ukrainian experience, one can make the following statements: The Ukrainian institutional framework for an approximation to EU law can hardly be recognized as stable. There are few promising signs for the effective development of legislative approximation. At the same time there are many challenges for Ukraine which cover the legal area and the institutional framework, e.g. the choice of the appropriate approximation techniques which should depend on the type of *acquis communautaire*; the lack of qualified specialists in areas related to the process of approximation; the 'frozen state' of some authorities which were originally created to take an active part in the process of approximation; the dynamism of the *acquis communautaire*. These challenges may become significant obstacles for Ukraine in further approximation of its law to EU standards.

B. Trade and Investment Aspects: the DCFTAs within the three Association Agreements

Marta Zakharko

The DCFTAs in the Context of the Association Agreements of the Three Countries: Overview, Basic principles, Comparison

I. Introduction

On 27 June 2014 Moldova, Georgia and Ukraine signed the Association Agreements with the European Union, which include provisions on a Deep and Comprehensive Free Trade Area (also called Deep and Comprehensive Free Trade Agreements, DCFTAs). These DCFTAs are anticipated to have a positive impact on the economies of both parties as well as to transform the legislative framework.

The paper will focus on three main issues: firstly, the nature of DCFTAs and their main features; secondly, basic principles on which the provisions of DCFTAs are based; and finally, the comparison of the three DCFTAs.

II. Overview of the DCFTAs

DCFTAs are incorporated in the Association Agreements (AAs) between the European Union and Moldova, Georgia and Ukraine. In the Georgian and Ukrainian AAs it is Chapter IV to deal with Trade and trade-related matters, in the EU-Moldovan AA it is Chapter V. All DCFTAs at hand consist of 15 Chapters, three protocols and Annexes. Each DCFTA consists of a considerable amount of articles[176] which is an indication of the importance of economic cooperation for all sides.

1. Place of DCFTAs in the world trade system

The nature of the DCFTAs, which are included in the AAs between the EU and Ukraine, Moldova and Georgia, cannot be analyzed without a proper insight into the world trade system and the place of those DCFTAs among other WTO Agreements and Regional Trade Agreements (RTAs).There are numerous barriers to international trade, which can be classified into several groups. The obstacles spread to trade the widest are tariff and non-tariff barriers, border and domestic, barriers regarding market access and market regulation, and finally, governmental and private measures.[177] The main task of the world trade system is to eliminate or at least lower those barriers. The World Trade Organization (WTO) provides countries with the opportunities to ne-

[176] Georgian DCFTA includes articles 254 articles out of 432, Moldovan – 269 of 465, and Ukrainian – 311 out of 486.

[177] See more on trade barriers: Basic legal instruments for the liberalization of trade: comparative analysis of EC and WTO law / Federico Ortino Oxford [u.a.]: Hart, 2004, p. 7-16.

gotiate trade agreements. Three main agreements exist within the WTO system: the General Agreement on Tariffs and Trade (GATT), the General Agreement on Trade in Services (GATS) and the Agreement on Trade-Related Aspects of Intellectual Property Rights (TRIPS),[178] However, due to the difficulties in negotiation of sensitive issues on a global level, the countries are encouraged to conclude regional (or preferential) trade agreements,[179] 84% of all RTAs are Free Trade Agreements (FTAs)[180], the agreements between two or more countries to remove border restrictions on goods among themselves but each country reserves the right to maintain the external trade policy it wishes in respect to non-member states,[181] FTAs can be a part of broader AAs (as in case of the Euro-Mediterranean AA[182] between the EU and Egypt).

The European Union (EU) has already concluded more than 40 preferential trade agreements. Nonetheless, taking into account the insignificant tariffs, the EU is willing to conclude a new generation of agreements - Deep and Comprehensive Free Trade Agreements,[183] These agreements do not only address tariff barriers and trade in goods but they also regulate trade in services and aim at reducing non-trade barriers. Therefore, DCFTAs between the EU and Ukraine, Georgia and Moldova are part of the new generation of FTAs.

III. Preconditions of concluding DCFTAs

There were two main preconditions for concluding DCFTAs between the EU and Moldova, Georgia and Ukraine: political and economic ones.

The DCFTAs are the logical conclusion of the whole EU policy towards neighborhood countries. The guiding EU initiative, the European Neighborhood Policy, was the beginning of a process of political and economic cooperation and integration.[184] In 2009 to the ENP was added the Eastern Partnership initiative, the goal of which is to "deepen and strengthen relations" between the EU

178 See more in the official publication of WTO "Understanding the WTO", https://www.wto.org/english/thewto_e/whatis_e/tif_e/understanding_e.pdf, last accessed 3 Feb 2015.

179 The term regional trade agreements is used in WTO Agreements. However, some scholars supports the definition preferential trade agreements, since it reflects the nature of these agreements, namely to gran the preferential market access for goods between two countries (see more in The regulation of international trade / Michael Trebilcock, Robert Howse and Antonia Eliason4. ed. London [u.a.] : Routledge, 2013, p. 83; The World Trade Organization : law, practice, and policy / Mitsuo Matsushita; Thomas J. Schoenbaum and Pe tros C. Mavroidis2. ed. Oxford [u.a.] : Oxford Univ. Press, 2006, p. 548-549.

180 The Oxford handbook of international trade law/ ed. by Daniel BethlehemOxford [u.a.]: Oxford Univ. Press, 2009, p. 238.

181 Understanding trade law / Michael J. Trebilcock Cheltenham [u.a.] : Elgar, 2011, p.15.

182 The text is available at http://eeas.europa.eu/egypt/aa/06_aaa_en.pdf , last accessed 13 Jan 2015.

183 See official website http://ec.europa.eu/trade/policy/countries-and-regions/agreements/last accessed 13 Jan 2015.

184 See more about ENP on official website http://eeas.europa.eu/enp/index_en.htm/last accessed 13 Jan 2015.

and Eastern neighborhood countries.[185] From the prospective of Eastern countries, a DCFTA with the EU was the possibility to rebuild their economy and put an end to Soviet means of administration.[186] Therefore, it is evident, that the main precondition for concluding DCFTAs was the political will of the parties.

Another precondition set by the EU for the conclusion of a DCFTA was the membership of a partner country in the WTO. Negotiations with Ukraine on a DCFTA started in February 2008, while negotiations on an AA commenced in March 2007. The delay was due to the confirmation of Ukraine's accession to the WTO.[187] From an economic prospective, the EU was the first partner in both import and export for Moldova and Georgia in 2010, and as for Ukraine, the EU was the second largest trade partner after the Russian Federation.[188] According to the State Statistics Service, the amount of investments in Ukraine was tantamount to 80% of the total investments into the Ukrainian economy.[189] Considering the existence of such close trade relations between the parties, the conclusion of the new Agreement, which would replace the outdated PCAs[190] was essential for further effective cooperation.

IV. Peculiarities of DCFTAs with Moldova, Ukraine and Georgia

1. "Deep" and "comprehensive" character

Unlike simple FTAs, DCFTAs include the words "deep" and "comprehensive". "Deep" means the obligation of Moldova, Ukraine and Georgia to approximate their legislation according to the EU acquis.[191] In the preamble of the three AAs, despite their different wording,[192] all three coun-

185 See more about Eastern Partnership on official website http://ec.europa.eu/europeaid/regions/eu-neighbourhood-region-and-russia/introduction-0_enlast accessed 13 Jan 2015.

186 Similarly, Mitsuo Matsushita in the book "The World Trade Organization: law, practice, and policy" indicated that preferential trade agreements have not only commercial purpose; they have a goal to fix the direction towards new standards and to end up with the past.

187 EU-Ukraine Free trade agreement: Deep and comprehensive. G. Van der Loo. Law of Ukraine: Legal Journal, Vol. 2013 Issue 3(2013). P 223-232, p. 225 (afterwards referred as G. Van der Loo).

188 EU-Ukraine DCFTA: the Model for Eastern Partnership Regional Trade Cooperation p.6.

189 Olexandr Sushko, Olga Zelinska, Robert Khorolskyy, VeronilaMovchan, IrynaSolonenko, Victoria Gumeniuk, VadymTriukhan // EU-Ukraine Association Agreement: Guideline for Reforms < http://www.kas.de/wf/doc/kas_32048-1522-1-30.pdf?120912140435 > p. 23; last accessed 08 Mar 2015

190 G. Van der Loo, ft. 12 p. 224.

191 G. Van der Loo, ft. 12 p. 226.

192 Moldovan AA: WILLING to create a Deep and Comprehensive Free Trade Area, which will provide *for far-reaching* regulatory approximation and market access liberalization, in compliance with the rights and obligations arising out of the World Trade Organization (WTO) membership of the Parties and the transparent application of those rights and obligations; Ukrainian AA: DESIROUS of achieving economic integration, *inter alia* through a Deep and Comprehensive Free Trade Area (DCFTA) as an integral part of this Agreement, in compliance with rights and obligations arising out of the World Trade Organization (WTO) membership of the Parties, and through *exte sive* regulatory approximation; Georgian AA: COMMITTED to achieve economic integration in particular through a Deep and Comprehensive Free Trade Area (DCFTA), as an integral part of this Agreement *including* regulatory approximation and in compliance with the rights and obligations arising out of the membership of the Parties in the World Trade Organization (WTO).

tries have a commitment of approximation of their legislation in order to achieve the economic integration in the EU market. Moreover, there are separate articles related to different spheres of regulation, which prescribe the approximation of legislation (for instance, with regard to sanitary and phytosanitary measures there are art. 181 of the EU-Moldova AA, art. 64 of the EU-Ukraine AA, and art. 55 of the EU-Georgia AA). Furthermore, the Annexes include a list of regulatory acts which should be implemented into the Ukrainian, Moldovan and Georgian legislation.

However, taking into account the dynamics of the development of EU legislation, some problems might arise. According to the wording of AAs, the approximation of laws is gradual, and the Annexes contain a timetable for implementation. Some measures must be implemented until the end of 2020 (construction products in Annex III to Chapter 3, for instance). Within the timetable, some changes or even new acts which regulate the same sphere can be adopted. Additionally, there are indications of time such as "during the [number] year period after the Agreement' coming into force". However, there might be a situation when those acts will no longer be valid at that time. The question which arises at this stage is whether States should implement only those acts, which were in force at the time of signing the Agreement, or should the States implement the subsequent modifications of those acts. As there are no clear answers to these questions within the Agreement, these issues will be solved by the mutual consent between the parties.

The term "comprehensive" of the DCFTA means that the Agreement covers all main aspects of trade relations[193]. DCFTAs are aimed not only at the elimination of tariff barriers and at the regulation of trade in goods. They also cover non-tariff barriers, such as technical barriers (chapter 3), sanitary and phytosanitary (SPS) measures (chapter 4), establishment, trade in services and electronic commerce (chapter 6), payments and movement of capital (chapter 7), public procurement (chapter 8), intellectual property (chapter 9), competition (chapter 10), energy law (chapter 11) etc. DCFTAs also include provisions about the transparency of regulation and sustainable development.

The motivation for parties to take such a vast amount of commitments in different spheres does not solely derive from economic reasons. The DCFTAs are incentives for the parties to upgrade their infrastructure and the level of processes and production methods with the help of the EU.[194]

193 G. Van der Loo, ft. 12 p. 226.

194 Conquering the EU market with new comprehensive trade agreements – Simulating DCFTAs between the EU and neighbour countries Marie-Luise Rau http://ageconsearch.umn.edu/bitstream/182655/2/Rau-Conqueing_the_EU _market_with_new_comprehensive_trade_agreements_%E2%80%93simulating_ DCFTAs_between_the_EU_and_n_a.pdf>, p. 4; last accessed 08 Mar 2015.

2. DCFTAs in the framework of the AAs

Another peculiarity of the mentioned DCFTAs is their incorporation into broader Association Agreements. Therefore, these DCFTAs cannot be considered separately from other provisions of the AAs, particularly from the preamble and the general principles of the Agreement. Furthermore, since the Agreements have a political nature, the basic precondition for concluding the DCFTAs was the political will. Moreover, some spheres are regulated both under the DCFTA and under the Chapter of the AA on Economic and Sectoral Cooperation. Energy law is one of those spheres. Despite the fact that these chapters refer to the same issue, particularly to energy law, they regulate different aspects. At the same time, being a part of a single Agreement, these provisions should be interpreted in conjunction with each other.

Basic principles of the three DCFTAs

The analysis of the DCFTAs indicates that there are three groups of principles: general principles of international trade, principles of AAs that apply to DCFTAs and specific principles of DCFTAs. The role of the principles must not be underestimated. All provisions of the DCFTAs and their application should be interpreted in the light of the above-mentioned principles.

I. General principles of international trade

As has been already mentioned in the first part of this paper, the DCFTAs between the EU and Moldova, Georgia and Ukraine are incorporated in the world trade system. Therefore, principles of international trade law, especially WTO principles, are applicable to the DCFTAs as well. The main principle is the principle of trade liberalization, which can be achieved by the reduction of trade barriers. The preamble of the WTO Treaty proclaims that this agreement is "directed to the substantial reduction of tariffs and other barriers to trade and to the elimination of discriminatory treatment".[195] The provisions of DCFTAs indicate that the main aim of DCFTAs is the liberalization.The second main principle of international trade law, which is implemented in the DCFTAs, is the principle of non-discrimination. Non-discrimination exists on two levels. Firstly, if there was some advantage granted to one country, it should be granted to other countries immediately and unconditionally (most-favored nation treatment). Secondly, the treatment of imported products should not be less favorable than the treatment of domestic products (national treatment).

---

195 Preamble of the GATT, <https://www.wto.org/english/res_e/booksp_e/analytic_index_e/gatt1994_01_e.htm #p> , last accessed 28 Feb 2015.

The core issue of these principles is to provide equal competitive opportunities for the products.[196] They are included in all three DCFTAs in Chapter 1.

Specific principles in the DCFTAs between the EU and Moldova, Georgia and Ukraine

Title I of all AAs prescribes the general principles, among which are the following: free market economy, effective multilateralism, fight against corruption etc. These principles are general and relate to the whole Agreement.

Furthermore, all DCFTAs focus on the principle of transparency and sustainable development. There are specific provisions on transparency in different chapters of the DCFTAs (competition, intellectual property, public procurement etc.). Additionally, the separate chapter 12 is dedicated to transparency issues. The main objective of that clause is to provide a "predictable regulatory environment for economic operators, taking into account the requirements of legal certainty and proportionality".[197] The underlying reason for such a particular attention can be the Soviet past of all countries with the lack of transparency. Moreover, due to Transparency International in 2013, among 175 countries, Ukraine has only the 144th place, Georgia – the 55th and Moldova – the 102nd.[198] Therefore, transparency issues are of utmost importance for all countries, and especially for Moldova and Ukraine.

The next specific principle is the sustainable development. The concept of sustainable development derives from international environmental law and has not yet achieved the status of a strict principle of international law.[199] However, there is a separate chapter 13 under the title "Trade and sustainable development" in all three DCFTAs, which demonstrates its importance in EU trade relations. Moreover, sustainable development is indicated as a common policy objective of the EU in Art. 10 A of the Lisbon Treaty.[200] Therefore, sustainable development constitutes an integral part of the external relations between the EU and other countries.

---

196 Principles of international economic law / Matthias HerdegenOxford: Oxford Univ. Press, 2013, p. 55.

197 Art. 220 of Georgian AA, Art. 282 of Ukrainian AA, Art. 356 of Moldovan AA.

198 Corruption perceptions index 2013 https://www.transparency.org/cpi2013/results; last accessed 03 Mar 2015.

199 Principles of international economic law ft. 21; p. 62.

200 Lisbon Treaty http://eur-lex.europa.eu/LexUriServ/LexUriServ.do?uri=OJ:C:2007:306:FULL:EN:PDF last accessed 15 Feb 2015.

Comparison of the DCFTAs

I. Similarities

At the very outset, it should be emphasized that the three DCFTAs have more similarities than differences. Firstly, they cover the same range of issues (tariff and non-tariff barriers, trade in services, intellectual property rights etc.). Secondly, they all have the same structure (15 chapters, 3 protocols and annexes). Furthermore, even the wording of many articles is the same. All DCFTAs reaffirm the WTO commitments of their parties. Even the preamble of the three DCFTAs includes the statement about the compliance with rights and obligations arising out of WTO Agreements. Finally, all three DCFTAs are reciprocal. Previously, Eastern Partnership countries enjoyed some preferences in access to the EU market. These preferences stem from programs like the Generalized System of Preferences (GSP), for which Moldova, Ukraine and Georgia were eligible. Moreover, Georgia even enjoyed preferences provided by the GSP+[201]. On the contrary, the DCFTAs are reciprocal: both parties open the access to each other's market. At the same time, due to the economic situation Ukraine currently is in negotiations in order to impose an import duty, which is inconsistent with its DCFTA.[202]

II. Differences of the DCFTAs

In spite of so many similarities, all three DCFTAs are different concerning the ambitions and the intentions of the parties. Georgia, for instance, was willing to liberalize as much as possible in the shortest period. Ukraine and Moldova, on the contrary, negotiated on some sectors of economy which they considered to be important and sensitive. However, the main differences are in the Annexes to DCFTAs.

For instance, the Moldovan DCFTA, unlike the two other DCFTAs, focused significantly on the approximation of legislation in chemicals and cosmetics (ANNEX XVI to Moldovan AA). Moreover, according to the Annexes, the Moldovan DCFTA prescribes a gradual liberalization with total elimination duties on 99.2% from the side of Moldova, and 99.9%from the side of the EU.[203] As for Ukraine, on the contrary, this state and the EU will respectively eliminate 99.1% and

201 Veronika Movchan/Shportyuk N0 445 / 2012. CASE Network Studies & Analyses No.445 – EU-Ukraine DCFTA: the Model for Eastern Partnership Regional Trade Cooperation.

202 Ukraine, EU to hold consultations on new import duties <http://www.kyivpost.com/content/ukraine/ukraine-eu-to-hold-consultations-on-new-import-duties 376707.html>last accessed 08 Mar 2015.

203 Forty-sixth Report of Session 2013–14 of House of Commons European Scrutiny Committee <http://www.publications.parliament.uk/pa/cm201314/cmselect/cmeuleg/83-xli/83xli.pdf> last accessed 06 Mar 2015.

98.1% of the duties in trade value.[204] The Georgian DCFTA provides the highest rate of elimination - 100 % (Georgia) and 99.9 % (EU).

The EU-Ukrainian DCFTA differs from the other DCFTAs in structure, as it has a separate chapter dedicated to mediation procedures. The probable reason for the highlighting of mediation procedures can be its underdevelopment in Ukraine. Furthermore, the Ukrainian DCFTA includes safeguard measures on cars and second-hand clothes, which are not prescribed in any other DCFTA.

As for the intellectual property rights, there are peculiarities in the regulation of geographical indications. For a transitional period of ten years Ukrainian products can use such geographical indications as champagne, cognac, calvados, Jeres Sherry etc. Parmigiano Reggiano, Roquefort and Feta enjoy the transitional period of seven years (according to Article 208 of the EU-Ukraine AA).

In addition, Ukraine is the only country mentioned which prescribes custom duties on export (Article 31). According to Annex 1-C of the Agreement, there is a transitional period for up to ten years for such groups of products as live animals, seeds of some types of oil-yielding crops, alloyed ferrous metal scrap, nonferrous metal scrap and semi-manufactured goods of that sort, waste products and scrap of ferrous metals etc. On the contrary, the Georgian DCFTA (Art. 29) and the Moldovan DCFTA (Art. 150) prohibit custom duties on export.

Finally, differences are present in the scope of reservations made by different countries. In the case of Ukraine (ANNEX XVI-A), Croatia made a reservation to national treatment and to the most favorable treatment obligations with respect to agricultural activities. Austria, Hungary, Malta and Romania made the same reservation for Georgia (ANNEX XIV-A), and all above-mentioned countries made the same reservation in the EU-Moldova AA (ANNEX XXVII-A).

Consequently, despite the very similar provisions in all three DCFTAs, each of the documents is unique.

III. Conclusion

To conclude, DCFTAs constitute today a significant part of the current regional trade system. They are the agreements of a new generation aimed at complete liberalization and economic inte-

[204] Panagiota Manoli. Political Economy aspects of Deep and Comprehensive Free Trade Agreements // Eastern Journal of European Studies, Vol. 4, Issue 2 December 2013, p. 56, http://www.ejes.uaic.ro/articles/ EJES2013 0 402MAN pdf> last accessed 8 Mar 2015.

gration. However, irrespective of the economic constituent, they are also political documents whose main aim is to confirm a new way of countries` development. Moreover, the three DCFTAs analyzed in this paper are means not only for an elimination and reduction of tariff and non-tariff barriers to trade, but also for the reconstruction of the economies of the partner countries. Due to their similar past and similar current problems, all three DCFTAs have a lot in common. Yet, there are significant differences which are mostly hidden in the Annexes to the DCFTAs. The DCFTAs at issue are expected to contribute to the development of the economies of all countries. The level of this contribution, however, depends on the fulfillment of the countries' obligations (approximation to the EU acquis and actual application of EU standards) and on the political situation.

Anastasiia Romanchenko

The Deep and Comprehensive Free Trade Area Parts of the Association Agreements with Georgia, Moldova and Ukraine: a Comparison of the Provisions on Technical Barriers and National Legislation

I. Introduction

The so-called economic parts of the EU Association Agreements (AAs) with Georgia, Moldova and Ukraine[205] provide for the creation of a "deep and comprehensive free trade area" of these countries with the European Union. This includes, in Title IV Chapter 3 of the Agreements with Georgia and Ukraine and Title V Chapter 4 of the EU-Moldova Agreement, provisions on regulations in the field of technical barriers to trade (Art. 53-58 EU-Ukraine AA, Art. 44-49 EU-Georgia AA; Art. 170-175 EU-Moldova AA), which are complemented by an Annex to the AAs (e.g. Annex III to Chapter 3 of Title IV EU-Ukraine AA, Annexes III-A and III-B EU-Georgia AA, Annex XVI EU-Moldova AA). In addition, the Parties have agreed to add in the future another Protocol, dealing with Conformity Assessment and Acceptance of Industrial Products.[206]

The structure of these quite short chapters is as follows: They start with a definition of technical barriers to trade and the regulatory scope of the chapter (e.g. Art. 53 EU-Ukraine AA), continue with an affirmation of the rights and duties of the Contracting Parties under WTO law (e.g. Art. 54 EU-Ukraine AA). Then follow two broad articles on technical cooperation and approximation of standards (e.g. Art. 55 and 56 EU-Ukraine AA). Specifically addressed are future agreements between the Parties on conformity assessments and acceptance of industrial products (e.g. Art. 57 EU-Ukraine AA) and the issue of marking and labelling (Art. 58 EU-Ukraine AA). The most difficult task in implementing these Chapters in the future is probably the legislative work on the long list of EU acquis communautaire provisions, which are listed in the Annexes to the Agreements.

According to the introductory provision of this Chapter (e.g. Art. 53 EU-Ukraine AA),the Chapter applies to the preparation, adoption and application of technical regulations, standards, and of the conformity assessment procedures as defined in the Agreement on Technical Barriers to Trade (TBT Agreement), contained in Annex 1A to the WTO Agreement[207] that may affect trade in goods between the parties. Technical barriers to trade, a category of nontariff barriers to trade,

---

205 Title IV of the AAs with Georgia and Ukraine, Title V EU-Moldova AA.
206 Art. 57 EU-Ukraine AA, Art. 48 EU-Georgia AA, Art. 177 EU-Moldova AA.
207 https://www.wto.org/english/docs_e/legal_e/17-tbt_e.htm.

are widely divergent measures which countries use to regulate markets, to protect their consumers or to preserve their natural resources (among other objectives), but they also can be used (or perceived by foreign countries) to discriminate against imports in order to protect domestic industries. The WTO TBT Agreement sets rules for the use of such barriers. However, trade experts predominantly consider TBTs to have great potential for being misused by importing countries as nontransparent - disguised or unclear - obstacles to trade. Global processes of economic globalization and the development of international trade cause a rapid process of internationalization of quality as a key element of the competitiveness of firms and their products. Due to these processes increasingly common standards, technical regulations, quality management system and environment, certification procedures and other are used in different countries.[208]

Barriers to international trade can be divided into two separate kinds and can be distinguished by the nature of their impact on trade flows. The first are natural barriers, in particular, the geographical distance between countries, the infrastructure, transportation, etc. With the strengthening of the processes of globalization, the coverage of an increasing number of countries, the development of modern communications comes a reduction of "distances" and the unification of the natural environment, which reduces the influence of this group of non-tariff barriers on the volume of trade flows. The second group of barriers includes various tools of foreign policy that are created by governments and which directly affect the level of import and export of goods. This category includes all commonly used measures of tariff and non-tariff regulation of foreign trade. [209] Standard-related measures serve an important function in facilitating international trade, also by enabling small and medium sized enterprises (SMEs) to obtain greater access to foreign markets. Standard-related measures also enable governments to pursue legitimate objectives such as protecting human health and the environment and preventing deceptive practices. Such measures can, however, pose a particular problem for SMEs, which often do not have the resources to address these problems on their own.[210]

II. Basic aspects relating to technical barriers to trade

The chapters of the three Association Agreements start with a definition of technical barriers to trade and with the determination of the regulatory scope of these chapters. Generally speaking,

---

208 See Ruzevicius, Technical barriers in international trade in the context of standardization and quality (in Russian), Стандарты и качество 2010, Nr. 11, pp.92-95.

209 Melnik/Pugaczewska, Non-tariff regulations in the EU (in Ukrainian), Bulletin of Kiev National Trade and Economic University 2014. No. 2, pp.15-28, accessible at http://nbuv.gov.ua/j-pdf/Vknteu_2014_2_3.pdf.

210 See Office of the United States Trade Representative, 2014 Report on technical barriers to trade, p.6, accessible at https://ustr.gov/sites/default/files/2014_TBT_Report.pdf.

the AAs largely and expressly refer to the corresponding WTO provisions (see e.g. Art. 54 EU-Ukraine AA, Art. 171 EU-Moldova AA).

1. Definition of technical barriers to trade

The term "technical barriers to trade" (TBT) refers to mandatory technical regulations and voluntary standards that define specific characteristics that a product should have, such as its size, shape, design, labelling/marking/packaging, functionality or performance (cf. Art.53 para.1 EU-Ukraine AA). The specific procedures used to check whether a product is in compliance with these requirements are also covered by the definition of TBT. These so-called "conformity assessment procedures" can for example include product testing, the inspection and certification of activities. TBTs are usually introduced by government authorities with a legitimate public policy objective in mind –for example, protecting human health and safety, animal and plant life and health or the environment, or safeguarding consumers from deceptive practices[211].The WTO TBT Agreement seeks to assure that mandatory product regulations, voluntary product standards, and conformity assessment procedures do not become unnecessary obstacles to international trade and are not employed to obstruct trade. The TBT Agreement seeks to balance two competing policy objectives, the prevention of protectionism and the right of States to enact product regulations for legitimate public policy purposes.

2. Scope of application of the TBT provisions of the AAs

All three Association Agreements apply to the preparation, adoption and application of technical regulations, standards, and conformity assessment procedures as defined in the WTO TBT Agreement.[212] It is expressly stated that the AAs' chapters on TBT do not apply to sanitary and phytosanitary measures which are the subject of separate chapters of the Agreements (like in the WTO) nor to purchasing specifications prepared by public authorities for their own production or consumption requirements.

III. Technical requirements of EU law

Over the years, the EU has passed an enormous amount of legislation, mostly directives, dealing with technical requirements. About 700 directives regulate technical standards for certain industrial products, but since the famous judgment of the European Court of Justice of 20 February

[211] See, Technical barriers to trade. – 3 p. - Mode of access: chrome extension: http://trade.ec.europa.eu/doclib/docs/2013/april/tradoc_150987.pdf, p. 1.

[212] See, e.g., Art. 170 EU-Moldova AA.

1979 in the Cassis de Dijon case[213], which permitted intra-EU imports of goods even without a formal harmonization of product-related standards the Commission changed its policy in the field of technical standards. The so-called "new approach" legislative technique approved by the Council of Ministers on 7 May 1985 is built on the following principles: 1) Legislative harmonization should be limited to the essential requirements (preferably performance or functional requirements) that products placed on the EU market must meet if they are to benefit from free movement within the EU. 2) Technical specifications for products meeting the essential requirements set out in legislation should be laid down in harmonized standards which can be applied alongside the legislation. 3) Products manufactured in compliance with harmonized standards benefit from a presumption of conformity with the corresponding essential requirements of the applicable legislation, and, in some cases, the manufacturer may benefit from a simplified conformity assessment procedure. 4) The application of harmonized or other standards remains voluntary, and the manufacturer can always apply other technical specifications to meet the requirements.

On the basis of new approach about 27 directives have been adopted on the basis of the New Approach, although traditional directives in the field of industrial products continue to exist and are also further developed. However, the new approach with a wide hazard-based scope has meant that entire industrial sectors have benefited from free movement of goods within the EU. Also the new approach directives more often use the support of the established standardization bodies, CEN, CENELEC and national standard bodies. Thus, standardization work is achieved in a more efficient way, is easier to update and involves greater participation from industry. A further feature of the new approach is the use of market surveillance and the choice of attestation methods that are available: by self-certification against the essential requirements, by using generic standards or by using notified bodies for type approval and testing of conformity of type.[214] Furthermore, the EU has passed a considerable number of horizontal directives applying to basically all products, in particular with regard to marketing, e.g. the Directive 2001/95/EC of 3 December 2001 on general product safety or the Directive 85/374/EEC of 25 July 1985 on the approximation of the laws concerning liability for defective products. Most of these directives are listed in the Annexes to the AA as topics for legal approximation.

---

213 Accessible at http://eur-lex.europa.eu/legal-content/DE/TXT/?uri=CELEX%3A61978CJ0120.

214 See also Brenton/Sheehy/Vancauteren, Technical Barriers to Trade in the European Union: Importance for Accession Countries, CEPS Working Document No. 144. – 2000. – 27 p., pg. 5.

IV. Legislation in Ukraine in the field of technical regulation with a view to approximation to EU Law

Even in the past, Ukraine has started to approximate its technical legislation to EU standards. In 2010-2011, three laws of Ukraine “On state market surveillance and control of non-food products”, “About General security non-food products” and “On liability for damage caused by defect in the products created a legislative basis for a modern system of market surveillance in accordance with the European standards. More concretely, the law of Ukraine “On state market surveillance and control of non-food products” of 2 December 2010 No. 2735-VI introduced a system of market supervision and complies with the requirements of EU legislation. The law eliminated market control of industrial products and focus of regulatory authorities on products with a high degree of risk for society and environment. The system of market surveillance eliminated the duplication controlling functions by public authorities and becomes transparent. The law of Ukraine “On General safety of non-food products” from 2 December 2010 No. 2736-VI is based on the EU Directive No.2001/95/EU. The law of Ukraine “On responsibility for damage caused by a defect in the product of 19 May 2011 No. 3390-VI provides for the full functioning of the market surveillance. Also, administrative reforms began to resolve conflicts of interest that existed in the State.[215]

Under the new Association Agreement, Ukraine will have to harmonize its legislation with the EU much more fundamentally than before. Art. 55 to 58 of the Association Agreement and its Annex III provide for a gradual harmonization of Ukrainian legislation in the area of technical regulation with the EU. Annex III to the Agreement provides that 5 "horizontal" regulations, as well as 27 "vertical" regulations should be harmonized within 5 years. At the end of 2013 more than forty technical regulations were approved, more than a dozen of them are directly or indirectly connected with the manufacture of food products, in particular: the conformity assessment modules, rules regarding labeling of food products with environmental labelling, packaging materials and packaging waste, safety of machines and equipment, security equipment, working under pressure, and other At the same time, none of the technical regulations on the production of a specific food product so far not been approved, although about a dozen projects TR has been developed.[216] Ukraine has developed a draft Strategy for the development of technical regulation until 2018. The draft Strategy identifies the plan of measures on implementation of Ukraine's

215 See, Kristof, Public administration reform in the system of technical regulation - the key to ensuring the access of Ukrainian products to foreign market (in Ukrainian), pp.113-123.

216 Cf. Krisanov, System of technical regulations of the European Union, Ukraine and the Customs Union for the agricultural and food field: directions for their converging, opportunities for contradictions' reduction and asymmetry minimization (in Ukrainian), Challenges of time 2014 № 2, p.7.

commitments defined in the text of the Association Agreement and Annex III thereto. Thus, Ukraine is facing a complex and lengthy task on harmonization of technical regulation system. On the basis of the development Strategy it is expected that by 2018, the Ukraine and the EU will have reached a mutual recognition of the results of the robot conformity assessment of industrial products that will allow for a mutually-recognized groups of products of Ukrainian producers to enter the market in the EU on the same terms that apply to manufacturers of member countries of the EU, the Ukrainian manufacturer cannot wait state reform of technical regulation for export to the EU, and to directly study the requirements applicable in the EU to its products. Ensuring the conformity of production requirements of the EU (eliminating technical barriers), the Ukrainian manufacturer now may enter the EU markets.

V. Conclusion

The removal of technical barriers to trade between Georgia, Moldova and Ukraine on the one side, the EU on the other, is an extremely important factor affecting trade between them. To date there has been little attempt to assess the importance of such barriers to trade between the EU and its Eastern European neighbors, but approximation of the legal systems of the three associated countries in this sphere does not start from zero and is a difficult und cumbersome, but realistic task. The question is how countries like Georgia, Moldova and Ukraine can find the necessary number of highly qualified specialists who understand both the technicalities and the legal requirements to fulfil this task according to the expectations of the EU.

Kseniya Smyrnova

Issues of Competition Law in the EU-Ukraine, EU-Moldova and EU-Georgia Association Agreements: Comparative Aspects

I. General background

Comparing Ukraine with other countries with competition protection systems, UNCTAD has noted in 2013 that Ukraine has begun the process of adoption of competition legislation and the formation of its implementation policy in very difficult initial conditions. Economic and political circumstances in Ukraine, as well as in other former Soviet republics, have been particularly tough. Ukraine adopted its competition legislation at the beginning of a period of rapid growth in the number of jurisdictions with competition laws throughout the world. As the experts of UNCTAD rightly observed, the journey towards an effective competition policy system in Ukraine has been arduous.[217] In the early 2000s, various market reforms and de-monopolization measures were taken. Despite various market reforms and de-monopolization measures, Ukraine's economy still features exceptionally high levels of concentration unrelated to superior economic performance.

Nevertheless, the process of harmonization of national competition legislation with EU law was and remains one of the key areas of cooperation between Ukraine and the EU. Harmonization defines the conditions for further deepening of economic and sectorial cooperation and creates legal preconditions for the next stage of European economic integration. The rules in this matter, which were contained in the EU-Ukraine Partnership and Cooperation Agreement[218] (PCA) of 1994, had only'soft law' character – the PCA did not place Ukraine under a strict obligation to harmonization of itscompetition legislation. At the same time, however, the special Article 51 of the PCA stressed that competition was one of the priorities of harmonization. The EU-Ukraine Association Agreement (AA), which was ratified by the European Parliament and the Verhovna Rada of Ukraine in September 2014 will replace – as soon as it has fully entered into force[219] - the PCA as the basic legal framework of EU-Ukraine relations (Art. 479 EU-Ukraine AA). Upon its entry into force the Association Agreement will be considered as a part of national legislation

217 See Voluntary Peer Review of Competition Law and Policy: Ukraine Overview, UNCTAD, 2013 // http://unctad.org/en/PublicationsLibrary/ditcclp2013d3_overview_en.pdf

218 The Partnership and Cooperation Agreement between EC and its Member States and Ukraine was concluded in 1994 and entered into force in March 1998. The PCA formed the legal basis of EU-Ukraine relations, providing for cooperation in a wide range of areas. It was concluded for the term of 10 years, but Art. 101 PCA provided the process of its automatic prolongation in case of denunciation notice absence.

219 For the time being, the EU-Ukraine AA is still in the phase of provisional application, see http://eur-lex.Europa.eu/legal-content/EN/TXT/HTML/?uri=CELEX:22014X1031(01)&from=DE.

(ch. 1, Art. 9 of the Constitution of Ukraine[220]) and in case of conflict with norms of current legislation is subject to priority application (ch. 2, Art. 19 of the Law of Ukraine "On international agreements of Ukraine").

Due to Ukraine's integration policy, its accession to the WTO in 2008[221], entering into force of the Free Trade Agreement with EFTA countries in 2012[222], signing and ratification of the Association Agreement with the EU, the open free trade areas opened their doors for Ukraine. Due to this fact the most important issue related to liberalized trade is competition rules that become increasingly crucial forUkraine.

Comparing the current Association Aagreement with Ukraine with analogue acts signed by the EU with others countries, it can be said that this is a 'fourth generation agreement'. It is the first of a new generation of Association Agreements between the EU and countries of the Eastern Partnership that covers a deep and comprehensive free trade area (DCFTA). Considering further the 'deep' and 'comprehensive' character of the FTA, it can be concluded that the EU-Ukraine DCFTA is the first of a new generation of FTAs concluded by the EU which will, once in force, gradually and partially integrate the economy of Ukraine into the EU Internal Market. Its integration into the Internal Market will take place, however, only under the condition that Ukraine approximates its legislation to the EU *acquis communautaire*.

On the other hand, the 'deep' character of the DCFTA refers also to Ukraine's commitment to approximate its legislation to the *acquis communautaire* in order to achieve its economic integration with the EU Internal Market. The DCFTA part of the AA (Title IV) contains numerous legislative approximation clauses according to which Ukraine must approximate its domestic legislation or standards to the EU *acquis*. Title IV of the Association Agreement shows that the EU-Ukraine AA not only covers traditional FTA areas, such as market access for goods, but also includes public procurement, intellectual property, energy etc. and – particularly relevant for this contribution: competition (Title IV Chapter 10 of the EU-Ukraine AA, same Chapter in the EU-Georgia AA; in the EU-Moldova AA the matter is regulated in Chapter 10 of Title V of the Agreement).

---

220 Article 9 of the Ukrainian Constitution of 1996 provides that: "International treaties in force, consented by the Verhovna Rada of Ukraine [Ukrainian Parliament] as binding, shall be an integral part of the national legislation of Ukraine. Conclusion of international treaties, contravening the Constitution of Ukraine, shall be possible only after introducing relevant amendments to the Constitution of Ukraine".

221 Law of Ukraine "On ratification of Protocol of Ukraine's accession to the WTO" dated 10.04.2008 No 250-VI, Verhovna Rada Bulletin 2008.№ 23, p. 213.

222 Law of Ukraine "On ratification of Free Trade Agreement between Ukraine and Member States of EFTA" dated 07.12.2011 No 4091-VI, Official Journal of Ukraine.of 13.01.2012.№ 1, p.. 9.

II. Provisions on competition in the three Association Agreements in comparison

The EU-Ukraine, EU-Georgia and EU-Moldova FTAs were announced as being the first in a series of so-called Deep and Comprehensive Free Trade Agreements (DCFTAs).[223] Within this category, the competition chapters are nevertheless very diverse.[224]

The competition chapter in the AA/DCFTA with Georgia is very superficial.[225] Cooperation provisions are not foreseen. Principles governing anti-competitive business practices and state interventions as well as subsidies provide that parties should maintain comprehensive and effective competition laws, and implement such legislation via a functioning authority, respecting the principles of transparency, non-discrimination, procedural fairness and respect for the rights of defence. Some provisions deal with the regulation of state monopolies, state enterprises and enterprises entrusted with special or exclusive rights, mainly requiring transparency. One provision regulates subsidies, which is not excluded from the DSM, in contrast to the rest of the competition chapter. There is no prejudice to the rights and obligations in the WTO agreement, and parties should 'take into account the limitations imposed by the requirements of professional and business secrecy in their respective jurisdictions'[226].

The EU-Moldova AA/DCFTA's competition chapter is comprised of two sections, one dealing with antitrust and mergers, and one revolving around state aid.[227] Again the obligation of maintaining competition laws and operational authorities is included. The provision on the implementation of competition laws emphasizes the independence of the competition authorities, a feature that is not present in any of the other DCFTAs. Again, state monopolies, public undertakings and undertakings entrusted with special or exclusive rights are regulated, in the sense that they should be subject to competition laws. Furthermore, cooperation and exchange of information is foreseen. However, the relevant provision is rather weak, merely stating that 'each competition authority may inform the other competition authority of its willingness to cooperate with respect to the enforcement activity of any of the Parties'.[228] Exchange of non-confidential information is allowed, subject to the confidentiality laws of each party and limited by the national requirements of professional and business secrecy. The entire section is excluded from dispute settlement. The

---

223 European Commission, The EU's Association Agreements with Georgia, the Republic of Moldova and Ukraine, Brussels, 23 Jun. 2014, MEMO/14/430.

224 Demedts. Which Future for Competition in the Global Trade System: Competition Chapters in FTAs, Journal of World Trade 49 (2015), no. 3, pp. 407–436.

225 Art. 203-209 EU-Georgia AA.

226 Art. 209 EU-Georgia AA.

227 Art. 333-344 EU-Moldova AA.

228 Art. 337 EU-Moldova AA.

section on state aid does not apply to fisheries and agriculture. The assessment of state aid is regulated, referring back to Article 107 TFEU, and the parties are to establish and maintain state aid legislation and an authority, thereby adhering to the transparency-principle. Again parties should 'take into account' limitations following from professional and business secrecy obligations, and a rather unique review clause is included.

Finally, the AA/DCFTA with Ukraine is somewhat particular. The competition chapter is much longer than in the other two AAs and is again divided in two sections[229]: antitrust and mergers; and state aid. The first section on antitrust and mergers traditionally elaborates on the importance of regulating anti-competitive behaviour, and indicates the practices that are considered inconsistent with the agreement. The AA focuses on the main principles of an undertaking's conduct on the market that can impede, restrict or distort competition (including conduct prohibited under Article 101 para.1 TFEU, abuse of a dominant position and certain concentrations that result in monopolization or a substantial restriction of competition in the market in the territory of either Party). The Association Agreement identifies the key practices and economic transactions that could potentially adversely affect the functioning of markets and undermine the benefits of trade liberalization established between the parties. These anti-competitive practices include: a) agreements and concerted practices between undertakings, which have the purpose or effect of impeding, restricting, distorting or substantially lessening competition in the territory of either Party; b) the abuse by one or more undertakings of a dominant position in the territory of either Party; c) concentrations between undertakings, which result in monopolization or a substantial restriction of competition in the market in the territory of either Party[230]. What is characteristic of the EU-Ukraine DCFTA is the provision on approximation of law and enforcement practice, with strict deadlines and hard obligations. Parties should exchange information and cooperate on enforcement matters, although the obligations are again particularly weak, stating that 'the competition authority of a Party may inform the competition authority of the other Party of its willingness to cooperate with respect to enforcement activity. This cooperation shall not prevent the Parties from taking independent decisions'[231]. The agreement foresees that the parties should consult each other, but this is not regulated in detail, nor is it mandatory.

The EU-Ukraine AA pays special attention to state aid, which remains unregulated in Ukraine. The principle of transparency is again central, and this time is made tangible via concrete obligations. Articles 106, 107 and 93TFEU shall serve as sources of interpretation. Finally, concrete

229 Art. 253-267 EU-Ukraine AA.
230 Article 254 AA.
231 Art. 259 para.2 EU-Ukraine AA.

changes to the domestic system of state aid control are required and listed in the agreement. What sets the EU-Ukraine DCFTA apart from the other DCFTAs is that Ukraine will align its competition law and enforcement practice to that of the EU acquis in a number of fields. As a result, there are actual substantive requirements for the domestic regime. This type of commitment cannot be found in other post-global-Europe FTAs. What is remarkable is that the scope of the EU acquis to which Ukraine should approximate its laws is not included in an annex, but in the main text of the agreement. This of course has consequences for the procedure to change this content. A formal treaty change will be required, which is rigid and burdensome. Furthermore, Ukraine commits itself to adopting a system of control of state aid similar to that in the EU and inspired by TFEU articles, including an independent authority. The level of detail in these provisions can also be considered quite novel.

III. Conclusion

The DCFTA is one of the most ambitious bilateral agreements that the EU has ever negotiated with a trading partner and should offer Ukraine a framework for modernization of bilateral trade and investment relations and a model for economic development.

Anastasiia Rogozina

Investment Protection in the Framework of the Three EU Association Agreements: Substantive Issues

The EU is the largest investor and recipient of FDI worldwide with 1400 bilateral agreements entered into by EU Member States since the late 1960s with Germany being a pioneer country which concluded the first BIT with Pakistan. After the Treaty of Lisbon the EU has become an independent «player» in the field of FDI and enjoys the freedom to conclude international agreements on this matter. However, the investment provisions in Association Agreements with Eastern Partnership countries are quite limited. The content of the specific provisions dealing with foreign investment, viewed comparatively, is discussed firstly, using significant differences of Association Agreements in comparison to BITs. Contrary to Member States' BITs, which provide standards of treatments of foreign investors at the post-establishment phase, the Association Agreements contain special provisions regarding the admission and establishment of FDI.

I. Overview of EU investment policy

1. History

The European Union is a supranational organization with limited, attributable powers. The EU's explicit external competences include the competence to conclude association agreements.[232] However, the European Union's competence to enter into an international agreement in a specific domain is not absolutely restricted to explicitly mentioned Treaty provisions.[233] Following its decision in the AETR case, the CJEU in the Kramer Case reaffirmed that the authority to act may as well "flow implicitly from other provisions of the Treaty, from the Act of Accession and from measures adopted within the framework of those provisions, by the Community institutions"[234]. Further, the Court declared that the conferral of an implied external power shall be assumed, provided that the EC disposes of the complementary internal competence in that specific domain "for the purpose of attaining a specific objective"; and that the Community's participation is necessary for the realization of that objective[235]. A EU competence in the field of foreign direct investment did not appear in the Treaty texts until the Treaty of Lisbon (TFEU). However, the broad interpretation[236] of the Common Commercial Policy (CCP) under Article 133 TEC opened the door to a

232 Ex-Article 310 TEC (now Article 226 Consolidated version of the Treaty on the Functioning of the European Union, OJ, 2012, C 326, hereinafter TFEU).
233 ECJ Case 22/70, Commission v. Council (AETR) (1971), ECR 263, para. 16.
234 ECJ Cases 3, 4 and 6/76, Kramer (1976), ECR 1279, paras. 19-20.
235 Opinion 1/76, European Laying-Up Fund for Inland Waterway Vessels (1977), ECR 741, paras. 3-4.
236 Opinion 1/78, International Agreement on Natural Rubber (1979), ECR 2871, para. 45: the CCP's enumeration

possible inclusion of FDI. The question whether the CCP would expand its scope to include matters related to foreign investment was finally settled, when the Court of Justice (CJEC) elaborated that the CCP's competence only included those aspects in the trade of services which are comparable to trades in goods.[237] The Court thereby excluded an authority over issues related to the free movement of persons and their rights of establishment, both of which represent indispensable aspects for an investment venture. Opinion 2/92 and the Treaty of Amsterdam later reaffirmed the above-said.[238] Thereafter, the Treaty of Nice appeared as a leap forward by adding the notions of trade in services and commercial aspects of intellectual property.[239] Articles 57, 43, 44 and 47 of the EC Treaty (free movement of capital and the freedom of establishment) conferred EC with an internal normative authority, which, in accordance with the principle of parallelism, may in pursuance of the specific action be realized by measures on the external sphere. ECJ Opinion 2/92 affirmed that an external competence derives from Article 57 II[240], but according to the Directive 88/361/EEC and the Court ruling in the Case 464/98, the scope of the notion «movement of capital» and thus the margin of action conferred upon the Community in Article 57 only encompass those investment related competences with regard to market access and pre-establishment phase of foreign investment. This excludes disposition over post-establishment regulations.[241] As for the freedom of establishment (Articles 43, 44 and 47 TEC) the Court found that in order to attain exclusive external competence over the domain of establishment provided for on the internal side, a complete intra-Community harmonization concerning the provisions on access to self-employed activity had to be attained first.[242]

Therefore, EU action in investment matters was quite limited. «Before the entry into force of the Lisbon Treaty, the competence on foreign direct investment (FDI) had been mixed; liberalization and protection were divided up between the EC and its Member States. Two layers of rules with regard to FDI co-existed[243]», namely, the bilateral investment treaties (BITs) of Member States and trade agreements of the EU with third countries. The latter were «focused on market access

of competences in the Treaty should be considered non-exhaustive; in order to fully exert its functions and to promote international trade the Community shall not be restricted solely to the traditional aspects of external trade (i.e. the removal of customs duties or quantitative restrictions) but should be enabled to make use of more sophisticated means.

237 ECJ Opinion 1/94, WTO Agreement: GATS and TRIPS (1994), ECR I-5267, paras. 41-47.

238 Kazimirek, Kevin, The New EU Competence over Foreign Direct Investment and its Impact on the EU´s Role as a Global Player, 2012, Available at http://www.uni-oldenburg.de/cetro/31251.html (date of accession: 01.03.2015), p. 19.

239 Article 133 V TEC.

240 ECJ Opinion 2/92, paragraph V, paras. 6-7.

241 Kazimirek, op. cit. 7, p. 21.

242 ECJ Opinion 2/92, OECD Decision on National Treatment (1995), ECR I-521, paras. 95-97.

243 Reclaiming Public Interest in Europe's International Investment Policy. EU Investment Agreements in the Lisbon Treaty Era: A Reader. Published by: the Transnational Institute on behalf of the Investment Working Group of the Seattle to Brussels Network, p. 19.

and non-discrimination for committed investments, with enforcement mechanisms through a State-to-State dispute settlement mechanism that applied to the whole agreement»[244].

2. Current investment competences of the EU

With the coming into force of the Lisbon Treaty on 1 December 2009, FDI has been incorporated into the issues belonging to the exclusive EU competence. Article 207 TFEU provides that the CCP covers FDI. This implies that EU Member States cannot continue concluding BITs and the EU can now negotiate trade and investment treaties by itself, on behalf of all members States.

The EU's investment policy is outlined in its Communication «Towards a comprehensive European investment policy» (2010).[245] It describes two features of IIAs concluded by the Member States: "not all Member States have concluded such agreements, and not all agreements provide for the same high standards (…) Another feature of the agreements of Member States is that they relate to the treatment of investors «post-entry» or «post-admission» only. (…) Gradually, the European Union has started filling the gap of «entry» or «admission» through both multilateral and bilateral agreements at EU level covering investment market access and investment liberalization[246]". The Communication 2010 also refers to research data, confirming that "substantive investment provisions in broad trade agreements impact trade and FDI flows more profoundly, or that the combination of substantive investment rules and provisions liberalizing other parts of the economy jointly impact trade and investment more significantly." [247]

The new competence of the EU gave rise to multiple questions, in particular, about the scope of the EU investment protection and its correlation to the exclusive competences of Member States in other fields (problems in case of overlapping, if business activities relate to more than one policy field), the lack of treaty FDI definition, and the fate of intra- and extra-EU BITs.[248] Some guidance on the FDI is given in the Annex to an old Council Directive and the ECJ jurisprudence: "the establishment and extension of branches or new undertakings belonging solely to the person providing the capital and the acquisition in full of existing undertakings, participation in new or existing undertakings with a view to establishing or maintaining lasting economic links, long-term loans with a view to establishing or maintaining lasting economic links, and reinvestment of

---

244 Ibid.

245 Towards a comprehensive European international investment policy: Communication from the Commission to the Council, the European Parliament, the European Economic and Social Committee and the Committee of the Regions COM (2010) 343 final, 7 July 2010.

246 Ibid, p. 5.

247 Ibid.

248 The problem of extra-EU BITs will be addressed in Section Investment commitments under the AAs with respective countries and the bilateral investment agreements of Ukraine with the EU countries (on the example of Germany-Ukraine BIT).

profits with a view to maintaining lasting economic links.[249]" As that list and the relative explanatory notes show, the concept of direct investments concerns investments of any kind undertaken by natural or legal persons and which serve to establish or maintain lasting and direct links between the persons providing the capital and the undertakings to which that capital is made available in order to carry out an economic activity.

II. The EU Association Agreements with Georgia, Moldova and Ukraine

The legal base for the conclusion of the association agreements is provided by art. 217 TFEU. The distinctive features of AAs[250] inter alia include offering the Most Favoured Nation (MFN) treatment and the intention to establish close economic and political cooperation (more than simple cooperation). Although the Partnership and Cooperation Agreements (PCAs) with the «western» post-Soviet countries (i.e. Russia, Ukraine and Moldova) already foresaw the possibility to establish a Free Trade Area (FTA),these agreements were limited in their scope and contents and have become, especially after those countries accessed the World Trade Organization (WTO), outdated[251]. The Communication «Global Europe: Competing in the World[252]» (2006) emphasized the need to pursue a «far-reaching liberalization of services and investment». The European Commission explicitly stated that it aims for «WTO-plus commitments in FTAs»[253]. In November 2006, the Council adopted the «Minimum Platform on Investment for EU FTAs», a template for future investment FTA negotiations. It placed emphasis on services and investment liberalization within the context of the 'Global Europe' strategy. The Minimum Platform is used as a basis for negotiations on trade in services and establishment (i.e. investment) in practically all EU FTAs, with the objective of strengthening EC enterprises' access to foreign markets.

1. Legal framework of EU relations with three countries

The EU adopted the European Neighborhood Policy (ENP) in 2003 «with the main objective to avoid the emergence of new dividing lines between the enlarged EU and its neighbors and to strengthen instead the prosperity, stability and security of the EU's neighborhood. In 2008, within

249 Annex I to Council Directive 88/361/EEC of 24 June 1988 for the implementation of Article 67 of the Treaty [article repealed by the Treaty of Amsterdam] (OJ 1988 L 178), p. 5, and ECJ Case C-446/04, Test Claimants in the FII Litigation (2006), ECR I-11814, paras. 180-182.

250 See „Association Agreements" at the EU External Action website: http://eeas.europa.eu/association/ (date of accession: 01.03.2015)

251 Van der Loo, Guillaume, The New EU-Ukraine FTA: Deep and Comprehensive?, Law of Ukraine: Legal Journal 2013, p. 224.

252 European Commission, 'Global Europe: Competing in the World', COM (2006) 567 final, 4 October 2006, available at http://eur-lex.europa.eu/legal-content/EN/TXT/PDF/?uri=CELEX:52006DC0567&from=EN, date of accession: 01.03.2015).

253 Ibid, p.19.

the context of the ENP, the EU established a specific Eastern Partnership (EaP) initiative aiming at a political association and further economic integration between the EU and its eastern neighbors[254]». Generally speaking, the AAs have an «integration without membership» objective. On 27th June 2014 the Association Agreements between the EU and three countries were signed[255] in Brussels. «The conclusion of an AA, which must include such a Deep and Comprehensive Free Trade Area (DCFTA), was first offered to Ukraine in 2008, and then to the other Eastern Neighbors in 2009in the framework of the EaP[256]». On 18th July 2014 the Georgian Parliament, on 2nd July 2014[257] the Parliament of Moldova, and on 16th September 2014 the Ukrainian Verkhovna Rada[258] ratified the respective AAs. It is noteworthy that «the European Commission defines [also] several other recently concluded trade agreements as comprehensive such as the FTA with Colombia and Peru (signed in 2012), Chili (entered into force in 2003) and Mexico (entered into force in 2000). Especially the new generation of FTAs who are the result of the Global Europe Strategy are labeled as 'comprehensive' (e.g. the FTA with Korea (entered into force in 2011)».[259] According to the new AAs, the previous PCAs are to be replaced by the new generation AAs.[260]

a) Georgia

Since 1st July 1999 a PCA of Georgia[261] and the EU (former EC) / Euratom / former ECSC and their Member States is in force. Georgia and the European Union have maintained relations since the 1990s, using different fora, e.g. since 2006 the INOGATE framework (an international energy co-operation program between the EU and some states of the Caspian and Black seas and their neighbors). On 2 October 2006, a joint statement on the agreed text of a Georgia-European Union Action Plan within the ENP was issued. The Action Plan was formally approved at the EU-

254 Communication from the Commission to the European Parliament and the Council - Eastern Partnership, COM (2008) 0823 final, 3. December 2008, available at http://eeas.europa.eu/eastern/docs/com08_823_en.pdf, (date of accession: 01.03.2015), p. 2.

255 See European Commission Press release, MEMO/14/430 of 23 June 2014, available at http://europa.eu/rapid/press-release_MEMO-14-430_en.htm (date of accession: 01.03.2015).

256 Van der Loo, op. cit. 20, pp. 224 – 225.

257 Release by the Ministry of the Foreign Affairs and European Integration of Moldova, http://www.mfa.gov.md/comunicate-presa-md/498082/ (date of accession: 01.03.2015).

258 Release by Verkhovna Rada of Ukraine, http://rada.gov.ua/en/news/News/News/97871.html, (date of accession: 01.03.2015).

259 Van der Loo, op. cit. 20, p. 227.

260 See Article 479 Association Agreement between the European Union and its Member States, of the one part, and Ukraine of the other part, OJ, 2014, L 161.

261 Council and Commission Decision of 31 May 1999 on the conclusion of the Partnership and Cooperation Agreement between the European Communities and their Member States, of the one part, and Georgia, of the other part,1999/515/EC, ECSC, Euratom, OJ L 205, 4.8.1999, available at http://eur-lex.europa.eu/legal-content/EN/TXT/ PDF/?uri=CELEX:31999D0515&qid=1473698001426&from=en, (date of accession: 01.03.2015), pp. 1 – 2.

Georgia Cooperation Council session on 14th November 2006 in Brussels. On 22nd July 2013 the EU reported on the successful completion of the negotiations with Georgia about an AA.[262]

b) Moldova

Similarly, the EU and Moldova concluded a PCA on 28th November 1994, which entered into force on 1st July 1998. Like in EU-Georgia relations, this treaty provides for a basis of cooperation with the EU in the political, commercial, economic, legal, cultural and scientific areas. Moldova and the EU began negotiating an AA, which was to replace the PCA, in January 2010.

c) Ukraine

A political dialogue of the EU with Ukraine started in 1994 with the signature of a PCA which entered into force in 1998. «Negotiations with Ukraine were first launched only on the AA in March 2007 and then on the DCFTA in February 2008, after the confirmation of the country's WTO accession. At the Paris Summit in 2008 the leaders of the EU and Ukraine agreed that an AA should be the successor agreement to the PCA. In October 2011, the EU and Ukraine finalized the political negotiations on the DCFTA. The AA was initialed in March 2012, but the DCFTA was only initialed, after legal scrubbing, in July 2012. On 15 May 2013, the Commission adopted the proposals for a Council Decisions on the signing and the conclusion of the EU-Ukraine AA».[263] On 21st November 2013 the former Ukrainian Government suspended the signing of the AA.[264] However, at an Extraordinary EU-Ukraine Summit on 21st March 2014 representatives of Ukraine and the EU signed the Preamble, Article 1 and Titles I, II and VII (the so-called political parts of the Agreement).[265] Title 4 of the AA (which establishes the DCFTA) entered into force on 1st January 2016, for the time being only on a provisional basis. In order to express its support for Ukrainian exporters, the EU also granted Ukraine in 2014 and 2015 autonomous trade facilitation.[266] Provisional application of the Association Agreement, inter alia, involves the entire title on General Principles (Title I) and Financial Cooperation (Title VI), almost the entire DCFTA (Title IV), Institutional, General and Final Provisions (Title VII) and several provisions regarding political dialogue (Arts. 4-6), Justice, Freedom and Security (Arts. 14 and

262 Association Agenda between the European Union and Georgia, available at https://eeas.europa.eu/delegations/georgia/documents/eap_aa/associationagenda_2014_en.pdf (date of accession: 01.03.2015), p. 1.

263 Van der Loo, op. cit. 20, p. 225.

264 See Statement by Ukrainian Department of Information and Communication of the Secretariat of the CMU, 21 November 2013, available at http://www.kmu.gov.ua/control/en/publish/article?art_id=246864641&cat_id=246866213 (date of accession: 01.03.2015).

265 See text of the Final Act of a Summit between the European Union and its Member States, of the one part, and Ukraine, of the other part, as regards the Association Agreement, FA/EU/UA/en 4, available at: http://eeas.europa. eu/delegations/ukraine/documents/association_agreement/final_act_text_en.pdf (date of accession: 01.03.2015).

266 „Association Agreement" at the Delegation of the EU to Ukraine website, http://eeas.europa.eu/ delegations/ukraine/eu_ukraine/association_agreement/index_en.htm (date of accession: 01.03.2015).

19) and economic and sectoral cooperation «without prejudice to the division of competences between the Union and the Member States».[267]

2. Models of EU agreements with Eastern Partnership countries

The investment regulation under the AAs points both to the investment liberation[268] and to the investment protection. "A controlled entry model that reserves the right of the host state to regulate the entry of foreign investments into its territory and a 'full liberalization' model that extends the nondiscrimination standard (both national treatment (NT) and MFN) in the agreement to the pre-entry stage of the investment. If a host State grants the entry rights, it usually extends treatment obligations to the admission and establishment phase of the investment, with no specific obligations on its part toward the admission itself".[269]

The General Agreement on Trade Tariffs (GATT) and, therefore, the Trade-related Investment Measures Agreement (TRIMS)[270] cover trade in all goods and thus subject all TRIMs on goods trade to the basic rules of national treatment and the prohibition on quantitative restrictions. To the contrary, the General Agreement on Trade in Services (GATS) distinguishes between four so-called modes of providing services and the mode that is relevant for our discussion is the third mode, namely «the supply of a service (...) by a service supplier of one Member, through commercial presence in the territory of any other Member[271]». This mode of service supply essentially operates by the establishment of a subsidiary or a branch in another WTO Member and therefore constitutes an investment within the meaning of most definition clauses of most BITs.

The MFN and NT obligations require that service suppliers are granted treatment not less favorable than that afforded service suppliers of any other WTO Member or domestic service supplier. However, there is a sectoral difference: MFN applies to all sectors covered by the agreement, except where particular exemptions were inscribed by each Member; NT – only applies to those

---

267 Article 486 EU-Ukraine AA, and Latrille, Pierre/ Lee, Juneyoung, Services rules in regional trade agreements How diverse and how creative as compared to the GATS multilateral rules?, 2012, available at https://www.wto. org/english/res_e/reser_e/ersd201219_e.pdf, (date of accession: 01.03.2015), pp. 14-15.

268 Gomez-Palacio, Ignacio/ Muchlinski, Peter, in; Muchlinski, Peter T./Ortino, Federico/Schreuer, Christoph (Ed.), The Oxford Handbook of International Investment Law, 2013. p. 240.

269 Molinuevo, Martin, Protecting Investment in Services. Investor-State Arbitration versus WTO Dispute Settlement, 2012. pp. 86-87.

270 Article 2 of TRIMs prescribes that no Member shall apply TRIMs that are inconsistent with the Articles III and XI of GATT and then refers to the illustrative list of such TRIMs contained in Annex 1 to the agreement.

271 Article I:2(c) of the General Agreement on Trade in Services, Apr. 15, 1994, Marrakesh Agreement Establishing the World Trade Organization, Annex 1B, THE LEGAL TEXTS: THE RESULTS OF THE URUGUAY ROUND OF MULTILATERAL TRADE NEGOTIATIONS 284 (1999), 1869 U.N.T.S. 183, 33 I.L.M. 1167 (1994).

sectors where Members have undertaken specific commitments, and according to the conditions or qualifications set out there in.[272]

There are three models of regional trade agreements[273]: the first model is based on GATS[274], the second – on NAFTA[275], and the third follows neither[276]. AAs with the Eastern Neighbors belong to the third model where "establishment" chapter covers mode 3 and go much further in many respects (for instance, by covering all “economic activities”)[277].

The chosen model of agreement influences the interpretation in case of a conflict between the service and the investment regulation. Nearly all NAFTA-type agreements give priority to the services chapter in case of a conflict. In GATS-type agreements the basic pattern is that the investment provisions apply to both services and to investment in services except for NT and MFN treatment, market access, and sometimes prohibition of performance requirements where the services chapter prevails or has exclusivity. Within the «others» category, the EU inspired agreements that encompass both the equivalent of mode 3 for services and investment in manufacturing, mining and agriculture in their establishment chapters.

3. Structure of the Association Agreements

Contrary to the classical FTAs, which only cover trade in goods, «comprehensive» trade agreements also cover other trade areas, «foreseeing not only the mutual opening of markets for most goods but also the partial and gradual liberalization of services and binding provisions on all other main trade area's such as sanitary and phytosanitary (SPS) rules, intellectual property rights

272 GATS Articles XVII: 1, XX: 1(b).

273 Latrille, Pierre/ Lee, Juneyoung, Services rules in regional trade agreements. How diverse and how creative as compared to the GATS multilateral rules? 2012, available at https://www.wto.org/english/res_e/reser_e/ersd201219_e.htm, (date of accession: 01.03.2015), p. 7.

274 The GATS-type agreements have the following features: positive listing of commitments, four modes of delivery, in principle no separate investment chapter covering services, a market access clause based on the quantitative restrictions in Article XVI of the GATS, a national treatment clause with like services and like services suppliers as a benchmark, no status quo or ratchet obligation, transparency obligation limited to publication, no explicit provisions on performance requirements, etc.

275 The NAFTA-type agreements include negative listing of commitments, distinction between a cross-border chapter covering mutatis mutandis modes 1, 2 and 4 and an investment chapter covering all investment including in services i.e. mutatis mutandis mode 3, a national treatment clause based on the "like circumstances" test instead of the "like services and like services suppliers" test, advance notifications, status quo and ratchet principles, explicit coverage of performance requirements, etc.

276 The "other" category includes seven EU related agreements and agreements that do not fit into the GATS or NAFTA categories. Their objective is deeper economic and political integration, while the other two types of agreements only aim to liberalize trade. The common features of EC/EU types of agreements are a "neither nor" approach to the scheduling of commitments, no modes and the use of alternative concepts such as freedom to provide services and establishment, a domestic regulation policy geared towards integration and harmonization and provisions on natural persons going much further than the GATS or the NAFTA models, notably in terms of access to employment and social security and of the status of dependents.

277 Latrille, Pierre/ Lee, Juneyoung, op. cit. 42, p. 9.

(IPR), trade facilitation, public procurement, energy, transport and competition[278]». «The «deep» character of the DCFTA on the other hand refers to commitment to approximate its legislation to the *acquis communautaire* in order to achieve economic integration in the EU Internal ket[279]». Unlike the previous soft-law instruments of the EU, such as the Action Plan and Association Agenda, this legislative approximation has a legally binding nature under the AAs.

The three AAs show some similarities in structure and nature of mutual commitments, with EU-Ukraine standing out due to excessive legislative approximation obligations on the part of Ukraine. Key differences between the EU-Ukraine AA and the Moldova or Georgia AAs are, for example, that Georgia is referred to in the preamble of the Georgia AA as an Eastern European country and that both the Georgian and Moldovan AAs do not include a non-discrimination clause for the treatment and the mobility of workers, corresponding to Articles 17 and 18 of the EU-Ukraine AA. In the trade part, important differences are, inter alia, that approximation clauses in the area of competition and "internal market treatment" in the area of establishment are not foreseen in the Georgia and Moldova DCFTAs.[280] The provisions on trade-related energy and intellectual property rights are less detailed in the Moldova and Georgia DCFTAs. The AA with Ukraine starts with a Preamble, in which the Parties express their commitments to develop "a new climate conducive to economic relations between the Parties, and above all for the development of trade and investment and stimulating competition, factors which are crucial to economic restructuring and modernization". Then follow seven Titles (with Title IV devoted to trade and trade-related matters), 3 Annexes; and 3 Protocols. The AAs with Georgia and the AA with Moldova show a similar pattern.

III. Comparison of investment commitments under the Association Agreements and other investment agreements

1. Overview of investment commitments under the Association Agreements

The investment provisions in the AAs are almost identical. Therefore, it is possible to consider only one AA (with Ukraine) and to make references to other two AAs in case of, if any, considerable differences.

According to official footnotes in the AAs,[281] investment protection is not included in the Chapter 6 «Establishment, trade in services and electronic commerce» except for the relevant provisions

278 Van der Loo, op. cit. 20, p. 226.

279 Ibid.

280 Latrille, Pierre/ Lee, Juneyoung, op. cit. 42, p. 1.

281 See footnote to Article 88 EU-Ukraine AA, Article 79 Association Agreement between the European Union

on MFN and NT for both before- and after-establishment. Moreover, the Agreements stipulate two restrictions: a non-preclusion clause for the pre-establishment phase ("The provisions of Article 88 do not preclude the application by a Party of particular rules concerning the establishment and operation in its territory of branches and representative offices of legal persons of the other Party not incorporated in the territory of the first Party…") and the negative lists of exceptions for both Parties (Annexes XVI-A and XVI-D to the Agreement).

The AAs, however, contain a specific definition of the term "investor" ("any natural or legal person of a Party that seeks to perform or performs an economic activity through setting up an establishment[282]") and of establishment[283] ("(a) as regards legal persons of the EU Party or of Ukraine, the right to take up and pursue economic activities by means of setting up, including the acquisition of, a legal person and/or create a branch or a representative office in Ukraine or in the EU Party respectively; (b) as regards natural persons, the right of natural persons of the EU Party or of Ukraine to take up and pursue economic activities as self-employed persons, and to set up undertakings, in particular companies, which they effectively control") but no definition of (foreign direct) investment.

Investment liberalization involves two kinds of provisions. The first is a provision which typically provides for rights of entry and establishment for investment in at least certain sectors of the economy. The second is a market access provision that generally provides for a right to provide services in at least certain sectors through a commercial presence in the host country.[284] The provisions on market access in AA can be found in Section 3 ("Cross-border supply of services").[285] Here the question whether the investment in a form of services is double regulated by Section 3 and Section 4 (both involve specific National Treatment commitments) arises.

In an investment doctrine, "where FDI is seen as a short-term commitment, then a clear separation can be made, between the right of admission – which deals only with the right of entry, that is, the rules set for admission – and the right of establishment – which deals with the way the ac-

and the European Atomic Energy Community and their Member States, of the one part, and Georgia, of the other part, OJ, 2014, L 261, and Article 205 Association Agreement between the European Union and the European Atomic Energy Community and their Member States, of the one part, and the Republic of Moldova, of the other part, OJ, 2014, L 260.

282 Article 86 EU-Ukraine AA.

283 According to Annexes XVI-A the EU made the following reservation: Treatment accorded to subsidiaries (of Ukraine companies) formed in accordance with the law of a Member State and having their registered office, central administration or principal place of business within the Union is not extended to branches or agencies established in a Member State by a Ukrainian company.

284 UNCTAD, Investment Provisions in Economic Integration Agreements, 2006, available at http://unctad.org/en/Docs/iteiit200510_en.pdf (date of accession: 01.03.2015), p. 76.

285 Article 84 EU-Georgia AA, Article 210 EU-Moldova AA.

tivity of the investor will take place over the duration of the investment and also with the protection of the type of presence that may be permitted". The lack of investment definition leaves the question open, because the duration of investment can serve as the criterion for granting rights under an investment treaty. In the latter case the services regulation and investment establishment in AAs could be distinguished on the basis of duration.

According to the AA, Ukraine enjoys an «internal market treatment». This unprecedented access to the EU Internal Market means that the Ukrainian legal persons will have the same freedom of establishment and will be able to provide services in the EU as juridical persons of EU Member States.[286] Regulatory approximation[287] commitments (specific for the EU-Ukraine AA and not for the other two AAs) play a significant role for the treatment in general. Among AA's peculiarities the explicit "market access" conditionality shall be mentioned. According to the requirements of DCFTA, Ukraine would have an additional access to a section of the EU Internal Market, only if the EU decides, after a strict monitoring procedure, that Ukraine successfully implemented its legislative approximation commitments. In those areas where the full internal market treatment is foreseen, such as in services and establishment, the arrangement is comparable to the mechanism for legislative approximation under the EEA[288]. However, this provision is irreciprocal in nature, and it makes possible for the EU to retract from the protection granted for Ukrainian investors.

Moreover, the AA drafters set up the standards of review ("the Parties shall regularly review the establishment legal framework and the establishment climate, consistent with their commitments under international agreements") and the references to the existing investment instruments[289] that are applicable if they offer a more favorable treatment to the investors, but only with regard to the pre-establishment phase (investment liberalization). Addressing public policy considerations, the AAs concern the relation between foreign investment and labor or environmental standards ("Upholding levels of protection"[290]). Besides, the AAs broaden the scope of public policy concerns linked with foreign investment, including social, health and cultural concerns.

Although the AAs contain special Chapters on Dispute Settlement and Mediation, the Parties did not provide for the investor-state dispute settlement mechanism.[291] If the provisions on investors' behavior and the maintenance of standards are breached, the persons who are directly affected are not provided by the AAs with any means for demanding the enforcement of these provisions.

286 Latrille, Pierre/ Lee, Juneyoung, op. cit. 42, p. 20.
287 Article 114 EU-Ukraine AA.
288 Latrille, Pierre/ Lee, Juneyoung, op. cit. 42, p. 20.
289 Articles 88-90 EU-Ukraine AA, 79-81 EU-Georgia AA, 205-207 EU-Moldova AA.
290 Articles 296 EU-Ukraine AA, 235 EU-Georgia AA, 371 EU-Moldova AA.
291 See Article 89 (2) EU-Ukraine AA.

2. Investment commitments under the AAs with respective countries and the bilateral investment agreements of Ukraine with the EU countries (on the example of Germany-Ukraine BIT)

The Germany-Ukraine BIT is an extra-EU BITs which was signed on 15th February 1993 and entered into force 29th June 1996. After the ECJ ruling[292] that Member State BITs may also be deemed to be in violation of the EC Treaty to the extent that they contain particular free transfer provisions, the fate of the extra-EU BITs remained undecided. However, Regulation No.1219/2012 (2012) establishing transitional arrangements for bilateral investment agreements between Member States and third countries confirms not to replace the investment promotion efforts of MSs, as long as they fit with the CCP and remain consistent with EU law.

The Germany-Ukraine BIT consists of 13 articles and a Protocol, and belongs to an old generation BITs with comparably abstract provisions. The definition of investment based on a notion of property holdings with an illustrative list of possible investment forms incorporates, inter alia, property, corporate rights, the right to monetary claims, intellectual property, contract rights, etc. Art. 3 of the respective BIT deals with the MFN and NT („each Party ensures on its territory with regard to investments owned by or under control of the natural or legal persons of the other Party and are allowed and made in accordance with the Party's current legislation, the treatment no less favorable than that the one offered to its own natural or legal persons or the ones of the third countries"). Therefore, the MFN and NT provisions are applicable to the investment already established "in accordance with a Party's legislation"[293]. The BIT might be interpreted in favor of an investor. However, the BIT is silent for the pre-establishment phase, and according to Article 90 of the EU-Ukraine AA the relevant provisions of AA on investment liberalization are applicable. In summary, the establishment of a Ukrainian subsidiary in Germany (depending on the qualification as an investor under the Treaties) would be covered by:

- EU-Ukraine AA with regard to establishment,
- EU-Ukraine AA and Germany-Ukraine BIT, with regard to NT and MFN treatment,
- EU law and Germany-Ukraine BIT with regard to other post-establishment investment protection.

In this case, the BIT regulations could arguably challenge the non-discrimination principle under EU law. Possible implications and questions also arise, when:

---

292 The ECJ ruled that its findings were 'not limited to the Member State which is the defendant in the present case', see Case C-205/06, Commission v Austria and Case C- 249/06, Commission v Sweden, judgments (Grand Chamber) of 3 March 2009, for both para. 43.

293 Article 2 Germany-Ukraine BIT.

- a subsidiary is investing in more than one European country (bearing in mind that Ukraine has 23 BITs with countries that are currently members of the EU[294])
- a subsidiary is providing services covered by EU-Ukraine AA and GATS.

3. Investment commitments under the AAs with the respective countries and CETA

On December 3, 2013, the European Commission issued a document concerning the investment provisions in the EU-Canada free trade agreement (CETA). «It is the first agreement that puts all EU investors on the same, equal footing[295]». Unlike the AAs with three countries, the innovative Canada-EU Trade Agreement has a special chapter on Investment (Chapter 10), where parties agreed upon certain limitations to the scope of the agreement. For the EU, the Section on Establishment of Investments and Section on Non-Discriminatory Treatment do not apply to measures with respect to audiovisual services. For Canada, the respective sections do not apply to cultural industries.

CETA offers a traditional asset-based[296] definition of investment with an open-ended list of possible forms of investment. In order to qualify for protection under the treaty, investments do not need to fulfill all listed requirements (i.e., the phrase "such as"). There are three groups of investors that can be distinguished with regard to CETA:

- national investors (investing in the Member State where they were established);
- European investors (established within a EU Member State but investing across boarders in other Member States); and
- third country (foreign) investors (established outside the EU but making investments in one or more of the Member States; they are protected under Article 63 (1) TFEU and under international law (customary minimal legal standards for the treatment of aliens or BITs)).[297]

NT provisions in Member States' BITs allow for "automatic"[298] treatment in accordance with Article 54 TFEU, as a European investor regarding its investments in other Member States and

[294] According to the UNCTAD IIAs Navigatorhttp://investmentpolicyhub.unctad.org/IIA/CountryBits/219 #iiaInnerMenu (date of accession: 01.03.2015).
[295] Investment Provisions in the EU-Canada Free Trade Agreement (CETA), Available at trade.ec.europ a.eu/doclib/docs/2013/november/tradoc_151918.pdf (date of accession: 01.03.2015).
[296] As opposed to an enterprise-based definition (which requires the establishment or acquisition of an enterprise in the host state), or a closed asset-based definition (which sets out an exhaustive and limited list of situations that constitute an investment).
[297] Directorate-General for External Policies, Policy Department. Investor-State Dispute Settlement provisions in the EU's international investment agreements. Volume 2-Studies.EXPO/B/INTA/2014/08-09-10 (2014), available at http://www.europarl.europa.eu/RegData/etudes/STUD/2014/534979/EXPO_STU(2014)534979(ANN 01)_EN.pdf (date of accession: 01.03.2015), pp. 143-144.
[298] Ibid.

therefore benefits from the principle of mutual recognition and from the secondary EU legislation facilitating intra-EU transactions. According to Article 62 TFEU this assimilation applies to the freedom of establishment as well as to services. NT granted in an IPA between the EU and a third country extends this guarantee to third country nationals established in one of the EU Member States. It follows that third country nationals would enjoy the same rights as Member States nationals regarding establishment, providing services as well as for participation in the capital of companies in other Member States under Article 55 TFEU.

The Agreement encompasses relevant provisions on market access[299] with a list of otherwise consistent measures. Unlike AAs, market access and right to establishment, expressly belong to the Investment Chapter. Articles X.6 and X.7 offer NT and MFN, respectively (unlike the AAs, the reference in these provisions is made to the "like situations") and cover "the establishment, acquisition, expansion, conduct, operation, management, maintenance, use, enjoyment and sale or disposal of their investments in its territory". The MFN clause is not applicable to ISDS. But far more important is the reservation clause that exempts from MFN and NT is "an existing non-conforming measure that is maintained by a Party", which can stem from the EU, Member States, a provincial, territorial, or regional government, or even a local government.[300] Together with the Prudential Carve-outs clause,[301] this provision shields the EU legal order and Member States' right to regulate. Reversely, the Germany-Ukraine BIT is silent on this matter.

IV. Conclusion

The EU had just gained the exclusive competence in the field of FDI when the Association Agreements (AAs) were signed. Therefore, the AAs neither offer a "fresh" regulatory perspective nor eliminate the legal uncertainty in the field of FDI. However, the AAs still go beyond the existing extra-EU BITs (some of them, like the Germany-Ukraine BIT, are rather obsolete). The undecided nature of market access and interrelation with the investment regulation arguably jeopardize an effective application of the provisions. Similar interpretational problems arise out of the double trade and investment regulation in the WTO system for investments in the form of services. This problem could be solved by adopting a separate chapter on investment in the respective AAs (like in CETA).

---

299 Article X.4: Neither Party shall adopt or maintain with regard to market access through establishment by an investor of a Party, either on the basis of its entire territory or on the basis of the territory of a national, provincial, territorial, regional or local level of government, certain measures or restrict or require specific types of legal entity.

300 Article X.14 EU-Canada Comprehensive Economic and Trade Agreement, text available at http://trade.ec.europa.eu/doclib/docs/2014/september/tradoc_152806.pdf(date of accession: 01.03.2015).

301 Article 15 Ibid.

C. Economic and Sectoral Cooperation within the three Association Agreements - Overview and Examples

Alexander Trunk

Introduction

All three Association Agreements contain extensive Titles on Economic and Sectoral Cooperation, following or preceding the DCFTA Title[302]. They are of a comparable size (roughly 120 articles each), about half of the size of the Titles on Trade and Trade-Related Measures (DCFTA Titles). The EU-Moldova AA and the EU-Ukraine AAs contain each 28 Chapters, the EU-Georgia AA is a bit more diversified (27 Chapters), but the subject-matters covered in these Titles are largely identical[303]. Nevertheless they differ in certain aspects. For example, the EU-Ukraine AA starts with the Chapter on Energy cooperation[304], which was apparently regarded by the Contracting Parties as of particular importance. This is understandable in view of the role of Ukraine as a highly important energy transit country between Russia, the Caucasus, Central Asia and the EU and in view of the disputes which arose between Ukraine and Russia in this respect in the last years and had an effect on the energy supply to EU countries. In contrast the EU-Moldova AA starts with a unique Chapter on Public Administration Reform[305], which shows the importance given by both sides to this structural topic. The EU-Georgia AA begins with a general Chapter on Economic Dialogue[306] (similar Chapters exist also in the two AAs), which seems systematically convincing in this context of the AAs and can be regarded as a sign that there was no necessity to put any specific issue at the top of this Title – arguably a positive element of "normality" in the EU-Georgia relationship.

There are close links between the DCFTA Titles of the Agreements and the Titles on Economic and Sectoral Cooperation. Sometimes the same economic sectors are specifically addressed in both Titles, e.g. the energy sector, financial services, the transport industry, agriculture and the information technology sector. Although the DCFTA title addresses these sectors from the trade perspective, while the Economic and Sectoral Cooperation Title have a broader cooperation-oriented approach, the contents of the provisions in both types of Titles is sometime very similar. This is due to the "deep and comprehensive" character of the new FTA approach, which includes

302 In the EU-Ukraine AA: Title IV (Art. 337 – 452), in the EU-Moldova AA Title V (Art. 21 – 142), in the EU-Georgia the matters have been distributed to two Titles: Title V "Economic Cooperation" (Art. 277 – 291) and Title VI "Other Cooperation Policies" (Art. 292 – 382)

303 Like the DCFTA Titles, the Economic and Sectoral Cooperation are also supplemented with various Annexes to the AAs, specifying, for example, the provisions of the EU acquis to which an approximation by the associated countries has been agreed in which time-frames and with which – if any - specifications.

304 Art. 337 – 342 EU-Ukraine AA.

305 Art. 21 - 23 EU-Moldova AA.

306 Art. 277 – 278 EU-Georgia AA.

cooperation and approximation of standards elements in the trade context, although they are also addressed in the broader cooperation Titles of the AAs. As a tendency one can state that the provisions in the DCFTA Titles usually fall under the exclusive competence of the EU, while the matters covered in the Economic and Sectoral Cooperation Titles are often characterized by mixed competences of the EU and its Member States. This is reflected by the differentiated approach as to the provisional application of the AAs[307]. In practice, the DCFTA Titles and the Economic and Sectoral Cooperation Titles will often have to be read in conjunction to understand the full content of the AAs.

The Titles on Economic and Sectoral Cooperation usually contain in each Chapter provisions on cooperation between the two sides (including information and dialogue) and approximation of law (with separately mentioned administrative practice). Mutual recognition of standards, administrative acts or judicial decisions, academic degrees etc. is not expressly addressed in the Chapters, but is certainly one of the aspects to be covered by the agreed dialogue and would seem to be a logical consequence of the process of approximation of the laws of the three associate countries to the EU acquis.

[307] Cf. In detail, see http://eurlex.europa.eu/legalcontent/EN/TXT/HTML/?uri=CELEX:22014X1031(01)&from=DE.

Ana Tokhadze

Enhancement of Corporate Social Responsibility – An Analysis from the Perspective of Economic and Sectoral Cooperation under the Three Association Agreements

This article is set up in order to clarify the main course of Corporate Governance upon social responsibility and to give general lines and remarks, which are stipulated by the three Association Agreements of Georgia, Moldova and Ukraine. At the outset, some terminological definitions will be discussed. Afterwards, the mainstream of Georgian, Moldavian and Ukrainian Corporate Governance will be described in a nutshell. A clarification of the main positions on this subject in the three AAs is also of high relevance, as well as, mentioning probable reforms in the name of attaining legal maturity in the field of company law and corporate governance.

I. Definition of Corporate Governance, Systems and Models

1. Corporate Governance (CG)

There is no official definition of CG. Corporations are governed in various manners.[308] This is affected from the key factors as follows: inner management system, industry (where the business is conducted), geographic location, economic, legal, social environment (etc.) of corporations. Precisely, all these inherent features vary in many respects; however, in a very concise manner, still, CG can be identified as an administrative process of "improving economic efficiency and growth as well as enhancing investor confidence. Corporate governance involves a set of relationships between a company's management, its board, its shareholders and other stakeholders"[309]. Thus, the relation between control (whether it's internal or external) and management, balancing interests between organizational bodies, proceeding business in the legal frameworks, holding responsibilities and obligations upon the society – all of these are subjected to the sound CG.

2. CG System

Identification of the CG system depends whether the corporation has either one-tier or two-tier governance system. Both of them evolve recruitment of controlling management through the certain organizational bodies, as for example: in one-tier system Board of Directors consists of inde-

---

308 As for example, there is a high dimension between the system of corporate governance of companies operating in financial industry and companies with a purpose of producing a certain product, Roth M., Conflict of Interest: compliance and its contribution to corporate governance in the financial services sector (Peters A., Handschin L. (eds.)), Conflict of Interest in Global, Public and Corporate Governance,Cambridge University Press, NY., 2012, 257.

309 OECD Principles of Corporate Governance, 2004, Preamble, 12.

pendent directors, who look after the performance of executive directors solving and managing the company on the daily basis; however, two-tier system separates supervisor board with responsibilities and duties to carry on control over the directors (coterminous to the German *Vorstand*[310]). Indeed, system identifies whether there is one-tier or two-tier corporate governance, therefore the main structure of the organization.

3. CG Model

The Model of a CG system in support of determination of the major orientation, focus of management; who's interests are mainly pursued and who will benefit or suffer a loss from (ir)relevant decision-making[311]. "There is no single model of good corporate governance"[312]. In every model balancing principal-agent's interests[313] increases the latitude of profitability for the corporation itself. Habitually, principal amounts for the shareholder and therefore director is in charge of agent. For the said, shareholders rely on specialized, but not self-interested agents.[314] However, dimension of interests, so called – conflict of various interests among shareholders, related parties, third parties, creditors, generally, stakeholder – hinders the process of considering only stockholder's material intentions.

A big variety of models derive from the incentives of management and purposes of the corporation: a manager-oriented model, shareholder primacy model, state-oriented model, labor-centered model[315], economic model, politic model, etc.[316] Manager-oriented model yield massive power and authority for the directors, which resulted in director's misbehavior in their professional activities by breaching fiduciary duties and therefore disregarding all moral or legal clauses. Even though, patterns of this model was liked according to the American Company Law, however, by

---

310 Chanturia L.,Korporatsiulimartva da direktortapasukhismgeblobakorporaciulmarTvashi [Corporate Governance and Liability of the Directors in the Corporate Governance], "Meridiani", Tbilisi, 2006, 127; Burduli I.,Konebriviurtiertobasaaktsosazogadoebashi [Property Relation in the Joint Stock Company], TSU House Publication, Tbilisi, 2008, 79, footnote 219; Schulz M., Wasmeier O., The law of Business Organizations, Berlin, 2012, 41-45.

311 Freeman E., Wicks A., ParmarB., Stakeholder Theory and The Corporate Objective Revisited, Organization, Science, Vol. 15, No. 3, 2011, 53.

312 OECD Principles of Corporate Governance, 2004, Preamble, 12.

313 This happens to be a current issue whenever one has to act on another's behalf, p. 258-259. Usually, principal is a shareholder and agent refers to the director, who performs in the name of the stockholder with a motivation of material gain, see, Kraakman R., Armour J., Davies P., Enriques L., Hansmann H., Hertig G., Hopt K., Kanda H., Rock E., The Anatomy of Corporate Law, 2nd ed., NY, 2009, 35.

314 Peters A., Managing Conflict of Interest: Lessons from Multiple Disciplines and Settings, (Peters A., Handschin L. (eds.)), Conflict of Interest in Global, Public and Corporate Governance, Cambridge University Press, New York, 2012, 362.

315 Hansmann H., Kraakman R., The End of History For Corporate Law, Yale Law School Working Paper, N 235, NYU Working Paper N 013, Harvard Las School Discussion Paper N 280, Yale SOM Working PaperN. ICF – 00-09, 2000, 5-11.

316 Tully St., International Corporate Legal Responsibility (Tully St. (ed.)), Walter Kluwer Law & Business, Netherlands, 2012, 111-112.

1970s, managerially-centered governance came to an end[317]. Once American managerial approach became a no-go, a new era in CG took up by enhancement of shareholder's primacy, which would increase so called 'shareholder's value'[318]. This type of model was expected to decrease 'Agency Cost'[319] and encourage incentives for financial standing of shareholders. However, shareholder-centered model, in a way, contradicts state-oriented model, also, named as labor-oriented model. This extends from the aim of particulars of this model, which is more social like, rather focused on shareholder's material gains. This is a model, which casts social responsibility for big corporations operating and developing economy. Therefore, corporations are obliged to concern social requirements (such as: environment protection, human rights protection, etc.) while conducting.[320] Thus, socially responsible corporation is at high level active in social way, which strengthens financial performance[321], glorifies a good reputation.[322]

II. General Review of Corporate Governance Models and Assessment of Corporate Social Responsibility in Georgia, Moldova and Ukraine

1. General Overview of CG Legislation in Georgia, Moldova and Ukraine

The adopted CG codes in all of the three countries – Georgia, Moldova, Ukraine – are quite effective and consistent with international standards and principles.[323] CG codes of named countries are not mandatory, but voluntarily applicable. General meeting of shareholders is a relevant organizational body, which decides whether 'comply or explain'[324] deviation from the CG codes. Exceptional is a Georgian CG code, which is in force for only Commercial Banks, but capable of being subscribed (on the voluntarily basis) for the rest companies.

---

317 Hansmann H., Kraakman R., The End of History For Corporate Law, Yale Law School Working Paper, N 235, NYU Working Paper N 013, Harvard Las School Discussion Paper N 280, Yale SOM Working PaperN. ICF – 00-09, 2000, 4.

318 Burduli I.,Saaktsiosamartlissafudzvlebi [Fundaments of Joint Stock Company], Vol. II, "Meridiani", Tbilisi, 2013, 370-374.

319 Bainbridge St., The New Corporate Governance in Theory and Practice, Oxford University Press, NY, 2008, 73-75.

320 Tully St., International Corporate Legal Responsibility (Tully St. (ed.)), Walter Kluwer Law & Business, Netherlands, 2012, 20-28.

321 Corporate Social Responsibility does not cause a financial decay, See, Rahim M. M., Legal Regulation of Corporate Social Responsibility, CSR, Sustainability, Ethics & Governance, Springer-Verlag, Berlin, Heidelberg, 2013, 14-15.

322 "Good Corporate citizenship, in the form of a well-developed plan and well-implemented program of product, service, and philanthropy, is the best form of reputation insurance you can get." See, Rubenst D., Good Corporate Citizen, A Practical Guide, John Wiley & Sons, Inc., New Jersey, Canada, 2004, 14.

323 See, Georgian Corporate Governance Code for the Commercial Banks, 2009, Forward; Corporate Governance Code of Republic of Moldova, 2007, Introduction; Ukrainian Corporate Governance Principles, 2003, Introduction.

324 In the same vein as is prescribed by the 'soft law', Hopt K. J., Corporate Governance in Europe: New Model of Regulation and "Soft Law" (Georgian translation by Burduli I.), Journal of Law, TSU, N. 1, 2009, 243- 245.

The CG system in Georgia, Moldova and Ukraine is of a hybrid type, since in existence of certain legal preconditions; a corporation is required to beget supervisory board. These requisites differ in each country. As for example: in Georgia according to the 'Law on Entrepreneurship' authority to the supervisory board should be conferred if the corporation is operating on the capital market, if the amount of shareholders exceeds 100, if the corporation has gained an accountability by the National Bank of Georgia.[325] If a total amount of shareholders in the joint stock company exceeds 50, general meeting of shareholders are electing the supervisory board due to the Moldavian legislation.[326] The same approach is in Ukraine, but the difference is in the amount of shareholders, which is cut down to 10.[327] Therefore, shareholder engagement (though their representatives in the supervisory board) in the process of CG is eventually envisaged.[328]

It is hard enough to single out one certain model, that is in action for Georgian, Moldavian or Ukrainian model, but as far as legislation perceives a board as a body performing with the best interests of shareholders, shareholder-oriented system is meant to be a bedrock of legislation.[329] Corporation is aligned to generate profit through any lawful way[330], however, in the name of social institution,[331] corporation has a moral responsibility. With reference to the economic approach of transaction cost, moral hazard plays an immense role to hold business conducts in the frames of morality and law. Consequently, Corporate Social Responsibility is meant to be a moral or legal constraint on operations conducted by the business-makers; precisely, it handles conflicts of interest between financial goals (whether in behalf of shareholders or corporation itself) and social targets.[332] After all, historically, corporations were established with an aim to accomplish social purposes (e.g.: railway construction in 1800s in America).[333]

---

325 See, 'Law on Entrepreneurship', Article 55, section 1.

326 'Law on Joint Stock Companies', Article 50(3) and Article 66.

327 'Law of Ukraine "On Joint Stock Companies", Article 51, section 1.

328 With this regards compliance with the requirement of AAs has been being more provided during last period. See, Georgian AA, Article 316, Sec. (a); Moldavian AA, Article 27, Sec. (A), Ukrainian AA, Article 387, Sec. (a).

329 Ukrainian Corporate Governance Principles, 2003, Introduction, 3, "Good corporate governance allows investors to be certain that their investment is used prudently by management to increase the company's financial and business activity and, therefore, to create shareholder value."; Corporate Governance Code of Republic of Moldova, 2007, Chapter VI, Associated Parties, 12, "Protecting the rights of the associated parties and establishing with them relations that will encourage value creation is for the benefit of the company and shareholders.".

330 This was a essence of the article written by Milton Friedman regarding CSR, see, Friedman M., The Social Responsibility of Business is to Increase Its Profits, New York Times Magazine, 1970, http://graphics8.nytimes.com/packages/pdf/business/miltonfriedman1970.pdf, [5.10.2014].

331 Tully St., International Corporate Legal Responsibility (Tully St. (ed.)), Walter Kluwer Law & Business, Netherlands, 2012, 3, cited: P. Ducker, The concept of the Corporation, The New American Library (Harper & Row, New York, 2nd ed., 1964), 137.

332 BeisinghoffN., Corporations and Human Rights, An Analysis of ATCA Litigation against Corporations, Peter Lang, Band 81, InternationalerVerlag der Wissenschaften, Frankfurt, 2009 85-87.

333 Tully St., International Corporate Legal Responsibility (Tully St. (ed.)), Walter Kluwer Law & Business, Neth-

2. Experience in Corporate Social Responsibility

Among the Ukrainian corporations 'Astrata' was nominated as the most successful organization, which managed to get the highest assessment and rate.[334] In the name of sustainable development as a basic principal of the mentioned organization is high social responsibility.[335] 'Astarta' has created a CSR program in reference to main areas, such as: environmental protection, giving support to rural community, conducting voluntarily social activities.[336]

From the Georgian perspective law firms frequently give financial support to the law students.[337] But due to the lamentable economic past, Georgian companies still find it hard to get additional funds to donate; therefore they simply abstain from such activities. Mainly commercial banks keep up the pace and set up quite appealing Corporate Social Responsibility programs.[338]

Among Moldovan companies, as in Georgia, the commercial banks are more active. They represent the most advanced sector as related to social responsibility of the domestic companies due to the significant material gains through publicly articulated information about the social responsibility.[339]

III. Main Statements of three AA's held in Common regarding Socially Responsible Corporate Governance

1. Highlighted Topics

In Georgian AA the field of Company Law mostly emphasizes protection of shareholders, creditors, stakeholders. According to the Georgian legislation shareholders may sue against the directors (derivative suit), they are entitled to the right to vote and therefore participate in the process of management. Besides, right of getting information in timely fashion, provision of investigation

erlands, 2012, 4-5, 22.

334 See, Corporate Governance in Ukraine, USAID, pfs, Cocorde Capital, October, 2011, 2, 6.

335 Regarding "Astrata's" CSR, see http://www.astartaholding.com/en/slaider-na-glavnoi/vysokaja-socialnajaotvetstvennost.htm, [12.12.14], 'Astrata' was found in 1993 in Ukraine, it operates with a focus on sugar production, crop growing, and cattle farming, see, Annual Repost of Astrata, 2013, 5, http://www.astartaholding.com/modules/ pages/files/139927237521_1033.pdf, [12.12.14].

336 Named corporation has invested a sufficient amount of money in support of kindergartens, schools, medical centers, also, by the end of 2013 year has employed 8960 workers, besides Environmental and Social Management Program (recognized by the IFC, the EBRD, the FMO and the EIB, furthermore see the link:) has been implemented in 2013, See, Annual Repost of Astrata, 2013, 23-24, http://www.astartaholding.com/modules/pages/ files/139927237521_1033.pdf, [12.12.14].

337 Stipendum funded by the Georgian law firm 'MKD',http://tsu.edu.ge/ge/faculties/law/news/V808294_HLZdcZA1l/?p=4, [12.12.14].

338 As for example, TBC Bank, which is a listed company on the London Exchange Stock ever since 2014. TBC is funding areas such as: tourism, take part in various social projects. Full list of activities can be found on TBC Bank's official site: http://www.tbcbank.ge/web/en/csr, [25.01.2015].

339 Oprunenco A., Prohnitchi V., Rusu M., Assessing Corporate Social Responsibility in Moldova, September-November, 2005, 21-22.

of corporate documents is also a sufficient remedy. Stakeholders are protected under the 'Law on Environment', which was highly de-regulated and abandoned from all the mandatory legal constraints.[340] Upon the AA of Georgia management policy of the corporation should be in compliance with EU regulations on corporate governance. By adoption of international guidelines Corporate Social Responsibility will be promoted by high sense of awareness.[341]

In the EU-Moldavian AA protections of shareholder's, creditor's and stakeholder's rights are as well of high importance, since it comes to be a key factor for fostering trade. In addition, management of corporation should be handed so, that social needs were satisfied (through the social responsibility), international standards were not breached (e.g. UN Global, OECD). It is essential to make information transparent during the process of incorporation. Business performance should conform to the standards and principles of International Acts and guidelines.[342]

The EU-Ukrainian AA involves relevant stakeholder's and shareholder's participation in the Corporate Governance. By enhancement of corporate governance policies, social responsibility and it is remedy will be fostered and resulted from sharing information regarding internal conducts. Social aims must be accomplished by adoption of international regulations.[343]

2. Promotion of Corporate Social Responsibility

Mentioned articles of three countries' AA's are constructed with the same idea of favoring social welfare, accommodating sustainable development of economy, encouraging business performance by evolvement of national legislation and through compliance with EU Directives, as well as standards defined by international organizations. Notwithstanding the fact, that, mostly, all these articles do not vary in many respects, individual approaches are needed for evolution of named fields of each country.

Indeed, all of these countries have attempted to fully implement OECD CG Principles and frame legislation accordingly. Albeit, standards endorsed by UN Global Combat (on human rights, labor, environment protection, anti-corruption),[344] the International Labour Organization (ILO) Tripartite Declaration of Principles concerning Multinational Enterprises and Social Policy[345] (which regards protection of employees, health care, conditions of working, etc.) are also of high

---

340 See, web-site of investing in Georgia, http://www.investingeorgia.org/, [15.12.14].
341 See, AA of Georgia, Articles as follows: 231 (e), 239(g), 316-319, 348, 349 (i), 352.
342 See, AA of Moldova, Articles as follows:27-30, 35, 367(e), 377(g).
343 See, AA of Ukraine, Articles as follows: 387-388, 293, 422.
344 UN Global Combat 10 Principles, https://www.unglobalcompact.org/AboutTheGC/TheTenPrinciples/index.html, [12.12.14].
345 See, web-site: http://www.ilo.org/wcmsp5/groups/public/---ed_emp/---emp_ent/-multi/documents/publication/wcms_094386.pdf, [15.12.14].

relevance and should be undertaken by the national regulatory environment. This shall need supplementary financial sources as well.

IV. Future Strategies and Action Plans with an Attempt of Implementation of the Provisions in the Association Agreements on Corporate Governance

In the framework of the business development "the Commission [is] ready to work with the Ukrainian authorities to provide support for issues such as corporate governance, the so-called corporate raids, lack of transparency". So, it's essential to deal with Corporate raids and the lack of transparency.[346] Improvement of the investment climate will result from strengthening the rule of law, ceasing bureaucracy, developing sufficient tax administration, abolishment of corruption, which will, simultaneously, have a positive impact on small and medium sized enterprises (SME).[347]

So far, the Georgian regulatory system has been lightened in order to keep foreign direct investments flowing in. This had created an obnoxious effect by loosening control over environment protection and economic sanctions for pollution, quality of the product, reducing prices on licenses, etc. In Georgia legal reforms are already on the agenda regarding sophistication of the 'Law of Entrepreneurs'. Topics as follows: Environment and Climate Change, Industrial and Enterprise Policy, Company Law, Accounting and Auditing and Corporate Governance are set as one of the priorities in the "Association Agenda between the European Union and Georgia".[348] High prominence is given to ensuring simple regulations for establishment of legal companies, international auditing standards should be applied by all listed companies at national level.[349]

Moldova faces a number of environmental challenges, which should be tackled by supporting investments in rolling stock, as well as, the rehabilitation of railway and national road infrastruc-

---

346 EU-Ukraine A European Agenda for Reform, version: 4 July 2014, http://ec.europa.eu/commission_2010-2014/fule/docs/ukraine/a_european_agenda_for_reform.pdf, [12.12.14].

347 Giucci, Ricardo, Kirchner, Robert, Zachmann, Georg, Von Cramon-Taubadel, Stephan, Economic Reform Agenda for Ukraine, German Advisory Group, Institute for Economic Research and Policy Consulting, Berlin, Kyiv, 2014, 5-1 http://www.beratergruppe-ukraine.de/download Beraterpapiere/2014/Economic%20Reform%20Agenda%20for%20Ukraine_March%20 2014.pdf, [12.12.14].

348 See, an official print: http://eeas.europa.eu/delegations/georgia/ documents/eap_aa/associationagenda_2014_en.pdf, [25.02.2015].

349 See, an official print: http://eeas.europa.eu/delegations/georgia/documents/eap_aa/associationagenda_2014_en.pdf, [25.02.2015].

ture, also, promotion of development of Moldova's corporate sector.[350] In addition, the establishment of SMEs should be supported, which will lead to the creation of new jobs.[351]

V. Concluding Remarks

The post-Soviet countries Georgia, Moldova, Ukraine have for many years gone through a lamentable financial situation that has hampered the process of development of a sufficient and sophisticated approach in the field of corporate relations. Due to the Association Agreements changes in the regulatory policies are indispensable, a plausible legal reform regarding corporate law is on the agenda. This paper was dedicated to a topic of Corporate Social Responsibility and its awareness in the named countries. If Georgia, Moldova and Ukraine wish to comply with the modern EU requirements in this field, it will be necessary to conduct researches and studies in the academic area by taking into account the Georgian, Moldavian and Ukrainian legal culture and the social and economic conditions in these countries.

This present comparative study was carried out by proposing some new amendments to Corporate Social Responsibility and proposing next steps, which take into consideration the rights of stakeholders and society. A sustainable economic development will be inconceivable without complying with all general principles established by the Organization for Economic Co-operation and Development (OECD), reinforcing good corporate practice by giving better opportunities for small and medium-sized, domestic or foreign enterprises, holding up a profitable corporate governance system together with a better protection of customers. Therefore, it is crucial to assess the legal and economic factors on that path, which these three countries have to go in the process of a possible future of Georgia, Moldova and Ukraine as welcome, positive members of the EU.

350 Strategy for Moldova, Document of the European Bank for Reconstruction and Development, approved on 30th April, 2014, 22-23.

351 Strategy for Moldova, Document of the European Bank for Reconstruction and Development, approved on 30th April, 2014, 41-42.

Olena Serpukhovitina

Cooperation in the Framework of the Three Association Agreements: Intellectual Property Law - Geographical Indications and Liability of Intermediary Service Providers

The Association Agreements (AAs) between the EU and Ukraine, Moldova and Georgia contain separate chapters dedicated to provisions on intellectual property (IP). Such Chapters 9 (the number is identical for the three AAs) are included in Title IV "Trade and Trade Related Matters" for Georgia and Ukraine, while in the Georgian AA it can be found in Title IV of "Economic and Other Sectoral Cooperation". The provisions contain regulations for all objects of intellectual property including copyright, trademarks, geographical indications, designs and patents with a separate section for enforcement of intellectual property rights. Moreover, in the EU-Ukrainian AA the institute of liability of intermediary service providers is placed in Chapter 9, while in Georgian and Moldovan AAs the institute finds itself in Chapter 6 "Establishment, Trade in Services and Electronic Commerce". In any event, the regulations on the liability of intermediary service providers directly influence the way of enforcement of intellectual property rights, since it is crucial for the protection of these rights on the Internet to the extent that the activities of intermediaries may result in infringements or supporting of infringements by others.[352] Consequently, there is quite a list of regulations on IP law of the countries in the Association Agreements.

Moreover, the specific approach was chosen by the EU in regard to the sphere according to the statement of Ms. Joanna Miksa,[353] since the representatives were aware of the uniqueness of their system of IP law protection and did not pursue the aim of complete integration of Moldova, Ukraine and Georgia into the distinct European system. The EU decided to not simply let the list of directives be implemented by the parties (since its implementation would be unachievable), but to copy some essential articles from those directives in respectful areas of IP law into the AAs (most of the articles are identical for all three of them). Such an approach allows Ukraine, Moldova and Georgia to refer to the practice of the EU countries and the jurisprudence of the European Court of Justice (ECJ). Even though the practice and decisions of the latter do not have an obligatory character for non-EU members, they can still shed light on the most effective mechanisms for implementation of the legal norms found both in EU Directives and AAs. Due to the extensive number of objects to be regulated under IP law, the attention within the article is given

[352] Pedro A. De Miguel Asensio, Internet Intermediaries and the Law Applicable to Intellectual Property Infringements, 3 (2012) JIPITEC 3, 350, p. 350.

[353] Meeting with representatives of DG trade, in particular with Trade coordinators of the Eastern Partnership, 27 January, 2015, Brussels.

to institutions of geographical indications (GIs) and the liability of intermediary service providers (ISPs).

I. Geographical Indications (GIs)

In order to access the cooperation mechanism established under AAs in respect to geographical indications, one should define the meaning of GI as such, the mechanism of protection established under the agreements, analyze the creation and functioning of a specific body in the sphere and provide at least one example of implementation of the respectful provisions in an individual country.

1. Definition of GI

Firstly, the EU representatives have examined the legislation of Ukraine, Georgia and Moldova on the correspondence to the elements specifically set out for the purposes of AAs and included in Annexes to these agreements (and not the EU legislation). Such examination has also included the mentioning of a unified definition of GI in the Annex XVII-A (Georgian AA), Annex XXX-A, Part C (Moldovan AA) and Annex XXII-A, Part B (Ukrainian AA), according to which "geographical indication identify a good as originating in a territory, region or locality of one or more states, where a given quality, reputation or other characteristic of the good is essentially attributable to its geographical origin". In other words, the GIs indicate the place where the products were produced or come from, which distinguishes them from the other products on the market.

2. The Mechanism of Protection

The bilateral protection of GIs between EU and non-EU counties is common practice. Such protection can be formed either through specific agreements that only regulate the protection of GIs (for example, with China) or in the framework of broader agreements (Free Trade Agreements).[354] In the case of Ukraine, Moldova and Georgia, the DCFTA was included into AAs and thus constituted the relatively new form of protection for GIs on bilateral level.

a) The Standard Procedure

In order to access the intentions of the parties behind concluding the agreements on the protection of GIs, it is relevant to provide a brief overview of the standard procedure for registering GIs in the EU for non-EU products. The procedure, which is almost the same as for EU GIs, is laid down in Regulation 510/2006 for agricultural products and foodstuffs, Regulation 110/2008 for

354 European Commission Directorate-General for Trade. (n.d.). Retrieved March 2, 2015, from http://ec.europa.eu /trade/policy/accessing-markets/intellectual-property/geographical-indications/.

spirits and Regulation 1234/2007 for wines[355].For the purposes of demonstrating the process, the registration procedure for non-EU agricultural products and foodstuffs shall be shown. Firstly, the producers should define the GI of the specified product, which should be further examined by national authorities. These authorities should then send the application in one of the official languages (there are 22 of them) to the Commission of the European Communities located in Brussels with all required documents (the same list as for the EU agricultural products and foodstuffs). The application is then examined by Commission services, which either accepts and publishes it in the Official Journal or rejects if the application is not in conformity with EU legislation. If the positive scenario is pursued, a 6-month opposition period should pass after the publication before the GI can be registered. However, if any opposition occurs, the parties should conduct appropriate consultations as for GI. The procedure in these circumstances can easily last for several years.[356]

b) Mechanism Established under the AAs

The mechanism established under AAs, on the other hand, provides for Ukraine/Moldova/Georgia from one side and EU countries from another to create a list of GIs that are to come through the objection procedure. The duration for submitting "a duly substantiated statement"[357] is 2 months in case of Ukraine and Moldova and 3 months for Georgia. The reason for the extended objection period might be that Georgia`s GIs list is the largest among the three countries. According to the statement of Ms. Joanna Miksa,[358] the EU representatives did not impose any restrictions on the amount of GIs that could be included into the list from either side. Thus, it was for the states to conduct prior consultations with the producers, who were willing to have their GIs registered in the EU. For example, Moldova did not include any agricultural products and foodstuffs or aromatized wines in the list to be protected in the EU and has only listed two types of wines. This phenomenon is probably dependent on the companies` willingness and ability to reach and expend into the EU market. Consequently, the formation of lists of the products, geographic indications of which are to be protected, is a demonstration of how states protect private interests on the international scale. Thus, the whole process for private entities was significantly simplified through the usage of the mechanism established under the AAs. However, the parties agreed that the registration in the country of origin is an obligatory prerequisite for the

355 Thual, D. (2011). Q&A Manual European Legislation on Geographical Indications (p. 132), p. 27.
356 Thual, D. (2011). Q&A Manual European Legislation on Geographical Indications (p. 132), p. 22.
357 Annex XXII-B to Ukrainian AA, Annex XXX-B to Moldovan AA, Annex XVII-B to Georgian AA.
358 Meeting with representatives of DG trade, in particular with Trade coordinators of the Eastern Partnership, 27 January, 2015, Brussels.

protection under AAs. Thus, if the former ceases to exist, the parties have to notify each other of the fact and further are free of any obligation to protect such a GI.

3. Temporary Measures for Ukraine

Ukraine was able to negotiate an exception to the general rule of protection of EU GIs within its sovereign territory under article 208 of AA. According to the article, different types of temporary measures are applicable to Ukrainian products that were not in conformity with the Agreement, in particular with the Annexes including the lists of EU GIs. Firstly, the national products that no longer complied with the GI protection provisions established under AA, could be continued to be sold "until stocks run out"[359]. Secondly, Ukraine negotiated the transitional periods of 10 and 7 years for certain products (for example, "Champagne" (10 years) and "Feta" (7 years) that contradicted with GIs of the EU parties. Thus, these kinds of products could still be manufactured by Ukrainian producers under GIs that "infringe" the EU once for the limited period of time. Such provision can be found only in the AA with Ukraine. However, this can be explained by the fact that Moldova and Georgia did not have conflicting GIs with the EU member states.

4. Sub-Committee on Geographical Indications

a) Formation of Sub-Committee

The Sub-Committee on Geographical Indications is established in all three AAs under article 211 for Ukraine, article 306 for Moldova and article 179 for Georgia. The regulations for these institutions are almost identical (only minor differences in wording, but without distinctions in meaning), thus the mechanism can be characterized as one whole for all three cases with possible references even to one AA. The GI Sub-Committee should comprise of representatives of the EU and Ukraine (Moldova/Georgia), who should arrange the meeting upon the request of either party and mutually decide on the time and place for its conduction, however, the meeting should be arranged within 90 days upon the request. The very aim of functioning of this "ad hoc institution" is expressly provided in respectful articles of the AAs, according to which the GI Sub-Committee was created with the purpose of monitoring the development of the Sub-Section on GIs and to intensify cooperation and dialogue on geographical indications.[360]

359 Article 208 (1) of Ukrainian AA.

360 Art. 211 of the EU-Ukraine AA, Art. 306 of the EU-Moldova AA and Art. 179 of the EU-Georgia AA.

b) Functions of the Sub-Committee

The GI Sub-Committee has various functions according to the provisions of the articles, however, there are four major tasks that should be distinguished: amendment of law applicable to the parties; exchange of information; modification of Annexes; monitoring implementation.

aa) Amendment of legislation

Firstly, the Sub-Committee is empowered to amend the law applicable between the parties on the protection of GIs. The provision is of importance, since as was already mentioned, the EU with the purpose of integration into its law system decided to only copy some essential points from its legislation into the AAs. In such a way, Ukraine, Moldova and Georgia received the mechanism through which further harmonization of their legislature to European standards in the sphere of GIs can be pursued upon the willingness and readiness of the states.

bb) Exchange of Information

The parties have agreed that the Sub-Committee should be responsible for exchanging information "on legislative and policy developments on geographical indications and any other matter of mutual interest in the area of geographical indications"[361]. The provision also has the element for harmonization of legislation of Ukraine/Moldova/Georgia to EU norms. Nevertheless, the core of this function lays within the exchange of information on GIs for the purposes of their protection. Keeping in mind that the protection on the level of AAs is dependent on the registration in the country of its origin, it is essential for the parties to update each other in a promptly manner on any changes to the status of GIs. For this reason, the respectful articles in the three AAs specifically point out the opportunity to conduct the meeting of GI Sub-Committee through the videoconference.

cc) Modification of Annexes

The parties having formed and conducted the objection procedure created the list of GIs, which was included in form of Annexes to these agreements. However, those lists could not be static, since, for example, certain producers can finally decide to enter the EU market and thus require the protection. Moldova can serve as a bright example for such potential need, since according to its AA, only two Moldovan GIs are under protection in the EU. For this reason, the parties decided to allow for additional GIs, subject to the same level of protection that the already included GIs enjoy under the agreements. The new GIs are to follow the same objection procedure of 2 (Ukraine/Moldova) or 3 (Georgia) months periods. Consequently, the GI Sub-Committee con-

[361] Art. 306 (4(c)) of the EU-Moldova AA; Art. 179 (3(c)) of the EU-Georgia AA; Art. 211 (3(e)) of the EU-Ukraine AA.

tains a flexible mechanism for adding new GIs under the simplified procedure established under AAs.

dd) Monitoring the implementation

After the negotiation and ratification of the AAs from both sides have taken place, the provisions are to be implemented in both parties, including the articles on GIs. The countries are to legislate on the national level and bring appropriate changes consistent with the obligations undertaken in the AAs. Therefore, the GI Sub-Committee also performs the controlling function, which basically means that this is a forum for the parties to control each other`s performance of obligations, since the Sub-Committee itself comprises only of the representatives from both sides.

5. Implementation of the provisions on GIs (Ukraine)

The process of implementation of the provisions concerning the protection of GIs is similar to the application of other articles. However, the brief overview of the implementation of GIs protection provisions should be given in order to provide the full picture on the regulation of the institute on the example of Ukraine.

a) The General Framework for Implementation

The Ukrainian Government, the Cabinet of Ministers, adopted on 17 September 2014 an Action Plan for implementing the AA between Ukraine and EU for the years 2014-2017[362]. According to this plan (item #154), the draft law on the adaptation of Ukrainian legislation to the one of EU and according to the provisions of AA in the sphere of intellectual property should be developed no later than in July 2015. The plan also appoints the responsible body both on the national level and the partner body on the level of the EU, which is the Director General of European Commission "Trade" in the case of intellectual property. Within six month after adopting the mentioned law, the Ukrainian executive bodies (Ministry of Economic Development and State Service of Intellectual Property) are to develop further regulatory and legal framework for the implementation of provisions.

b) Protection of GIs

Moreover, in order to provide the protection to the GIs listed in the Annexes to the AA, the parties agreed that the EU would provide the technical support till March 2015, while the directors

[362] Plan sachodiv s implementaziiUgody pro acoziaziju, s odnijejistorony, ta s Jevropejskym Spivtovarystvom s inshoji, na 2014-2017 roky (The plan of actions for implementation of the Agreement on Association between Ukraine, from one side, and European Union, from the other for years of 2014-2017). Issued by Cabinet of Ministers of Ukraine. 17 Sept, 2014. Retrieved March 3, 2015, from http://zakon1.rada.gov.ua/laws/show/847-2014-%D1%80/ print1411489052577299.

general of European Commission "Trade" and "Agriculture and Development of Agricultural Territories" are responsible for the task. Only after the support is provided, Ukraine created the needed electronic data for the protection of EU GIs within five months.

c) The GI Sub-Committee

The creation of the GI Sub-Committee does not require changes into the internal law system of Ukraine. Thus, Ukraine undertook under item #160 of the plan to ensure the participation in co-operation and functioning of GI Sub-Committee and to exchange information and conduct dialogs during 2014-2017. However, the mentioned obligation constitutes only one of the functions of GI Sub-Committee discussed above, which can be explained by the fact that the performance of other functions requires the prior implementation of the articles on GIs protection. According to the timeframe provided in the previous section, this can be reached no sooner than in August 2015.

II. The Liability of Intermediary Service Providers

All three AAs contain the provisions on the exemptions of liability of intermediary service providers (ISP), even though the Moldovan and Georgian agreements contain these regulations in sections relating to the electronic commerce. However, EU has followed the same approach as for intellectual property section (while for Ukraine the provisions on liability of ISP are placed in IP section) for the drafting of provisions, since the articles on liability of ISP are mere restatements of parts of the E-Commerce Directive 2000/31/EC (Articles 12-15). The institute has become of high importance for the enforcement of IP rights due to the fast development of the Internet and the increased amount of infringements conducted online. The latter should be accessed in the light of the statement that "all online activities must be in contact with at least one ISP"[363]. Consequently, the institute having direct influence on enforcement of IP rights should be briefly looked upon with concentrating attention on the three kinds of activities of ISP that are exempted from liability, namely, "mere conduit", "cashing" and "hosting".

1. "Mere conduit"

According to the AAs[364] the "mere conduit" is an information society service "consists of the transmission in a communication network of information provided by a recipient of the service, or the provision of access to a communication network". Thus, the two types of activities are ex-

363 Baistrocchi, Liability of Intermediary Service Providers in the EU Directive on Electronic Commerce, 19 Santa Clara High Tech. L.J. 111 (2002). Retrieved March 8, 2015, from http://digitalcommons.law.scu.edu/chtlj/vol19/iss1/3, p. 118.

364 Art. 257 of the EU-Moldova AA; Art. 130 of the EU-Georgia AA; Art. 245 of the EU-Ukraine AA.

empted from the liability, however, are subject to three conditions: 1) the provider should not initiate a transmission; 2) the provider should not select the receiver of the transmission and 3) the provider should not select or modify the information contained in the transmission[365]. These provisions protect the ISPs, who act simply as the "carriers" of information and store it only for the purposes or transition and no longer.[366] The provision was designed to simply protect network operators for the consequences of traffic delivered via their networks if they have no control of its content.[367]

2. "Caching"

The "caching" is defined in the AAs[368] as an information society service that "consists of the transmission in a communication network of information provided by a recipient of the service" and there is "automatic, intermediate and temporary storage of that information, performed for the sole purpose of making more efficient the information's onward transmission to other recipients of the service at their request". The aim of the service is to avoid overloading the internet with repetitive high demand for certain materials, which can be reached by storing the copies of high demand data on the local servers to allow for the information to reach the end-users in the quickest way possible.[369] One of the necessary conditions for exemption from this kind of liability is the absence of modification of information by the ISP, which requires the provider to keep the original version of data from customers. Moreover, the ISP among other requirements shall comply with conditions on access to the information, which means all existing restrictions on the access imposed by the customer for the posted content are to be maintained. The same relates to the rules regarding the updating of the information, "specified in a manner widely recognized and used by industry".[370]

3. "Hosting"

According to the AAs[371] the information society service of "hosting" "consists of the storage of information provided by a recipient of the service". For the exemption for liability to be successfully invoked, the provider should not have the actual knowledge of illegal activity or should not be aware of the facts or circumstances, from which such an illegal activity can be apparent.

365 Ibid.
366 Lesiak, Comparative Analysis of the Liability of Internet Service Providers in the Context of Copyright Infringements in the U.S., European Union and Poland, 3 Masaryk U.J.L.&Tech. 287 (2009), p. 287.
367 Moller, Christian, Freedom of the media in social networks and social media. Retrieved March 8, 2015, from http://www.osce.org/fom/96523?download=true.
368 Article 258 of Moldovan AA; article 131 of Georgian AA; article 246 of Ukrainian AA.
369 Baistrocchi (ft. 12), p. 120.
370 Article 258 of the EU-Moldova AA; Art. 131 of the EU-Georgia AA; Art. 246 of the EU-Ukraine AA.
371 Art. 259 of the EU-Moldova AA; article 132 of the EU-Georgia AA; Art. 247 of the EU-Ukraine AA.

Moreover, after the ISP acquired such knowledge or awareness, the provider should act "expeditiously to remove or to disable access to the information".[372] In other words, "hosting" can be defined as a service, according to which individuals or entities can rent space online and incorporate any data on that space.[373] For example, in the Telecinco v. YouTube case decided by the Spanish court in 2010, which applied the provisions of EU Commerce Directive, the court found that YouTube was an intermediary service provider and could not and did not have an obligation to control all the videos that users uploaded. Moreover, the notice-and-take-down procedure existed on YouTube, which worked smoothly every time the Telecinco (claimant) requested for the removal of infringing content[374]. On the other hand, the ECJ in L'Oréal v eBay case clarified that for the host providers to be exempted from liability such activities should be technical, passive, neutral and automated, which was not the case for the online marketplace (eBay in the case before the UK court), if "it provides assistance which entails, in particular, optimizing the presentation of the offers for sale in question or promoting them".[375]

It should be noted that the exemption from liability does not preclude the issuance of orders by court to delete certain content or block domain names, which infringe the rights, including the intellectual property ones.

4. Implementation of the provisions on IPS (Ukraine)

The general framework already mentioned in part B, IV, 1 of this paper also applied for Ukraine in terms of implementation of the provisions, which relate to the liability of ISPs. No specific provisions relating specifically to this institute were established. However, it would be useful to take a look at the current state of legislation regarding the institute in order to identify the volume of provisions to be included into the law aimed at the implementation of the norms on IP of the AA between the Ukraine and the EU. The three information society services should be considered for the mentioned purposes.

The exemption of liability for "mere conduit" cannot be considered to be a completely new institute for Ukraine. The Law of Ukraine on Telecommunications while defining the ISP as an operator of telecommunications states that this is a commercial entity with the right to work in the sphere of telecommunications having the right to technical services and exploitation of telecom-

---

372 Ibid.

373 Baistrocchi (ft. 12), p. 122.

374 Miquel, Peguera. Telecinco v. YouTube: the ruling in its context. Retrieved March 8, 2015, from https://ispliability.wordpress.com/2010/09/26/telecinco-v-youtube-the-ruling-in-its-context/.

375 Barbieri/De Santis, ECJ rules on trademark protection online and intermediaries' liability – L'Oréal v eBay. Sept. 9, 2011. Retrieved March 8, 2015, from http://www.lexology.com/library/detail.aspx?g=a13ca6ad-94d5-43f2-bb51-6687358cc4be.

munication networks[376]. The mentioned law provides for exemptions from liability of ISPs for the materials transmitted through their networks, while pointing out the absence of the right for ISP to control the information sent or received from customers. If the latter condition is fulfilled, the ISP cannot be held liable for any damages to customers or third parties, which was caused through the use of Internet services. However, there are no detailed provisions on the possibility of storing information or the conditions, according to which the ISP providing the "mere conduit" would be considered as not controlling the information passed.

As for the service of "caching", there is no legislative protection for these types of information society services in Ukraine. Thus, in this regard, Ukraine will have to provide basic regulations in the sphere.

Finally, no safe harbor is established for providers of hosting services in Ukraine under current legislation. However, the state practice, which was formed recently, shows that the courts start to refuse the proceedings in case when the lawsuits is filed before the hosting service provider, but not before the actual infringer of the rights of the claimant. However, in order to comply with the requirements for implementation of the AA, the specific regulations should be introduced on the official level, since the national court practice is not binding in Ukraine.

III. Conclusion

The Association Agreements between Ukraine, Georgia and Moldova on one side and the EU on the other contain a Chapter dedicated to the approximation of the law of the contracting states in the sphere of intellectual property. Among other objects of IP law, the agreements contain a co-operation mechanism on geographical indications (GIs). The parties have agreed upon a unified definition of GI, established a simplified procedure for acquiring protection of GIs of all contracting parties within the territory of others and have created the Sub-Committee on GIs. The latter body comprising representatives of both parties is granted with the important functions of the amendment of law applicable to the parties (since the provisions of EU Directives were only partially incorporated into the AAs), of exchange of information (since the GIs protection under AAs is dependent on the validity of registration in the home country), of modification of the list of GIs in Annexes to be protected (allows the addition of new indications to be granted the same level of protection) and the function of monitoring the implementation of the provisions of the Sub-Section on GIs.

---

[376] Art. 40 para 4 of the Law of Ukraine on Telecommunications, VidomostiVerxovnoyiRadyUkrayiny of 8.3.2015, p 155, available at http://zakon4.rada.gov.ua/laws/show/1280-15.

The AAs also contain an essential section for the enforcement of IP rights relating to the exemption of intermediary service providers from liability. The agreements introduce the exemptions for the three types of activities: "mere conduit", "caching" and "hosting", within which the ISPs have no obligation to monitor the content transmitted or posted by the clients and cannot be held liable for it.

In regards to the implementation, each country (Ukraine/Moldova/Georgia) drafts a plan for implementation of the provisions of AAs into its national law systems. Moreover, the EU from its side supports the countries in the process by appointing the EU responsible body and by providing technical assistance. The example of the latter is the assistance in operation of data of GIs in Ukraine established under "The plan of actions for implementation of the Agreement on Association between Ukraine, from one side, and European Union, from the other for years of 2014-2017". The implementation of the provisions depends significantly on the condition of national legislation. For instance, only the exemption from liability of ISP providing the "mere conduit" service is regulated on the level of legislation, while the other two need the introduction of basic regulations in Ukraine.

Consequently, the AAs have established a cooperation mechanism in the sphere of intellectual property law and its enforcement is to be implemented in Ukraine, Georgia and Moldova from one side and EU from the other.

Solomon Menabdishvili

How Georgia has Fulfilled its Obligations Assumed under Article 204 of the Association Agreement

The Association Agreement between Georgia and EU was signed on June 27, 2014. Under Article 204 of the Agreement, Georgia has taken the obligation to adopt competition rules, which will be effectively directed against the economic agents' restrictive actions of competition. In addition, competition legislation should allow an effective control over the merger of the economic agents as well as it is supposed to avoid the abuse of a dominant position by a dominant economic agent. Georgia is also responsible for setting up of a competition authority responsible for the effective enforcement of competition law.

Before signing the Association Agreement the Government of Georgia assigned the Ministry of Economy and Sustainable Development to work on the amendments and supplements to the Law on Free Trade and Competition, which was speedily adopted by the Parliament of Georgia on 21 March 2014.[377] Significant amendments have been adopted in the law, which can be considered a step forward in terms of convergence with EU legislation. The title of the law has been changed and it is now named "Law on Competition of Georgia".

The aim of my paper is to show how Georgia has fulfilled its obligations assumed under Article 204 of the Association Agreement. First, I will discuss provisions of Competition Law of Georgia in terms of effectiveness and then Competition Agency's authority provided by the Law.

I. Regulation of bilateral behaviors of undertakings

1. Article 7 of the Law on Competition of Georgia

Modern Competition rules concerns with bilateral as well as unilateral behaviors of undertakings restricting competition on the market. Art. 7 of the Law on Competition of Georgia has an equivalent content as Art. 101 of the Treaty on the Functioning of the European Union (TFEU). Art. 7 para. 1 of the Law prohibits contracts, decisions or concerted practice of economic agents having the object or the effect to prevent, restrict and/or to distort competition within the relevant market. This article prohibits the following conducts: 1) direct or indirect fix purchase or selling prices or any other trading conditions; 2) limit or control production, markets, technical development, or investment; 3) share markets or sources of supply by consumers, location or other characteristics; 4) apply dissimilar conditions to equivalent transactions with other trading parties, thereby plac-

377 See, the Law on Competition of Georgia, <http://competition.ge/en/page2.php?p=4&m=62> [28.12.14].

ing them at a competitive disadvantage; 5) make the conclusion of contracts a subject to acceptance by the other parties of supplementary obligations which, by their nature or according to commercial usage, have no connection with the subject of such contracts; 6) setting agreed terms of tender (as to ensure material gain or advantage for concerted economic agents or other parties participating in the state procurements), which causes substantial damage to legal interests of the purchasing organization.

There are two serious objections concerning this Article: first of all, it prohibits contracts of the undertakings, while Art. 101 TFEU forbids agreements. The latter term is more general than the first one. The term "agreement" includes contracts. According to the existing case law of the European Union, the application of competition rules is not limited to legal contracts. Art. 101 applies to formal cooperation as well as to informal cooperation of undertakings. In the European Union a broad definition has been given to the term "agreements" as well as to the terms "decisions" and "concerted practice"[378]. The concept of an agreement provided by Art. 101 focuses on the existence of the concurrence of wills between the undertakings. Art. 101 deals with any type of cooperation among economic agents despite their form of expression. It does not matter if they happen in writing or in oral[379]. The term "agreement" includes "gentlemen's agreements", trade association's rules, standard contract terms as well as other forms of cooperation. The second objection is that the list of prohibited conducts is exhausted, while the list of Art. 101 TFEU is not exhausted.

2. Article 8 of the Law on Competition of Georgia

The first paragraph of this Article introduces the "de minimis rule" which is enshrined in the "soft law" of the EU. This provision is in compliance with the Notice on Agreements of Minor Importance which do not appreciably restrict competition under Art. 101 para.1 TFEU (de minimis notice)[380]. The main objection to this Article is that according to it hardcore restrictions are following the conducts: a) price fixing; b) market sharing; and c) collusive tendering. In the European Law whereas, collusive tendering in itself is not a hard core restriction. According to the EU case law, the third type of hardcore restriction is the control or the limitation of production.

---

378 See Whish/Bailey, Competition Law, 7th ed. (2012), pp. 99-100.
379 See, Ezrachi, EU Competition Law: An Analytical Guide to the Leading Cases, 3th ed. (2012), p.51.
380 See, the Notice, <http://eur-lex.europa.eu/legal-content/EN/TXT/HTML/?uri=OJ:C:2014:291:FULL& from=EN>, [09.01.2015], §§ 8-9.

3. Article 9 of the Law on Competition of Georgia

This Article has a similar provision to Art. 101 para.3 TFEU. It exempts agreements, decisions and concerted actions of undertakings if they fulfill the following four cumulative criteria: 1) improving the production or distribution of goods, promoting technical or economic progress; 2) while allowing consumers a fair share of the resulting benefit; *and provided they do not*3) impose restrictions on the concerned economic agents which are not indispensable to the attainment of these objectives; 4) afford the possibility of eliminating competition in respect of a substantial part of the products in question to such economic agents.

II. Regulation of unilateral behaviors of undertakings

1. Article 5 of the Competition Law of Georgia

According to Art. 5 para.1, determining an economic agent's dominant position certain factors shall be taken into account, in particular: the relevant market of the undertaking, the financial condition of the economic agent's competitor, barriers to entry to the market or barriers to expand production, the buyers' market power, the availability of raw material sources, the vertical integration degree, etc.

2. Article 6 of the Competition Law of Georgia

Under Art. 6 para.1 of the Law, only the misuse of a dominant position is prohibited. Holding of a dominant position is not per se illegal. The list of prohibited actions provided by Art. 6 para.2 is in compliance with Article 102 TFEU. It should be noticed that the list is not exhausted. According to the Article, dominant economic agents are not entitled: 1) To directly or indirectly impose unfair purchase or to sell prices or other unfair trading conditions; 2) to limit production, markets or technical development to the prejudice of consumers; 3) to apply dissimilar conditions to equivalent transactions with other trading parties, thereby placing them at a competitive disadvantage; 4) to make the conclusion of the contract's subject to acceptance by the other parties of supplementary obligations which, by their nature or according to commercial usage, have no connection with the subject of such contracts, and etc.

III. Merger/Concentration

According to Art. 11 of the Law on Competition of Georgia, concentration means: a merger of two or more independent economic agents; the gaining of direct or indirect control over the economic agent or any part of its business through a purchasing of the securities or of the asset. The control can be carried out by agreements or by other means; the participation of the same person in management boards of different economic agents; the establishment of a fully operational joint venture for a long period.

Under this Article, mergers resulting from acquiring or strengthening a dominant position are prohibited because they may substantially distort an effective competition on the relevant market of Georgia. Art. 11 is in compliance with the EU Merger Regulation #139/2004 and relevant guidelines.

Article 11^1 enshrines a compulsory advance notification rule on a planned concentration. The Agency examines the expected concentration within one month upon the submission of the notification. In complicated cases the term may be extended up to two additional weeks. If the Agency fails to give its answer within the term, it automatically means a positive answer. Time limits for studying the notified concentration is too short compared to the EU Merger Regulation #139/2004[381]. The Agency will not able to study the concentrations thoroughly in 45 days. Art. 10 of the Regulation entitles the Commission to carry out the examination for several months in exceptional cases.

As already mentioned Art. 11 obliges undertakings to notify their planned concentration in advance to the Agency. Though, Art.11^1 says that a concentration with the participation of economic agents of the regulated sphere of economy or a concentration with certain amounts of values of individual or aggregate assets or an annual turnover determined by the Rules for Submission and Consideration of Notification on Concentration, is no subject to prior notification to the Agency.

According to Art. 11^2 of the Law, notification of the concentration is not compulsory in case:

1. The undertakings' joint value of assets or annual turnover is less than 10 million GEL or 20 million GEL respectively;[382]
2. there is a "temporal" acquisition of shares;
3. of insolvency or liquidation;
4. of a merger between interdependent undertakings.

Nothing has been said on vertical mergers in the Law on Competition of Georgia or in the Rules on Submission and Consideration of Notification on Concentration. It is presumed that vertical

381 See, Council Regulation (EC) No 139/2004 of 20 January 2004 on the control of concentrations between undertakings (the EC Merger Regulation),<http://eur-lex.europa.eu/legal-content/EN/ALL/;ELX_SESSIONID=0LDnJwJKH16BVqLyrGhy2tdM5LxGzH1NGGByT1t5HKYJGnGkq16F!-1016348133?uri=CELEX:32004R0139>, [10.01.2015].

382 See, Article 3 of the Procedure on Submission and Consideration of Notification about Concentration. Available at <http://competition.ge/en/page2.php?p=4&m=141>, [10.01.2015].

mergers are not as harmful to competition and consumers as the horizontal ones. There are two guidelines on merger cases in the European Union. One of them concerns horizontal mergers and the other one covers vertical concentrations. According to the horizontal merger guidelines, there is the presumption that if the parties to the merger have joint market shares below 25 per cent, their concentration may not impede an effective competition on the market[383]. As for non-horizontal merger cases, according to the Commission's opinion, if the market share of the merged entity in each of the markets concerned is below 30 per cent, a competition concern is unlikely. Therefore, in the European Union the most important factor for the assessment of concentrations are the market shares of the parties to the concentration and it would be better to provide it in the Law on Competition of Georgia instead of providing it in the undertakings' value of assets or annual turnover.

IV. The Authority of the Agency

1. Investigation authority of the Agency

In accordance with Art. 16 para. 1of the Georgian Law on Competition, the Competition Agency is being formed to enforce the competition policy in Georgia. Its main task is the enforcement of the competition policy in Georgia, creating favorable conditions for the development of competition, protection and the exclusion, detection and suppression of all types of anti-competitive activities.

In international practice two systems of considering violations of competition law are widespread: the single-level approach, the so-called integrated system and the two-level approach – the separated system[384]. The two-level system is common in the United States, where, in case the antitrust law violation is ascertained as a result of an investigation, the Antitrust Division of Department of Justice hands the case to the Court for a final decision, and itself acts as the State Prosecutor. It should be noted that the Georgian Law on "Free Trade and Competition" adopted on 8 May 2012, envisaged the two-level procedure, namely, in accordance with Art. 29 in case the agency would have revealed a violation of the law as a result of investigation, it used to hand the case to the court for further consideration and the final decision.

383 See, paragraph 18 of the Guidelines on the assessment of horizontal mergers under the Council Regulation on the control of concentrations between undertakings, <http://europa.eu/legislation_summaries/competition/firms/l26107_ en.htm>, [10.01.2015].

384 See, Comprehensive Strategy in Competition Policy, Government of Georgia, <http://www.government.gov.ge/files/41_32357_225550_Comprehensive20StrategyinCompetitionPolicy.pdf>, [20.05.2014], p.27.

The administrative authority of the competition agency has been increased as a result of the amendments and supplements to the mentioned law adopted in 2014. Namely, in accordance with Art. 18 para.1 subpara."a" of the Law, the Agency inquests the case based on an application or/and on a complaint or on its own initiative; according to subparagraph "h", the administrative functions of the Agency have increased and it is entitled to impose penalties on economic agents based on the outcome of the investigation.

In accordance with Article 3 para. "m", the applicant shall be a person who has the information or the guaranty that the competition legislation of Georgia is being essentially violated, though its property is not directly affected and for this it applies to the competition agency. According to Article 22 para.1, the applicant cannot be considered as a party. Therefore, the consumer suffering from property damages from any breach of competition rules is not entitled to submit an application or complaint to the Agency. While in the European Union legal persons as well as natural persons are entitled to lodge a complaint provided they show a legitimate interest.

The plaintiff can also apply to the agency by submitting the complaint and the evidence. The latter is considered to be a party with an evidential burden (Art. 22 para.2 of the Law). According to Art. 3 para. "n" of the Law, the complainant may be an economic agent who believes that the competition legislation of Georgia is being violated, and its property is directly affected by this violation, for which it applies to the Competition Agency.

The Competition Agency carries out the administrative proceedings through two-level procedures:1) check of the admissibility of the application/complaint; 2) study-inspection of the application/complaint.

Upon registering the application and claim, the Competition Agency reviews the eligibility of the application and the claim through a simple proceeding. In case it is considered eligible, the Agency starts an investigation.

The Investigation usually lasts for 3 months. Based on the importance and the complicacy of the case, this term could be further prolonged, but to no more than 10 months.

The agency may request the case-related information and documentation from the interested parties and the relevant economic agents. It is also obliged to send the applications/claims registered against the relevant economic agents to them and to give them the period, not less than 5 days and prolonged up to 15 days, to provide their own notes, suggestions or additional information. Usually the competition agency invites the interested parties to the explanatory session. During the investigation, the Agency is entitled to invite an expert for a conclusion on some issues based on the parties' requests or on the Agency's own initiative.

In accordance with Art.25 para.8 of the Law, if necessary, the competition agency is entitled to apply the on-site inspection of the economic agent against which the application/claim is filed with a motivated solicitation and request to the court during the investigation. Based on the mentioned provision, we might assume that the Agency is not entitled to inspect the sites of those economic agents, against which the agency has launched an investigation on its own initiative.

According to Art.25 para.8 of the Law on Competition, the competent authority is entitled to inspect the economic agent on site in case: 1) the information and documentation requested by the agency and submitted by the economic agent is not sufficient to continue the investigation; 2) there is a danger of destruction or/and of hiding the case-related information; 3) the parties do not meet their obligation to provide the information and documentation; 4) it is necessary to visually inspect the material assets.

Under the Law on Competition, during the on-site inspection, the competition agency is entitled to get acquainted with the documentations related to the economic agent's activities, including the financial-economical documentations, it is further entitled to make copies, to get the explanations at the site and to enter to the legal and actual sites of activities of the economic agent. According to the "Law on Competition" the agency is not entitled to seal up or seize the property under the ownership or the use of the economic agent. It is neither permitted to detain a person, to inspect its correspondence or to eavesdrop its telephone conversations.

It should be noted that the economic agents' inspection procedures are regulated in details by the Administrative Procedure Code of Georgia. Art. 21^2 of the Code refers to the procedures of applying to the court with a solicitation about the on-site inspection of the company by the controlling organ and its consideration. According to the first section, the solicitation of the controlling body is presented to the judge before the inspection of the undertaking. According to the second section, if there is an immediate and direct danger of destruction of the evidence, the controlling agency may commence the inspection and submit the inspection request to the judge within 24 hours. Upon the submission of the request the controlling agency shall substantiate the urgent necessity of the inspection (third section). In addition, the solicitation should reflect the accurate information about the company to be inspected, the terms of the inspection, the nature and the limitations of the inspection.

According to Art. 21^3 para. 12 of the Administrative Procedure Code of Georgia, the inspection of the entrepreneur should be carried out only within 15 days. Though, as an exception, in case of a reasonable solicitation, the mentioned term could be prolonged for another 15 days. In addition, in case the turnover of the enterprise to be inspected is more than 1 million GEL, the mentioned 30 days period could be additionally extended for no more than up to 40 days.

Under Art. 21^2 para. 2 of the Administrative Procedure Code exceptional situations are stipulated in which the controlling body can start with the proceedings without the court's order. In this case as well, it is obliged to apply to the court within 24 hours and to substantiate what was the urgent need for the inspection. The controlling body can start the inspection without the prior consent from the court in the following cases: 1) it is impossible to suspend the enterprise activities; 2) it will considerably harm the enterprise; or 3) the entrepreneur asks for the inspection.

If the judge does not happen to legalize the launched inspection of the enterprise, the inspection has to be stopped immediately according to the section 6 of the 21^{st3} Article of the Administrative Procedure Code. In this case, the entrepreneur might claim the compensation for damages resulting from the illegal inspection.

Art. $21^3$of the Administrative Procedure Code describes in detail the procedural rules under which the court will consider the solicitation of a controlling body over the examination of the enterprise. The solicitation should be considered within 72 hours after its submission. As a rule, the judge individually reviews the case without a hearing. After receiving the solicitation, the judge is obliged to inform the enterprise concerned about the received solicitation no later than within 24 hours and to send the corresponding materials to the enterprise or to its representative. If the judge believes that a further inspection of the circumstances indicated in the solicitation is required, he can consider the case at an open court session, different from the cases related to the Law of Georgia on "The Operative - Investigation Activities" and the Criminal Procedure Code. The parties have to be informed about the session no later than 48 hours after the submission of the solicitation to the court. The entrepreneur or its representative is entitled to present its opinions in written to the judge within 24 hours after the notice about the inspection and the submission of the case materials have been handed to them. If the judge satisfies the solicitation of the agency, it is obliged to provide the parties with the copies. The entrepreneur is entitled to file an appeal to the court issuing the order for the cancellation of an order within 48 hours after receipt of a copy.

According to Art. 21^3 para. 14 of the Administrative Procedure Code, the order to inspect an enterprise shall take effect only upon expiry of the deadline for appealing the order. The appeal against the order suspends the action of the order.

In order to effectively enforce the rules of the Law of Competition of Georgia, under special conditions or so-called emergencies, the Competition Agency should have the authority to inspect the economic agents on site without the advanced permission of the court in exceptional cases. It is especially important to reveal the secret cartel agreements, because the unexpected inspection of the economic agents on site is more effective in terms of obtaining classified documents. If the Agency wants to carry out the inspection of the economic agent on site with the purpose to obtain the classified documents, it is desirable that it happens without the prior notice, as it is impossible to obtain the desired evidences if economic agents know in advance that the Competition Agency wants to inspect their premises. It is natural, that it can immediately destroy or hide the relevant evidence. Thus, if the competition agency wants to obtain information and/or evidence with the purpose of a case investigation, it is preferable to carry out this procedure without the Court's prior consent and to apply to the court only after the initial 24 hours, to legitimize the emergency inspections, otherwise it is highly unlikely to reach the desired goal.

2. Sanctions under the Law on Competition of Georgia

According to Art. 33 of the Georgian Law on Competition, if the agency ascertains a violation of Art. 6 (abuse of a dominant positions) or Art. 7 (cartel agreements), it can fine the offenders up to 5 percent of their annual turnover. If economic agents do not obey the decision of the agency or if they repeatedly commit offense, they might be fined up to 10 percent of annual turnover. In determining the penalty, the Agency should consider the harm caused by such violation as well as the duration and the severity of the violation. It should be noted that the sanctions stipulated in Article 33 may not be imposed on the economic agents functioning in the regulated fields of economy. As Art. 3 para. "r" of the Law determines, such fields are commercial banking activities, electronic communications, broadcasting, electricity, natural gas, etc.

In addition to the penalties stipulated in Article 33, the Agency may use sanctions against the dominant economic agent provided in Art. 18 para.1 subpara. "k". In particular, the Agency is authorized to raise the issue of the division of an economic agent by force to the relevant authorities, in case the dominant economic agent repeatedly abuses its dominant position.

On the economic agents who do not provide the requested information or who provide incomplete or deliberately misleading information to the agency, a penalty may be imposed by the latter in accordance with Art. 18 para.1 subpara. "f" and Art. 32 by thousand to three thousand GEL.

The Agency is not entitled to impose sanctions on those economic agents, which violate:

1. Article 11^1 of the Law, namely do not fulfill the obligation of prior notification of a planned concentration to the competition authority.
2. Conditions provided for in Article 11^3 of the law, namely involved in an unfair competition.

According to Art. 18 para.1 subpara. "g", the Agency may require of an economic agent to bring its activities into conformity with the requirements of the Law on Competition.

Fines must be severe in order to have a deterrent effect. The concept of deterrence has two key assumptions: the first is that specific punishments imposed on offenders will deter or prevent them from committing further infringements; the second is that the fear of punishment will prevent others from participating in similar infringements. In comparison to the sanctions existing in the European Union, which is provided by Regulation # 1/2003, the amount of fines enshrined in Competition Law of Georgia is weak. According to Art. 23 para. 2 of the Regulation, the Commission is entitled to impose fines up to 10 percent of its total turnover in the preceding business year on an undertaking breaching Articles 101 or 102 TFEU (equivalent to Art. 7 and 6 of the Law on Competition of Georgia). Under paragraph 1 of this Article, the Commission may impose fines not exceeding 1 per cent of the total turnover in the preceding business year on undertakings if they supply incorrect, incomplete or misleading information or if they do not supply information within the required time-limit or if seals affixed by officials have been broken, etc.

In addition to the penalties, Art. 24 of the Regulation provides for periodical penalty payments up to 5 % of the average daily turnover in the preceding business year per day. This type of sanction is enshrined in order to compel economic agents to comply with decisions of the Competition Authority and to put an end to the infringement of competition rules.

As we have seen above, the Law on Competition of Georgia does not provide all types of sanctions as the Regulation # 1/2003 and the amounts of fines enshrined in the Law are not as severe as in the EU. It should be noted that the infringements of competition rules are not penalized by the Criminal Code of Georgia. Only collusive tendering in state procurements is penalized under Art. 195^1 of the Code.

V. Conclusion

Thus, based on the proposed analysis of the Law on Competition of Georgia, it can be assumed that there are some serious flaws in the provisions and that the competition agency has limited power to enforce the law and cannot be regarded sufficiently effective.

First of all, it should be considered that competition law should apply to all sectors of economy, without any exception. Exclusions of the important sectors such as the banking sector, electronic communications, electricity, natural gas from the range of competition law seem unjustified, since these sectors have a significant role in the development of the national economy. The original version of the existing Law on Competition, which was adopted in May 2012, provided a gradual application of competition rule to the fields of regulated economy. Namely, Art. 34 of the Law concerning transactional and final provisions enshrined that the Law would be applicable to the following fields:

1. electronic communications from 1st January 2016 (Art. 34 para.1);
2. energy and natural gas from 1st January 2019 (Article 34 para.3).

The provisions on gradual applications of the competition rules to the different sectors of regulated economy were abolished upon the adoption of the significant amendments and supplements to the Law in March 2014. After the "Rose Revolution" the most important fields of regulated economy in Georgia have been dominated by statutory or natural monopolists[385] entailing high prices for different services and products provided by the monopolists. It would be better to provide common competition rules applicable to all fields of economy, without any exception, because it may promote free entry to the markets and enhance competition in the fields. As Simon Bishop and Mike Walker think, monopolies are bad for the consumer's welfare and therefore they should be regulated in order to protect the interests of consumers.[386]

Secondly, the prohibited list of behaviors of economic agents provided by Art. 7 should not be exhausted. The term "contract" must be replaced by the term "agreement", otherwise the Agency and then the Court will have problems concerning the qualification of the conducts of undertakings as a contract.

---

385 See Menabdishvili, Getting Closer Together: Georgian Competition Laws are being brought into line with EU rules, "Competition Insights", London, June Issue 2013, pp. 5-7.

386 See Bishop/Walker, The Economics of EC Competition Law: Concepts, Application and Measurement, 3td ed. 2010, p.15.

Thirdly, the Competition Agency should have more authority for an effective enforcement of competition law. When there is an immediate danger of destruction of evidence, the Agency should be able to inspect the site of the economic agents without the prior consent of the court. In addition to inspecting economic agents at the site, the agency also should have the authority to inspect the real and movable property of employees of the economic agent such as directors, lawyers and other employees. For example, it should have the authority of inspecting their vehicles. There are some cases in the EU case law in which it is vital to inspect the privately owned property of directors or lawyers to obtain crucial evidence. There were also cases in which the cartel arraignments were organized by a law firm which was hired by the members of the cartel. Naturally, obtaining information and evidence for the case would have been only possible as a result of the on-site inspection of this law firm.

Fourthly, for an effective enforcement of competition rules, it is important to have strict sanctions that the competition agency may impose on the economic agent breaking the law. As noted above, the Agency may impose fines up to 5 percent of the annual turnover in case of violations of Articles 6 and 7 on the economic agents. The amount of fines should be increased and harmonized with the amount enshrined in Regulation #1/2003. The penalty of up to 5 percent of the annual turnover for violating the provisions may be considered as an ineffective sanction because the offender may prefer to pay 5 % or 10 % of its annual turnover rather than fulfilling the decision of the Agency. Accordingly, it is desirable that periodical penalty payments are prescribed in the Law on Competition to compel economic agents to abide the decision. In addition, it should be noted that the Agency cannot impose a penalty if the economic agents have implemented a concentration without prior notice to the Competition Agency or that it cannot carry out unfair competition. Thus, the Law on Competition of Georgia in regard to the sanctions provided against the violation of the rules of the law might be considered inefficient since apart from the fact that it cannot force economic agents to stop violations, it also cannot have a preventive nature.

Finally, for the prevention of violations of competition rules, it is very important to criminalize them. According to Art. 195 of the Criminal Code of Georgia adopted in 1999 the violation of competition legislation was a crime and the law provided the penalties. The mentioned Article was abolished on 8 May 2012. It would be desirable to restore the article with the same content in the Criminal Code since, on the one hand, it might prove to be preventive and, on the other hand, on the basis of the change the investigation authority may apply effective measures in accordance with the Criminal Procedure Code of Georgia in the investigation of violations of competition law.

D. Cooperation in the Area of Justice, Freedom and Security in the Three Association Agreements and Related Issues

Ludmila Negritu

Cooperation in the Area of Justice, Freedom and Security in the Three Association Agreements in the Overview: Comparison between the AAs and with EU law

Association Agreements (AAs) are international agreements, which the European Community/European Union has concluded with third countries with the aim of setting up a general framework for relations with some third countries or groups of countries. Association Agreements are today the EU's main instrument to bring countries in the Eastern Partnership region closer to the EU, including EU standards and norms. In certain cases, AAs prepare for a future membership in the European Union. Association Agreements differ in their exact content and finality depending on the partner country. EU Association Agreements normally provide for a progressive liberalization of trade (at various degrees: Free Trade Area, Customs Union etc.) and political association.

One of the elements of the three AAs, which the EU has concluded in 2014 with Georgia, Moldova and Ukraine, is the creation of the area of freedom, security and justice between the Parties under Title III of each of the Agreements (Art. 13-21 of the EU-Georgia AA, Art. 12-20 EU-Moldova AA, Art. 14-24 EU-Ukraine AA). The presence of such provisions in the AAs is one of the important differences in comparison with the pre-existing PCAs of the three countries with the EU. Historically, this is due to the circumstance that at the time when the PCAs were concluded, the EU (then EC) did not have a competence to pass secondary legislation in this subject matter area[387].

I. Context: The Eastern Partnership of the EU and the System of AAs

The difference between those Association Agreements, which have recently been concluded with Eastern Partnership countries (Georgia, Moldova, Ukraine)[388] and other AAs. which the EU has struck with third countries, is the Deep and Comprehensive Free Trade Area (DCFTA) part included in the three AAs. In signing this, Eastern Partnership members have committed themselves to adopting specific parts of EU legislation in (mainly) trade, consumer protection and environmental regulation. Countries, which sign such a DCFTA, must adopt some 350 EU laws within a ten-year timeframe. Signatories of an AA/DCFTA will also have access to the EU's 500

387 This competence was created only under the 1997 Amsterdam Treaty, i.e. after the PCAs were negotiated, see https://en.wikipedia.org/wiki/Area_of_freedom,_security_and_justice#History.

388 Armenia backed away from an AA in 2013 due to political considerations.

million consumers market with a combined economy of 12.9 trillion Euros.[389] Association Agreements are international treaties, from the EU perspective they are part of the secondary legislation of the EU, i.e. under EU law they rank below the EU Treaties (primary EU law). They are binding for the EU and its Member States as well as for the associated countries and can – depending on their content – create direct rights and duties for citizens. In the EU, they are concluded in a legislative procedure laid down by Article 218 para.6 of the Treaty on the Functioning of the European Union.

II. Common Elements of the Three EU AAs in the Area of Justice, Freedom and Security

The Titles III of the EU Association Agreements with Moldova, Ukraine and Georgia cover a broad range of issues concerning the rule of law and respect for human rights; protection of personal data; cooperation on migration, asylum and border management; treatment of workers; mobility of workers; movement of persons; money laundering and terrorism financing; cooperation on the fight against illicit drugs; the fight against crime and corruption; cooperation in fighting terrorism and legal cooperation. The topics mentioned – as well as the heading of Title III - are derived from the corresponding Title V (Art.67-89) of the Treaty on the Functioning of the European Union, but they have a much more limited content.

The European Union's Area of Freedom, Security and Justice was created to ensure the free movement of persons and to offer a high level of protection to citizens. It covers policy areas that range from the management of the European Union's external borders (Schengen system) to judicial cooperation in civil and criminal matters and police cooperation. It also includes asylum and immigration policies (Dublin system) and the fight against crime (terrorism, organized crime, cybercrime, sexual exploitation of children, trafficking in human beings, illegal drugs, etc.).

In the AAs, the EU and Ukraine/Moldova/Georgia commit themselves to increase their dialogue and cooperation on migration, asylum and border management. The importance of the introduction of a visa free travel regime for the citizens of these countries in due course, provided that the conditions for well-managed and secure mobility are in place is recognized in the Agreement (see e.g. Art.15 EU-Moldova AA). Also, they have agreed to combat organized crime and money laundering, to reduce the supply of and demand for illicit drugs and to step up cooperation in the fight against terrorism. However cooperation between the Parties in civil and criminal is con-

389 Muravska/Berlin, The EU - Eastern Partnership Countries – Association Agreements and Transdisciplinarity in Studies, Training and Research, in: Baltic Journal of European Studies, vol.4 (2014): No 2(17), p.136.

strued rather weakly. The AAs mainly refer to cooperation in the frame of the Hague Conference for Private International Law (see e.g. Art. 20 para. 1 EU-Moldova AA) or the UN and the Council of Europe (see e.g. Art.20 para.2 EU-Moldova AA). No mention is made of an inclusion of Georgia, Moldova or Ukraine into whatever EU regulations in this field, e.g. the Brussels Regulations governing cross-border cooperation in civil matters within the EU.

III. Differences between the Three AAs in the Area of Justice, Freedom and Security

1. Data Protection

The Agreement with Georgia establishes special provisions regarding protection of personal data in the Annex I of title III - Freedom, Security and Justice.[390] Each Contracting Party shall ensure a legal level of data protection, which at least corresponds to that set out in the EU Directive 95/46/EC of 24 October 1995 on the protection of individuals with regard to the processing of personal data and on the free movement of such data. In the same context, the EU-Moldova Agreement establishes provisions on the protection of personal data making the connection with Directive No 2006/24/EC of 15 March 2006 on the retention of data generated or processed in connection with the provision of publicly available electronic communications services or of public communications networks and amending Directive No 2002/58/EC.[391] In the EU-Ukraine AA there is only a laconic provision about the protection of personal data, which states: „The Parties agree to cooperate in order to ensure an adequate level of protection of personal data in accordance with the highest European and international standards, including the relevant Council of Europe instruments. Cooperation on personal data protection may include, inter alia, the exchange of information and of experts".[392]

2. Migration

Regarding cooperation in migration, asylum and border management matters the AA with Ukraine contains a particular provision, namely that the Parties may have an exchange of views about any informal employment of migrants.[393] In the AAs with Georgia and Moldova (not in the EU-Ukraine AA) an implementation of the Working Arrangement on the establishment of operational cooperation between the European Agency for the Management of Operational Coopera-

---

390 See Art. 14 and Annex I to Title III of the EU-Georgia AA.
391 See Art. 14 and Annex to Title III - Justice, Freedom and Security of the EU-Moldova AA.
392 Art. 15 EU-Ukraine AA.
393 See Art. 16 EU-Ukraine AA.

tion at the External Borders of the Member States of the European Union (FRONTEX) and relevant state organs in Georgia and Moldova is established.[394]

3. Mobility of workers

Provisions concerning the treatment of workers[395] and mobility of workers[396] are laid down only into the Ukraine agreement in a more explicit version, namely subject to the laws, conditions and procedures applicable in the Member States and the EU, treatment accorded to workers who are Ukrainian nationals and who are legally employed in the territory of a Member State shall be free of any discrimination based on nationality as regards working conditions, remuneration or dismissal, compared to the nationals of that Member State. Ukraine shall - due to the laws, conditions and procedures in Ukraine - accord the treatment referred to in paragraph 1 of Article 17 to workers who are nationals of a Member State and who are legally employed in its territory.

4. Movement of persons

In the area of movement of persons, the EU-Moldova Agreement contains special stipulations, e.g. a reference to the Agreement between the European Community and the Republic of Moldova on the facilitation of the issuance of visas, which entered into force on 1 January 2008 as amended on 27 June 2012.[397] In the Georgian Association Agreement the same article is entitled Movement of persons and readmission. It states that the Parties will ensure the full implementation of the Agreement between the European Union and Georgia on the readmission of persons residing without authorization, which entered into force on 1 March 2011 as well as the agreement on the facilitation of the issuance of visas, which entered into force on 1 March 2011. In the same context, the EU-Ukrainian Agreement states that the Parties shall take gradual steps towards a visa-free regime in due course, provided that the conditions for well-managed and secure mobility, set out in the two-phase Action Plan on Visa Liberalization presented at the EU-Ukraine Summit of 22 November 2010, are in place.

5. Judicial cooperation

In contrast with the Agreements with Georgia and Moldova, the EU-Ukraine Agreement has slightly divergent provisions concerning legal cooperation. The Parties agree to enhance judicial cooperation in civil and criminal matters, making full use of the relevant international and bilateral instruments and basing themselves on the principles of legal certainty and the right to a fair

---

394 See Art. 14 EU-Moldova AA.
395 Ibid., Article 17.
396 Ibid., Article 18.
397 See Article 15 of the EU AA with Moldova, 27.06.14.

trial. In Georgia`s and Moldova`s Agreements the following is stated: „The Parties agree to develop judicial cooperation in civil and commercial matters as regards the negotiation, ratification and implementation of multilateral conventions on civil judicial cooperation and, in particular, the conventions of the Hague Conference on Private International Law in the field of international legal cooperation and litigation as well as the protection of children".[398] The provisions concerning legal cooperation and the other clauses laid down by the EU Association Agreements with the mentioned countries are basic and relatively common. Special requirements are embodied in the Action Plans to be executed by the States signatory to the Agreement in due time.

6. Interim summary

As a result of what has been described, Moldova, Georgia and Ukraine have to undertake all the above-mentioned actions that are fixed in the AAs for each signatory country, taken into consideration the outcomes of the negotiating process with EU. In the field of legal cooperation and home affairs, Moldova has to accomplish the following tasks provided by clause 2.5 of the EU-Moldova Action Plan[399] such as approximation of legislation to the EU law and standards relating to the status of refugees (paragraph 46) or to adopt and efficiently implement the legislation and measures for the development of arrangements under which judicial cooperation can be offered and obtained from other states, to explore the possibilities for cooperation between Moldovan agencies, Europol and Euro just in accordance with Europol Convention and the relevant Council decisions. Similarly, in the EU-Georgia[400] and EU-Ukraine Action Plans[401] different measures are stated, which must be undertaken by Ukraine (clause 2.4) and Georgia (clause 4.3) in the field of Freedom, Security and Justice.

IV. The Provisions of the Three EU Association Agreements on Cooperation in Civil Matters and the EU Law in this Field

The Treaty on the Functioning of the European Union as a source of European Law provides that the Union shall constitute an area of freedom, security and justice with respect for fundamental rights and the different legal systems and traditions of the Member States and that the Union shall facilitate access to justice, in particular through the principle of mutual recognition of judicial and extrajudicial decisions in civil matters.[402] European law concerning judicial cooperation in civil

398 See Article 20 of the EU AA with Moldova, 27.06.14.

399 EU-Moldova Action Plan, https://eeas.europa.eu/enp/pdf/pdf/action_plans/moldova_enp_ap_final_en.pdf, 19.08.16.

400 EU-Georgia Action Plan, https://eeas.europa.eu/enp/pdf/pdf/action_plans/georgia_enp_ap_final_en.pdf, 19.08.16.

401 EU-Ukraine Action Plan, http://www.enpi-info.eu/library/content/eu-ukraine-action-plan-0, 19.08.16.

402 See Article 67 TFEU.

matters contains very detailed and numerous provisions in this field; according to them the Union shall develop judicial cooperation in civil matters having cross-border implications, based on the principle of mutual recognition of judgments and of decisions in extrajudicial cases. At a European Council Meeting in Tampere/Finland in 1999 was decided that this principle should govern judicial cooperation in both civil and criminal matters within the EU.[403] For this purpose, EU countries should make use of e-justice (information and communication technologies in the field of justice), adopt common minimum rules to approximate criminal and civil standards, and strengthen mutual trust. The EU must also to obtain coherence with the international legal order as creating a secure legal environment for interacting with non-EU countries. Also, the European Parliament and the Council, acting in accordance with ordinary legislative procedure, were called-upon to adopt measures, particularly when necessary for the proper functioning of the internal market, aimed at ensuring: (a) the mutual recognition and enforcement between Member States of judgments and of decisions in extrajudicial cases; (b) the cross-border service of judicial and extrajudicial documents; (c) the compatibility of the rules applicable in the Member States concerning conflict of laws and of jurisdiction; (d) cooperation in the taking of evidence; (e) effective access to justice; (f) the elimination of obstacles to the proper functioning of civil proceedings, if necessary by promoting the compatibility of the rules on civil procedure applicable in the Member States; (g) the development of alternative methods of dispute settlement; (h) support for the training of the judiciary and judicial staff.[404] All three Association Agreements establish similar provisions, though in a very open and soft form, regarding the cooperation in civil matters: the parties agree to develop judicial cooperation in civil and commercial matters as regards the negotiation, ratification and implementation of multilateral conventions on civil judicial cooperation and, in particular, the Conventions of the Hague Conference on Private International Law in the field of international legal cooperation and litigation as well as the protection of children. This means that the Parties require a period of time, assistance to their approximation towards the relevant political and regulatory framework, before they can join the European legal framework.

V. The Provisions in the EU Association Agreements on Cooperation in Criminal Matters and EU Criminal Law

Today, Article 67 TFEU has established cooperation between EU Member States in criminal matters as a subject of intergovernmental cooperation. The common framework includes police and judicial cooperation in criminal matters and the prevention and combat against racism and xeno-

---

403 Tampere European Council, 15/16.10.1999, Presidency conclusions, B. A genuine European area of justice, http://www.consilium.europa.eu/en/search/?q=Presidency+conclusions&search=search, 18.08.2016.

404 See Title V – Area of Justice, Freedom and Security, Chapter III, Art. 81 TFEU.

phobia.[405] Under the TFEU a number of legal on harmonization of penal laws[406] with regard to certain areas considered as crucial in the fight against organized crime, were adopted. The main legal instruments to approximate national substantive criminal law in the EU were so-called framework decisions. Article 83 TFEU provides that the EU may establish minimum rules concerning the definition of criminal offences and sanctions in areas of particularly serious crimes with a cross-border dimension resulting from the nature or impact of such offences or from a special need to combat them on a common basis. Such crimes are, in particular: terrorism, trafficking in human beings and sexual exploitation of women and children, illicit drug trafficking, illicit arms trafficking, money laundering, corruption, counterfeiting of means of payment, computer crime and organized crime.

As regards judicial cooperation in criminal matters from the perspective of the Association Agreements, the Contracting Parties have stated – again in a very soft form - that they will seek to enhance cooperation on mutual legal assistance. This would include, where appropriate, accession to, and implementation of, the relevant international instruments of the United Nations and the Council of Europe and closer cooperation with Eurojust.[407] This will certainly be an area where concrete further proposals for cooperation will have to be developed.

VI. Conclusion

Joining the EU– the political dream in all of the three associated countries – means a transitional period, expenditure and not just profits and more concessions from both sides during any future negotiations. Georgia, Moldova and Ukraine can in this respect draw lessons from earlier EU accession by Central and Eastern European countries, mainly the principle of differentiation. However, before any idea about accession to the EU can become realistic, the EU and the associated countries will have much to do to make the Association Agreements work – the example of the Area of Freedom, Security and Justice shows that the AAs do not offer a blueprint in this field, but leave further steps to a large degree to future agreements between the Parties.

[405] See Article 67 TFEU.
[406] See Article 83 TFEU.
[407] Art. 20 of the EU-Moldova AA; Art. 21 EU-Georgia AA; Art. 24 EU-Ukraine AA.

Salome Kavtaradze

Elements of Freedom of Movement of Persons in the Three Association Agreements

After the signing of the Association Agreements between EU and Georgia, Moldova, Ukraine on 27 June2014 there are many hopes for the future of these countries. Important is to distinguish between reality and illusions, make clear goals and follow them in order to develop these three countries further. The main long-term objective of these three countries is to become members of the EU, but this certainly not to be realized very quickly. There are also many factors making further EU enlargement more and more difficult. But looking at countries which emerged from the communist rule in the early 1990s, but did not immediately start down the path of EU membership, it is reasonable to say that they have been less stable, secure and prosperous than those who have already become EU members (for example: Poland)[408]. Also, not each EU member state is at the same level developed, but at least they are in a better situation than most of the Eastern Partnership countries.

One of the very realistic objectives, however, is to obtain free movement within the European Union for citizens of Georgia and Ukraine, and Moldova has already achieved this standard. In this paper the issue of free movement of persons will be discussed not only in the context of the Association Agreements as this would be very insufficient. Negotiations about free movement of persons began much earlier with Georgia, Ukraine and Moldova, and there are other important documents such as Visa Facilitation Agreements and Readmission Agreements with regard to persons residing without authorization. After fulfilling the obligations of these documents free movement of Georgian or Ukrainian citizens within the EU can be discussed. The European Union divides the world into four categories in order to visa policies: 1) EU member state citizens, who can freely travel within EU without any permissions; 2) citizens of countries participating in the European Economic Area enjoying privileged relationships with the EU and having equivalent rights; 3) favoured third-countries, e.g. Israel, which are placed on the EU's 'positive' visa list of Council Regulation 539/2001 meaning that their nationals do not require a visa to enter the EU; 4) third-countries that a replaced on the 'negative' visa list of Council Regulation 539/2001 meaning that their citizens do require a visa to enter the EU[409]. Important is to move Ukraine and Georgia from the "negative" to the "positive" list. One step in direction to this aim is the imple-

408 Bond, EU Enlargement, Center for European Reform, 2014, p. 2.
409 Trauner/Kruse EU Eastern Neighbourhood: Economic Potential and Future Development, ENEPO, 2008, p. 6.

mentation of requirements of the Visa Liberalization Action Plan and the Readmission Agreement as well.

In this paper the necessary measures in all three countries to gain free movement of persons into the EU will be discussed on the basis of the AAs, the respective Visa Facilitation and Readmission Agreements and the Visa Liberalization Action Plans. There are many similarities between these documents in all three countries. At the example of Georgia these documents will be analyzed in a more detailed manner. With regard to Moldova and Ukraine only main issues and differences can be mentioned.

I. Georgia

1. Free Movement of Persons according to the Association Agreement

In the text of the EU-Georgia Association provisions on Freedom, Security and Justice are located in the Third Title. This title also includes provision on the free movement of persons, namely the free movement of Georgian citizens within the European Union. In article 16 of AA it is provided that the Contracting Parties will ensure a full implementation of the Agreement between the European Union and Georgia on the readmission of persons residing without authorization, which entered into force on 1 March 2011 and the Agreement between the European Union and Georgia on the facilitation of the issuance of visas, which entered into force on 1 March 2011. Also the Parties shall continue to endeavor to enhance the mobility of citizens and shall take gradual steps towards the shared objective of a visa-free regime in due course, provided that the conditions for well-managed and secure mobility set out in the two-phase Action Plan on Visa Liberalization are in place (Art. 16 para.2 of the AA).

There are no other specific rules about free movement of persons in the AA and the enforcement of the whole AA does not depend on enforcement of documents linked with visa liberalization. The agreements on the facilitation of the issuance of visas and readmission of persons residing without authorization are legally independent from the AA and their implementation does not depend on the implementation of the AA.

2. The Visa Facilitation Agreement

The Visa Facilitation Agreement states that the visa-free travel regime for Georgian citizens is a long-term goal, provided that the conditions for well-managed and secure mobility will be fulfilled. The parties recognize that visa facilitation should not lead to illegal migration and that special attention must be paid to security and readmission. The Visa Facilitation Agreement makes it easier and cheaper for Georgian citizens, in particular those who travel most, to acquire short stay visas for travels to and throughout the EU. A short stay visa is a visa for an intended stay of not more than 90 days in a period of 180 days. EU citizens are already exempted from the visa obligation when travelling to or transiting through Georgia since 1 June 2006. The agreement substantially simplifies the necessary supporting documents for a visa application for certain categories of persons, e.g. close relatives who are visiting Georgian citizens residing in the EU, businessmen, scientists, students and journalists. For some categories of frequent travelers and under certain conditions, member states are supposed to issue multi-entry visas with long periods of validity. Holders of diplomatic passports are exempted from the visa obligation.

As a general rule, the agreement stipulates that a decision upon the request to issue a visa must be taken within 10 calendar days. The agreement also reduces the visa handling fee from € 60 to € 35 for all Georgian citizens and provide a total exemption from the visa fee for certain categories of applicants, e.g. close relatives who are visiting Georgian citizens residing in the EU, pensioners, children below the age of 12, disabled persons, scientists, students and journalists.

On 28 November 2008, the Council gave the European Commission the mandate to start negotiations of the visa facilitation agreement with Georgia. They were concluded in the first half of 2010 and the agreement was signed in June 2010. The European Parliament gave its consent in December 2010. It must be noted that the United Kingdom, Denmark and Ireland are not taking part in the agreement. The agreement contains a list of documents which are necessary for particular categories of citizens (close relatives, members of officials' delegations, pupils, students, post-graduates, teachers, people travelling for medical reasons, journalists, participants in international sport events, business people and representatives of business organizations and etc.). On the whole there are 13 types[410] of persons who will get very concrete benefits from the Visa Facilitation Agreement. Important is that according to Art. 12 of the Visa Facilitation Agreement the parties shall set up a Joint Committee of experts composed of representatives of the Union and of Georgia. The Union shall be represented by the Commission, assisted by experts from the Member States. The Committee has several tasks: monitoring the implementation of the Agreement; suggesting amendments or additions; settling disputes arising out of the interpretation or application of the provisions of this agreement.

According to Art. 13 of the Agreement as from its entry into force this agreement shall take precedence over provisions of any bilateral or multilateral agreements or arrangements concluded between individual Member States and Georgia, in so far as the provisions of the latter agree-

410 EU-Georgia Visa facilitation agreement, Article 4, Official Journal of European Union, 25.2.2011.

ments or arrangements cover issues dealt with by these agreements. The Agreement contains only 13 articles, it is not large, but covers all necessary issues for such agreements. The Agreement has entered into force on 1 March 2011 and it functions very successfully in Georgia. But according to some reports made by some influential NGO's[411], there are also problems on the way of implementation of this agreement. For example some consulates of EU Member States still do not have visa information available in Georgian, which is of course a big challenge for some visa seekers.[412]

Despite all the positive steps made in this field among the Eastern Partnership (region) countries visa denial in Georgia has the highest percentage. For the year 2012 it was nearly 13.3%.[413] In comparison with 2011 when the visa denial rate was 14.8 % it is obviously reduced, but still remains to be too high for visa free regime requirements. One can list many reasons, e.g. the unstable political or social situation in Georgia because of internal or external factors, Georgia's biggest neighbor Russia, who is always a threat for its neighbors,[414] the high rate of unemployment etc. The Visa Facilitation Agreement is a very positive step to simplify travelling for Georgian citizens within the EU, but it is not a tool for obtaining a visa-free regime. It can be described as a necessary step toward a visa-free regime and a step in the Visa Liberalization Action Plan.

3) Readmission Agreement

Visa Facilitation Agreements go usually hand-in-hand with Readmission Agreements between the EU and third countries. The European Commission, as well as governments of its Member States, argued on various occasions that the credibility and integrity of the legal EU immigration system would be in danger without an efficient common return policy.[415]

On 28 November 2008, the Council gave the European Commission the mandate to start negotiations of the Readmission Agreement with Georgia. They were concluded in the second half of 2010 and the agreement was signed in November 2010. The European Parliament gave its consent in December 2010.The Readmission Agreement aims to enhance cooperation between Georgia and the EU in fighting against illegal migration. Readmission agreements set out clear obliga-

---

411 EU-Georgia Action Plan on Visa Liberalization monitoring of implementation, Transparency International Georgia, Interim Report 2013.

412 Eastern Partnership –Roadmap after Vilnius Summit, Policy Recommendations, KAS, 09.12.2014, Tbilisi, Georgia.

413 Visa Liberalization and Perspectives, Research Paper, European Initiative Liberal Academy Tbilisi, Open Society Georgia Foundation, 2013, p.25.

414 Eastern Partnership –Roadmap after Vilnius Summit, Policy Recommendations, KAS, 09.12.2014, Tbilisi, Georgia.

415 Trauner Florian, Kruse Imke, EUEasternNeighborhood: Economic Potentialand Future Development, ENEPO, 2008, p. 8.

tions and procedures for the authorities of EU member states and the third countries concerned as to when and how to take back people who are illegally residing on the territories of the parties. They do not cover only the illegal staying of nationals of both parties, but also of third country nationals and stateless persons being in an irregular situation provided they have a clear link with the requested party (e.g. visa or resident permit). After the Amsterdam Treaty had transferred competences for readmission to the EU, member states decided to sign only those Community readmission agreements that provide for there turn of citizens not only of contracting states but also third country nationals[416]. All the new Readmission Agreements also include readmission of third country national. The Agreement is based on the principles engrained in the European Convention on the Protection of Human Rights and Fundamental Freedoms. The Agreement also includes a number of other procedural rules, such as time-limits for the readmission applications, modalities for the transfer of the returnees, the cost of the transfer and the protection of personal data of the returnees. A Joint Readmission Committee is established so as to monitor the application of the agreement and decide on certain technical arrangements. As well as in the Visa Facilitation Agreement the UK, Ireland and Denmark do not take part in this Agreement. The Agreement on readmission obliges not only Georgia, but also the member states of the European Union. The agreement contains necessary procedures for readmission and also 6 annexes which also are part of agreement and parties shall apply them. In the framework of the Visa Facilitation Agreement and the Readmission Agreement, Georgia-EU joint Committees were created, which ensure the fulfillment of obligations and organize a regular exchange of information.

In accordance with a President's Decree of 26 April 2011, the Ministry of Internal Affairs of Georgia was determined as a competent authority for the implementation of the agreement. The Ministries of Foreign Affairs, Justice and Internally Displaced Persons from the Occupied Territories, Accommodation and Refugees were instructed to provide necessary assistance to the competent authority whenever needed. Based on the President's Decree, the Minister of Internal Affairs issued an order, which amended the Patrol Police Regulations to accommodate additional functions under the agreement.[417]

4) Visa Liberalization Action Plan (VLAP)

Despite the above listed benefits of the Visa Facilitation Agreement, even the full implementation of this Agreement cannot give Georgia visa free travel regime with the EU. The Visa Facilitation

416 Trauner Florian, Kruse Imke, EUEasternNeighborhood: Economic Potentialand Future Development, ENEPO, 2008, p. 8.

417 Further Information can be found on official web-site of Ministry of Internal Affairs of Georgia http://police.ge/en/ministry/structure-and-offices/international-relations-department/euro-atlantic-integration/european-union/ saqartvelosa-da-evrokavshirs-shoris- (last acceded on 28.02.2015).

Agreement is the best way to see how willing a country and its citizens are to get visa free travel regime. In the contrary VLAP can lead a country to desirable visa-free travel regime with the EU, but only after full implementation of its requirements. Georgia was granted a VLAP in early 2013, earlier than the Association Agreement was signed. That is why the Association Agreement is not repeated in the listed requirements of the VLAP. The visa liberalization dialogue between the EU and Georgia was launched in Brussels on 4 June 2012. On 25 February 2013 in Tbilisi the European Commission presented the Action Plan on Visa Liberalization to the Georgian authorities. The VLAP is structured around four blocks, namely 1) Document security, including biometrics; 2) Integrated border management, migration management, asylum; 3) Public order and security and 4) External relations and fundamental rights.

According to the VLAP there are two phases of liberalization. The first phase is dedicated to the policy framework, the second phase is more specific, but based on the first one. The first Progress Report from the European Commission to the European Parliament and the Council on implementation of the VLAP was already issued by the end of 2013. The evaluation mission focused on the blocks, the implementation of which was considered to be the most advanced, namely Block 1 and 2.[418] The Progress Report was very detailed and contained both aspects: what has been done and what has to be done in the nearest future for further implementation of VLAP.

In February, March and May 2014, Georgia submitted an updated Progress Report. An evaluation mission took place in spring 2014 with experts from EU Member States, assisted by the Commission services, the European External Action Service and the EU Delegation to Georgia. The mission focused on Block 3 and 4 of the VLAP. The second Progress Report was the final report on the first phase of the implementation of the VLAP. In the second phase the Commission will focus on assessing the effectiveness and the sustainability of the implementation of the second-phase VLAP benchmarks. It will also monitor the adequacy of the legislative and policy framework, as the two sets of benchmarks are closely linked. Members of the Commission already visited Georgia. The next report is to be presented in 2015. There are no specific time frameworks for the implementation and conclusion of the second phase. The process will be long and not easy, but there are also some very positive statements from high officials, e.g. German Foreign Minister Frank-Walter Steinmeier said in Tbilisi in December 2015 that Georgia would soon get a visa free regime with the EU. Of course such an announcement should not be perceived by the Georgian Government as a guarantee, but at the same time one should not forget that the visa-free

418 First progress report on the implementation by Georgia of the Action Plan on Visa Liberalization, COM (2013) 808 final, Brussels, 15.11.2013.

travel regime is more likely a political decision from the EU. Lots of work have to be done in direction of legislation approximation and their implementation and hopefully these reforms will continue also with success.

II. Ukraine

1. Association Agreement

The text of the Association Agreement between Ukraine and the EU in field of free movement of persons is very similar to the EU-Georgia AA. It is also located in Title III – Justice, Freedom and Security. Article 19 of Association Agreement (Movement of Persons) obliges the Parties to ensure a full implementation of the Agreement between the European Community and Ukraine on the Readmission of Persons of 18 June 2007 (through the joint readmission committee set up by its Article 15) and the Agreement between the European Community and Ukraine on the Facilitation of the Issuance of Visas of 18 June 2007 (through the joint committee for management of the agreement set up by its Article 12). Both Agreements entered into force on 1 January 2008. In the AA close attention is paid to ensuring the mobility of citizens, including through the introduction of visa-free regime after creating the appropriate conditions specified in the VLAP. At the same time, the Agreement does not substitute the said Action Plan and therefore the terms of introducing the visa-free regime do not depend on the timing of the Agreement's entry into force and implementation.[419]

In Ukraine the mobility of citizens is a key instrument of Ukraine's European integration policy and seen as an indicator of its success.[420]

The main difference between the EU-Georgia and EU-Ukraine AAs in this respect is that the EU-Ukraine AA also includes protection of Ukrainian workers who are legally employed in the member states and also free movement of workers. In this field the AA is not very specific, it is more general. But it is very important that the EU sees the need to regulate this subject. On the other hand such regulations cannot lead to specific results and this part of Agreement probably will find a specification in other documents. Ukraine is a very large and populous country, with more than 40 million citizens. This means that much workforce could migrate from Ukraine to EU countries for better work conditions and better salary. The Ukrainian crisis is not all over and it is very natural that people want to go away from war. But there are countries in the EU, which

[419] EU-Ukraine Association Agreement: Guideline for reforms, SushkoOleksandr, Zelinska Olga, Khorolskyy Robert, Movchan Veronika, SolonenkoIryna, GumeniukViktoria, Triukhan Vadim, KAS Policy Paper, p. 15.

[420] EU-Ukraine Association Agreement: Guideline for reforms, SushkoOleksandr, Zelinska Olga, Khorolskyy Robert, Movchan Veronika, SolonenkoIryna, GumeniukViktoria, Triukhan Vadim, KAS Policy Paper, p. 18.

are not very "kind" to foreigners. Not only people from non-EU space are seen as a danger from those countries (e.g. UK), but foreign workers in general, even from some EU member states.[421]

2. EU-Ukraine Visa Facilitation and Readmission Agreement

The Visa Facilitation Agreement and the Agreement on the Readmission of persons residing without authorization between EU and Ukraine entered into force in 2007. The amended version of the Visa Facilitation Agreement entered into force in 2013. The implementation of both documents is very important for the future relationship EU-Ukraine. Although these documents have been in force for seven years, the implementation phase is still ongoing. The Visa Facilitation Agreement and the Readmission Agreement with Ukraine and Georgia are quite similar with very few differences. The main aim of the Visa Facilitation Agreement is to make it easier for Ukrainian citizens to travel within the EU. The importance of the Agreement on Readmission of Persons is based on the need of a joint fight against illegal migration. Frequent travelling and illegal migration stand very close together. The implementation of both agreements at the same time has an immense meaning.

3. VLAP

The EU-Ukraine Visa Dialogue was launched on 29 October 2008. The VLAP was presented to Ukraine by the Commission on 22 November 2010. It sets a series of precise benchmarks for Ukraine in four blocks of relevant issues, with a view to the adoption of a legislative, policy and institutional framework and its effective and sustainable implementation. During the implementation of first phase requirements the Commission has reported three times in whole, so there are three Progress Reports. With the third Progress Report Ukraine closed the VLAP's first phase successfully and stepped into implementation of the second phase.

As above mentioned, Ukraine gained the VLAP in 2010, but it took too long to conclude the first phase of the VLAP. This had many politicaland other reasons. First of all Ukraine with a population of more than 40 million inhabitants is the largest country in the Eastern Partnership region and it is always more difficult to reform a big country than small countries. Of course, if there is political willingness of leading persons, reforms will be carried out and implemented. But this does not happen easily in the case of Ukraine. The new Government of Ukraine is trying very hard to get as many benefits from the EU as possible, but under war conditions it is very hard to carry out reforms and implement them successfully. Because of the war in some parts of Ukraine and because of the hard economic situation in the whole country it seems unrealistic for Ukraine

[421] Bond Ian, EU Enlargement, Center for European Reforms, July 2014.

to get visa free travel regime during the Riga summit in spring 2015. The VLAP also includes a number of domestic reforms[422], which are about document security, including biometrics, integrated border management, migration management, asylum, public order and security and external relations and fundamental rights.

III. Moldova

Moldova is the first country in the Eastern Partnership which already has a visa-free travel regime with the EU because of the full implementation of the VLAP requirements. Moldovan citizens having a biometric passport have been enjoying visa-free travel regime with EU (only short-stay visa)[423] since 28 April 2014. All countries in the Eastern Partnership are different, with different social, economic and political backgrounds. Nowadays all of them have territorial problems (Georgia – Abkhazia, South Ossetia; Moldova – Transnistria; Ukraine – Crimea; Eastern Ukraine) and almost every support from the EU is more than welcomed. Without doubt the visa-free travel regime will have a positive effect on Moldova´s further development.[424] It should be also mentioned that a large number of Moldovan citizens had already free travel possibility before, because they have Romanian passports.[425] An estimated seventh part of the population of 500.000 Moldovans holds Romanian (and therefore EU) passports.[426] Despite this factor visa-free travel regime and progress made by the Moldovan government is very important.

Moldova - as well as above discussed Georgia and Ukraine - has a Visa Facilitation and Readmission Agreement, also a VLAP. The Agreement between the European Community and the Republic of Moldova on the Readmission of persons residing without authorization and the Visa Facilitation Agreement (amended on 27 June 2012), entered into force on 1 January 2008. The Visa Liberalization Dialogue between the EU and Republic of Moldova was launched on 15 June 2010 and the Visa Liberalization Action Plan (VLAP) was presented to the Moldovan authorities in January 2011.[427] In its latest report on the implementation of the VLAP, the Commission considered that the Republic of Moldova met all the benchmarks needed.[428] As not-biometric pass-

422 EU-Ukraine Association Agreement: Guideline for reforms, Sushko Oleksandr, Zelinska Olga, Khorolskyy Robert, Movchan Veronika, Solonenko Iryna, GumeniukViktoria, Triukhan Vadim, KAS Policy Paper, p. 46.

423 European Commission, Statement, Brussels, 3 April 2014 http://europa.eu/rapid/press-release_STATEMENT-14-101_en.htm (last acceded on 28.02.2015).

424 Already in 2 month after 28 April the rate of travelers in compare with last year has risen with 9%, Irmer Sven-Joachim, Wolf Theodor, Das Assoziierungsabkommenzwischen der RepublikMoldau und der Europäischen Union istunterschrieben, Länderbericht, Juni 2014.

425 Stemmer Anna, The Republic of Moldova and the Migration, KAS International Reports, 9/10/2011, p. 48.

426 More information under: http://www.foreignaffairs.com/articles/141181/mitchell-a-orenstein-and-kalman-mizsei/moldova-in-the-middle (last acceded on 28.02.2015).

427 More information under: http://europa.eu/rapid/press-release_IP-11-59_en.htm?locale=fr (last acceded on 28.02.2015).

428 More information under: http://europa.eu/rapid/press-release_IP-13-1085_en.htm (last acceded on 28.02.2015).

ports are still in use partially in Moldova the Visa Facilitation Agreement still remains in force for these non-biometric passport holder citizens, as well as the Readmission Agreement.

Since it emerged from the Soviet Union Moldova has been in a hard economic, social and political situation; it is still the poorest country in Europe. The migration rate in the country with a population of 3.5 million people is high, approximately 700.000 people are abroad. Therefore a main concern was that once the borders will be open, citizens of a country affected by migration will take advantage and will depart abroad in large numbers. But in reality the situation is not so scary. In the first eight hours of free circulation, 200 Moldavians crossed the border with their biometric passports and in the first four months 201.714 citizens went to the European Union (according to the Border Police). Most of those people use the opportunity to travel for vacation, to explore European countries, to meet with emigrated relatives, to visit friends[429].The same struggle we can now see in Georgia and Ukraine. Of course there will always be some people willing to migrate into EU Member States or other richer countries, but Governments are obliged not only according to an Associations Agreement, but firstly according to their mandates to create better economic, social or political environment in each country.

IV. Conclusion

The aim of this article was a situation analysis of free movement of persons in Georgia, Ukraine and Moldova according to the newly signed Association Agreements with the EU and other related documents. It was an overview to the current obligations of the countries and future perspectives. Free movement of people is only one small part of a big Association Agreement. Enforcement of the whole Agreement will take years and the way towards economic growth, political stabilization etc. will not be easy. People, as well as the Governments of each country should take courage and make steps to a better future.

Visa liberalization and a visa-free regime are easier to obtain than other benefits from the EU. There are very concrete to-do-lists of reforms, which are of course better for each country to be implemented. As the article says, the three countries are doing well. Moldova already has a visa-free travel regime with EU for biometric passport holder Moldovans since 29 April 2014. Georgia and Ukraine also made significant improvements on document security, including biometrics; integrated border management, migration management, asylum; public order and security and external relations and fundamental rights issues, but the second phase of the VLAP is not yet

[429] More information under: http://forummigrantu.blog.idnes.cz/c/445937/Liberalization-of-visa-regime-for-citizens-of-Moldova.html (last acceded on 28.02.2015).

closed. There is no timetable for closing the first or the second phase of the VLAP, but it will be done as soon as possible in order to obtain the desirable visa-free regime with the EU. Without doubt that there will always be a certain fear in Europe of many migrants from Eastern Partnership countries because of the less developed social and economic environment, but if migration politics is planned wisely, migration of many Georgians or Ukrainians can be avoided. Globalization itself brought migration and it cannot be stopped, but it can be planned. Despite of some negative events happening now all over the world and also in Eastern Partnership countries, the Governments of these countries should be concentrated to do more for the improvement of the situation. One thing is clear, Georgia, Moldova and Ukraine have chosen the European path, a path of development, democracy, human rights protection, equality, and steps on this path should be done well.

E. Dispute Settlement under the Three Association Agreements

Yulia Khomyn

Settlement of Trade Disputes under the Three Association Agreements

Each Association Agreement between the European Union and Georgia, Moldova and Ukraine provides for a large Title on "Trade and Trade-Related Matters", which contains the core provisions on the agreed Deep and Comprehensive Free Trade Area (DCFTA). For an effective implementation of these provisions, which are supplemented by the numerous Annexes, Appendices and Protocols to the Agreement, a developed and clear dispute settlement mechanism ("DSM") is indispensable. The Association Agreements do provide for such DSMs[430], which are based on the model of the WTO Dispute Settlement Understanding. The basic advantages of the DSM in the AAs are said to be: faster procedures, a reduction of time-limits of the arbitration procedure in urgent cases, and further particularities for urgent energy disputes. The DSMs under the Association Agreements address inter-state trade disputes, not disputes between private parties or between a private party and a State. They provide for: 1) consultations and determinations by a group of experts regarding trade and sustainable development measures 2) arbitration; 3) mediation.

The purpose of this paper is to consider and compare the DSM mechanisms provided for in the AAs with regard to DCFTA disputes, analyze the procedures, in particular novelties of the arbitration procedure, and try an evaluation of possible consequences of these DSMs for the further development both of business and the public sector. The paper will mainly concentrate on the EU-Ukraine AA, but will draw some comparisons with the other AAs.

I. General observations on the mechanisms of dispute settlement in the Association Agreements (Ukraine, Moldova, Georgia)

Every international treaty can lead to disputes. In order to have a uniform interpretation of the treaty or to resolve disputes in a manner, which is specific to the subject-matter of the treaty, some treaties provide for a specific mechanism of dispute resolution. Such a mechanism can be more effective than merely political or diplomatic negotiations between the Contracting Parties or the use of non-specialized international courts or national courts. The Dispute Settlement Mechanism (DSM) in the World Trade Organization has demonstrated that in particular in trade disputes a specific dispute resolution system can have very positive result. It is therefore not surprising, that many modern trade or trade-related agreements include specific DSMs. The three Asso-

---

[430] Title IV Chapter 14 in the EU-Georgia and the EU-Ukraine AA, Title V Chapter 14 in the EU-Moldova AA.

ciation Agreements with Georgia, Moldova and Ukraine are thus in line with a general modern trend. Effective DSMs allow the Contracting Parties to show that they are committed to the agreed elimination of trade barriers. Moreover, in order to avoid a formal dispute, the Parties often do not commit unilateral actions in violation of the treaty. If the Parties have different political or economic power, a progressive and effective mechanism of dispute settlement can help them to resolve the disputes in an unbiased manner, which is acceptable to all sides and will probably lead to its effective implementation. In order to evaluate the effectiveness of these objectives, also the duration of the settlement procedure has to be considered since a long-lasting procedure could deter complainants from bringing their cases in the DSM.[431] A good settlement mechanism should provide for a range of measures which can help to avoid or solve disputes, e.g. which could establish a non-judiciary mechanism of dispute settlement, or create an advanced mechanism of consultation and arbitration, and ensure that sanctions could only be used as a measure of last resort.

The EU Association Agreements with Georgia, Moldova and Ukraine contain a number of legal provisions concerned with the resolution of disputes. Some of them deal with legal proceedings of private parties (e.g. Art. 414 EU-Georgia AA,Art.444 EU-Moldova AA, Art.471 EU- Ukraine AA), others with non-specified disputes between the Contracting Parties (see, e.g. Art.421 EU-Georgia AA).

However, the most important dispute settlement provisions of the AAs have been developed specifically for trade disputes between Contracting Parties (Art. 244 – 270 EU-Georgia AA, Art. 380 – 406 EU-Moldova AA, Art. 303 – 336 EU-Ukraine AA). They provide for: 1) consultations and determinations by a group of experts regarding trade and sustainable development measures 2) a two-tier system of resolving trade disputes through negotiation and arbitration; 3) mediation[432]. The Chapters are structured as follows: Objective and scope; consultations and mediation; arbitration and compliance; general provisions. In addition to the respective provisions in the main texts of the AAs there are three Annexes dealing with specific procedural aspects: rules of the procedure, rules of mediation, Code of conduct for arbitrators and mediator.

Generally speaking, the DSM under the AAs resembles the WTO DSM, but it is tailored to the specifics of the AAs as essentially bilateral (EU – associated country) treaties and the needs of the

---

431 Cf. Szepesi, Comparing EU free trade agreements: Dispute Settlement, available (http://ecdpm.org/wp-content/uploads/2013/11/IB-6G-Comparing-EU-Free-Trade-Agreements-Dispute-Settlement-2004.pdf) [24.02.2015].

432 See, the notice at http://www.law-now.com/ealerts/2014/09/ukraine-euukraine-association-agreement-ratified-by-ukraine?sc_lang=fr [24.02.2015].

Contracting Parties. For example, the DSM of the AAs is construed as being quicker than the WTO DSM. This is illustrated by the time-period for the AA/DFTA DSM, which adds up to 150 days maximally (approximately 5 months) excluding the stage of consultations. In contrast the time-period in the WTO DSM totals up to one year and three months.

II. The scope of the DSM in trade and trade-related matters under the three AAs

Each of the three EU Association Agreements includes a Title" Trade and trade-related matters", which is the core of the DCFTA part of the agreements and provides for trade liberalization in nearly all sectors of the economy[433]. Trade liberalization in the AAs go farther the WTO provisions, which are common to the EU and its Member States and the three associated countries. It refers both to trade in goods and, though in a somewhat more limited manner, to trade in services. Trade liberalization under the AAs includes, in particular, the abolishment or reduction of customs duties and other similar charges, the reduction of non-tariff barriers to trade, the granting of market access and the guarantee of National Treatment[434]. These guarantees are accompanied by far-going provisions on mutual cooperation in many economic matters, approximation of law and administrative practice and other detailed provisions, e.g. on trade remedies. The DCFTA parts of the AAs are closely related with the Titles of the AAs on Economic and Sector Cooperation[435], which also provide for cooperation and approximation of law and administrative practice.

The DCFTA Dispute Settlement Mechanism provisions cover in principle all aspects of the DCFTA parts of the three Agreements (Title IV EU-Georgia and EU-Ukraine AA, Title V EU-Moldova AA), however with some exceptions. For example, under Art. 37 para. 4 and under Art. 207 EU-Georgia AA the DSM is not applicable to the Chapters on trade remedies (Art. 37 – 43 of the AA), and most of the Chapter on Competition (Art.203 – 205 of the AA). It does not apply to other Titles of the Agreements.

III. Consultations

1. Overview

The stage of consultations between the parties is of great importance. This part of the DSM is not complicated and long-lasting, but it is compulsory, Before taking any other actions, the countries in dispute have to talk to each other to see if they can settle their differences by themselves. The

433 (Title IV) Art. 22 – 277 EU-Georgia AA, (Title IV) Art. 25 – 336 EU-Ukraine AA, (Title V) Art. 143 – 412 EU-Moldova AA

434 See, e.g. Arts.31 and 85 EU-Georgia AA.

435 E.g. (Title V) Art. 337 – 459 EU-Ukraine AA.

Parties should endeavor to resolve disputes regarding the interpretation and application of the provisions of the Titles "Trade and trade-related Matters" of the AAs (including any relevant Annexes and Protocols)by entering into consultations in good faith with the aim of reaching a mutually agreed solution[436]. The respective articles in eachof the three AAs have the same content. They will in the following be studied more closely at the example of the EU-Ukraine AA.

2. Procedure of consultations

The EU-Ukraine AA provides for several steps of the consultations between the parties. Firstly, the requesting party must submit an appropriately written request to the other party, and its copy to the AA Trade Committee. In this request the measure at issue and the provisions of this Agreement which a party considers to be applicable, should be indicated[437].

The next stage is a holding of consultations within 30 days since the receipt of the request. As a rule, the consultations shall take place in the territory of the party being accused, unless the parties agree differently. The stage of holding the consultations shall be concluded within 30 days unless both parties agree to continue the consultations. All confidential information disclosed during the consultations shall remain confidential[438]. In distinction to the provisions on consultations foreseen in the AAs, the WTO DSM provides for longer terms for resolving disputes. It provides for resolving disputes within 60 days after the date of receipt of the request for consultations[439]. However, there are some exceptions concerning matters of urgency, including those regarding perishable or seasonal goods. In this case, terms are reduced by half[440].When consultations concern the transport of energy through networks and one party considers there solution of the dispute particularly urgent because of an interruption, in full or in part, of the transport of natural gas, oil or electricity between Ukraine and a EU Party, they shall be held within three days from the date of submission of the request and shall be deemed concluded three days after the date of the request's submission unless both parties agree to continue consultations[441]. The established procedure of consultations concerning the transport of energy goods can, hopefully, prevent from establishing a 'manual mechanism' of dispute settlement, which took place in 2006 and 2009 between the Ukraine, Russia and EU related to gas conflicts[442].The last stage of consultations is a timeframe of holding the consultations and its effects. If consultations are not held with-

---

436 Art. 477 para.2 EU-Ukraine AA.
437 Art. 305 para.2 EU-Ukraine AA.
438 Art. 305 para.3 EU-Ukraine AA.
439 Art. 4 para.7 WTO:Understanding on rules and procedures governing the settlement of disputes available at https://www.wto.org/English/tratop_e/dispu_e/dsu_e.htm[25.02.2015].
440 Art. 305 para.4 EU-Ukraine AA.
441 Art. 305 para.5 EU-Ukraine AA.
442 Arts. 307 para.8) 308 para.4, 309, 310 para.3 and 314 EU-Ukraine AA.

in the timeframes or if consultations have been concluded and no agreement has been reached on a mutually agreed solution, the complaining party may request the establishment of an arbitration panel.[443]

IV. Arbitration

1. Overview

Arbitration is the most important part of the DSM and is regulated in the Agreements in great detail. More specifically, the AAs regulate the commencement of the arbitration proceedings, the establishment of an arbitration panel, the conduct of arbitration and finally ways to ensure compliance with the panels' decisions (rulings).

2. Procedure of arbitration

a) Commencement

After the unsuccessful stage of consultations between the parties, the complaining party may request the establishment of an arbitration panel.[444] The request for arbitration must be submitted in writing through diplomatic channels to the party complained against and the Trade Committee by indicating measures and describing a legal basis for the complaint. If the complaining party requests the establishment of a panel different from the standard terms of reference, the written request shall include the proposed text of special terms.[445] Within 10 days from the date of submission of the request, the parties should try to reach an agreement on the establishment of the arbitration panel.[446] If the parties could not reach an agreement on this issue, the arbitration panel shall be appointed by a lot from a list of fifteen people. Every party offers such a list of five people. Both parties have to choose five other persons who are citizens of neither of the parties and they are able to act as chairmen of the arbitration.[447] This list should be composed no later than six months after the entry into force of the AA.[448] Arbitrators must have special knowledge or experience in law and international trade. To guarantee their independence, they may only make use of their personal capacity and must not receive instructions or be affiliated with any organization or any Party's Government.[449]

443 Art. 305 para.6 EU-Ukraine AA.
444 Art. 306 para.1 EU-Ukraine AA.
445 Art. 306 para.2 EU-Ukraine AA.
446 Art. 307 para.2 EU-Ukraine AA.
447 Art. 307 EU-Ukraine AA.
448 Art. 323 para.1 EU-Ukraine AA.
449 Art. 323 para.3 EU-Ukraine AA.

The arbitration panel consists of three persons, who are elected by the chair of the Trade Committee or the chair`s delegate by lot. One person from each list is submitted by every party. One person proposed by the complaining party, one person proposed by the accused party, and one person selected by the parties to act as a chairman. The members of the panel are appointed within five days from the date of the application's filing[450]. In the case of a suspension of energy transit between one associated party (Georgia, Moldova, Ukraine) and an EU Party (or the threat of such a termination), this period is reduced to two days.[451] The representative of every party has a right to be present during the election process. The process of selecting one person to act as a chairperson is very important. In this case, the parties should choose an arbitrator, who must be independent and impartial and who is supposed to avoid creating an appearance of impropriety or bias and who shall not be influenced by self-interest, outside pressure, political considerations, public clamor, and loyalty to a Party or fear of criticism. The provisions which provide for the establishment of a tripartite arbitral panel and the selecting of unbiased persons are quite important. The Association Agreements also foresee a procedure for replacing arbitrators, if the members are unable to participate, have withdrawn or need to be replaced because they do not comply with the requirements of the Code of Conduct which is set out in one Annex to the Association Agreement. The procedure of replacement, which is set up in the provisions of on the establishment of the arbitration panel, is the same.

b) Conduct of the proceeding

Within five days from its composition the arbitration panel receives the right to examine the matter referred to in the request for arbitration and can rule on the compatibility of the measure in question with the provisions of this agreement.[452] Panel hearings are open to the public in accordance with the Rules of Procedure set out in the Annexes of the Agreements.[453] At the request of the party or on its own initiative, the arbitration panel may seek information from any source, including any information from the parties or experts' evaluations. The arbitration panel should endeavor to make decisions by achieving a consensus. If a consensus decision is not possible, the appropriate decision is made by the majority of vote.[454] Individual opinions of the arbitrators that differ from the approved decision, should not be disclosed in any way. Any decision of the arbitration panel shall be binding for the parties and it does not create any rights or obligations to individuals or entities.

---

450 Art. 307 EU-Ukraine AA.
451 Art. 307 para.8 EU-Ukraine AA.
452 Art. 306 para.3 EU-Ukraine AA.
453 Art. 308 para.2 EU-Ukraine AA.
454 Art. 321 para.1 EU-Ukraine AA.

The panel has to prepare a preliminary report on the arbitration case and submit it to the parties within 90 days after the date of appointment. This period may be extended by the arbitration panel if requested, but not to more than 120 days from the date of appointment of the arbitration panel. In addition, each party may submit a written request to receive a review by an arbitration panel on specific aspects of the preliminary report within 14 days from the date of distribution.[455] But there are some exceptions to this rule: 1) in cases of urgency, including those involving perishable or seasonal goods, the abovementioned terms are reduced by half. 2) in case of an interruption, in full or in part, of any transport of natural gas, oil or electricity, or a threat thereof between an associated country and a EU party, the interim report shall be issued after 20 days and any request shall be made within five days of the issuance of the written report[456]. Every party may request the chairperson of the panel to act as a conciliator concerning any matter relating to the dispute by making a request to the panel. If the dispute is not be resolved within 15 days, the conciliator shall recommend a resolution and shall decide on the terms and conditions, to be observed by the parties until dispute settlement.[457]

If written comments on the preliminary report have been made, the arbitration panel can amend it and continue the analysis of the arbitration proceeding. The final ruling of the arbitration panel shall include a discussion of the arguments that were presented at the stage of preliminary analysis.[458]

Upon expiry of a period of 120 days the arbitration panel sends a ruling to the parties and to the Committee. The AA/DCFTA procedure of dispute settlement is not long–lasting. In contrast with the WTO, there is no established Appellate Body in the DSM of the AAs. This could be an advantage for a quick resolution of a dispute.

<u>c) Compliance</u>

The parties should take any possible measures for the implementation of the ruling in good faith and agree on the time required for the execution of the ruling. The period may be extended up to 150 days after the written notice of the parties and the Committee, and the application of the reduced period of time for issuing resolution for: 1) In cases of urgency, including those involving perishable or seasonal goods - within 60 days but not longer than 75 days. The arbitration panel may give a preliminary ruling within 10 days from its establishment on depending on whether it deems the case to be urgent. 2) In case of an interruption of energy transit between an associated

455 Art. 308 para.1 EU-Ukraine AA.
456 Art. 308 paras.3 and 4 EU-Ukraine AA.
457 Art. 309 EU-Ukraine AA.
458 Art. 308 para.5 EU-Ukraine AA.

country and an EU Party (or the threat of such a termination) the resolution may be submitted within 40 days. No later than 30 days after the notification of the ruling arbitration panel to the parties, the party being complained against shall notify the complaining party and the Trade Committee of the time it considers it will require for a compliance. Are asonable period of time may be extended if it is agreed upon mutually.[459]

In order to verify the measures taken to implement the ruling of the arbitration panel, the Party complained against should submit information to the complaining party and to the Trade Committee about the implementing measures within a reasonable time.[460] If the parties cannot agree on the existence of compliance, the complaining party may file a written complaint to the arbitration panel, to publish its decision within 45 days from the date of such a request.[461]

In case of an application of measures which concern the interruption of energy transit between one of the associated countries and an EU Party, the complaining party may suspend obligations arising under the AAs to a level equivalent to the nullification or impairment caused by a party failing to bring itself into compliance with the panel`s findings within 15 days of their release.[462] This suspension may take effect immediately, and may be maintained for no longer than three months if the other party has not complied with the panel`s report. Further more the complaining party can support a suspension during the proceedings.[463]

If the party complained against does not give any information on implemented measures or if the arbitration panel rules that the notified measures are inconsistent with the provisions of AAs, the complaining party may request a temporary compensation, whereupon the accused party shall provide appropriate proposals.[464] If no agreement on compensation is reached within 30 days from the end of the reasonable period of time, the complaining party is entitled to suspend obligations at a level equivalent to the nullification or impairment caused by the violation.[465] Afterwards the complaining party may implement the suspension at any moment upon expiry of ten days after the day of notification.[466] The suspension of obligations shall be temporary and shall

[459] Art. 310 EU-Ukraine AA.

[460] Art. 311 EU-Ukraine AA.

[461] Art. 313 para.2 EU-Ukraine AA.

[462] Art. 315 para.2 EU-Ukraine AA. According to Art. 478 para.2 of the AA, the denunciation of the Agreement not sanctioned by the general rules of international law or the violation of the essential elements of Article 2 of the AA can also lead to the suspension of DCFTA rights or obligations.

[463] Art. 315 para.2 EU-Ukraine AA.

[464] Art. 315 para.1 EU-Ukraine AA.

[465] Art. 315 para.2 EU-Ukraine AA. According to Art. 478 para.2of the AA, the denunciation of the Agreement not sanctioned by the general rules of international law or the violation of the essential elements of Article 2 AA can also lead to the suspension of DCFTA rights or obligations.

[466] Art. 315 para.2 EU-Ukraine AA.

only be applied until measures considered to be inconsistent with the provisions of the AA have been withdrawn or amended or until the parties have agreed on settling the dispute[467]. The party complained against may appeal a suspension to the arbitration panel. The arbitration panel must notify its decision within 30 days after the date of request.[468]

The parties may reach a mutually agreed solution to a dispute at any time. The parties shall jointly notify the Trade Committee and the chairperson of the arbitration panel, if applicable, of all such solutions, and the corresponding stage of the arbitration procedure shall be terminated.[469]

3. Relations with WTO obligations

In principle, dispute settlement under the Association Agreements is without prejudice to the WTO dispute settlement procedure. However, there is an interesting provision in the AAs prohibiting to challenge the same measure under the WTO DSM and the AA/DCFTA DSM at the same time. The party which "instituted a dispute settlement proceeding, either under (...) this Agreement or under the WTO Agreement, (...) may not institute a dispute settlement proceeding regarding the same measure in the other forum until the first proceeding has been concluded"[470]. WTO and AA/DCFTA procedures are quite similar, and the parties are not allowed to seek redress of an obligation which is identical under the AA and WTO Treaties in the two fora. Such provisions provide for effectivity of the respective dispute resolution procedure, and are to avoid inconsistencies in the application of the law[471]. Nothing in this Chapter shall preclude a party from implementing the suspension of obligations authorized by the DSB. The WTO Agreement shall not be invoked to preclude a party from suspending obligations under this Chapter[472].

4. Regulatory approximation and referrals to the European Court of Justice

Another highly interesting particularity of the provisions onAA/DCFTA DSM is a duty of arbitration panels to refer questions to the European Court of Justice (ECJ). This relates to such provisions of the AA, which require an associated country to approximate its laws of administrative practices to the EU acquis (see Article 322 EU-Ukraine AA, Article 267 EU-Georgia AA, Article 403 EU- Moldova AA). It is interesting to analyze this procedure at the example of Ukraine. This procedure only applies to disputes concerning the interpretation and application of provisions relating to legislative approximation in a limited number of DCFTA Chapters: Chapter 3 (Tech-

467 Art. 315 para.6 EU-Ukraine AA.
468 Art. 316 para.2 EU-Ukraine AA.
469 Art. 317 EU-Ukraine AA.
470 Art. 324 para.2 EU-Ukraine AA.
471 See further Art. 324 para.2 EU-Ukraine AA.
472 Art. 324 para.4 EU-Ukraine AA.

nical Barriers to Trade), Chapter 4 (Sanitary and Phytosanitary Measures), Chapter 5 (Customs and Trade Facilitation), Chapter 6 (Establishment, Trade in Services and Electronic Commerce), Chapter 8 (Public Procurement) or Chapter 10 (Competition), or which "otherwise imposes an obligation defined by a reference to a provision of EU law upon a party".[473] If a dispute in relation to one of those chapters concerns a question of interpretation of a provision of EU law, the arbitration panel may not decide the question, but has to request the ECJ to give a ruling on the question, which will be binding for the arbitration panel.[474] There is no competence of arbitration panels to ask for a preliminary ruling to the ECJ in any other agreements concluded by the EU. The procedure of giving a ruling on the question by the ECJ is quite important. One of the main advantages of DCFTA DSM are reduced terms and procedure. But this factor recedes into the background, asit concerns the ruling of the European Court of Justice.'' In such cases, the deadlines applying to the rulings of the arbitration panel shall be suspended until the Court of Justice of the European Union has given its ruling. The ruling of the Court of Justice of the European Union shall be binding on the arbitration panel''.[475] The peculiarity of this provision in the EU-Ukraine AA is an obligation of a consistent interpretation of only one specific DCFTA chapter and not of the entire agreement.[476]

V. Mediation

1. Overview

All three EU Association Agreements with Georgia, Moldova and Ukraine allow also mediation as an alternative to arbitration and fixe provisions on mediation mechanisms. Mediation under the AA/DCFTA DSM has its own procedure and mechanism of implementation.

Mediation under the AA/DCFTA allows Contracting Parties to tackle adverse effects on trade in goods. The aim is not to review a measure's legality, but to find a quick and effective solution to market access problems. Mediation is one of a variety of procedures of resolving disputes. Mediation is based on the voluntary participation of the parties. It is a procedure, in which an intermediary without adjudicatory powers (the mediator) systematically facilitates the communication between the parties with the aim of enabling the parties themselves to take responsibility for resolv-

---

473 Art. 322 para.1 EU-Ukraine AA.

474 Art. 322 para.2 EU-Ukraine AA.

475 Art. 322 para.2 EU-Ukraine AA.

476 Two other DCFTA Chapters contain a similar provision on ECJ-case law conform interpretation (*i.e.* public procurement and competition), but without the same strict obligation. Ukraine must respectively take "due account" of (Art. 153 para.2) or use "as sources of inspiration" (Art. 264) the relevant case law of the ECJ.

ing their dispute. Additional core characteristics are the confidentiality of the procedure and the neutrality of the mediator.

Mediation can be differentiated from other types of alternative dispute resolution, among them arbitration, ombudsman procedures, conciliation and structured negotiation. Good guidelines to distinguish these procedures from mediation are the characteristic features of mediation: the voluntary and flexible nature, the mediator's lack of adjudicatory competence and the self-determination of the parties[477]. Whereas, for example, arbitrators have the competence to issue (at least partly) binding decisions, in mediation it is up to the parties and not to the mediator to decide whether and how to solve the conflict. A conciliator has greater influence on the outcome than a mediator as well by, for example, announcing a (nonbinding) conciliation decision. The mediator instead tries to empower the parties to solve their conflict themselves.[478]

2. Scope

It is important to mention the scope of the mediation mechanism in the AAs, as some differences between the three Agreements can be observed. Ukraine has devoted a separate Chapter XV to this mechanism. With regard to Georgia, a detailed mechanism is described in Annex XIX to the AA, and Moldova fixed this mechanism in Annex XXXII to the EU-Moldova AA. In Ukraine the mediation mechanism applies to any measure falling under the scope of Chapter 1 of Title IV of this Agreement (National Treatment and Market Access for Goods) adversely affecting trade between the parties.[479] On the other hand, mediation shall not apply to measures falling under Chapter 6 (Establishment, Trade in Services and Electronic Commerce), Chapter 7 (Current Payments and Movement of Capital), Chapter 8 (Public Procurement), Chapter 9 (Intellectual Property) and Chapter 13 (Trade and Sustainable Development) of this Agreement. The Trade Committee may, after a due consideration, decide that this mechanism should apply to any of these sectors.[480] In contrast, there is no special scope of the mediation mechanism in the AAs with Georgia and Moldova. Only the general scope of the Chapter "Dispute Settlement" in the AAs with Georgia and Moldova would seem to apply, i.e. in principle all matters of interpretation and application of the provisions of the DCFTA-Titles of the AA.[481]

---

477 Steffek, Mediation in the European Union: An Introduction (2012), accessible at http://www.diamesolavisi.net/kiosk/documentation/Steffek_Mediation_in_the_European_Union.pdf [25.02.2015].

478 Steffek, Mediation in the European Union: An Introduction, Cambridge June 2012 http://www.diamesolavisi.net/kiosk/documentation/Steffek_Mediation_in_the_European_Union.pdf [25.02.2015].

479 Art. 327 para.2 EU-Ukraine AA.

480 Art. 327 para.3 EU-Ukraine AA.

481 Art. 245 EU- Georgia AA.

3. Mediation procedure in the EU-Ukraine AA

a) Request for information

Before the initiation of the mediation procedure, a party may request information at any time regarding a measure adversely affecting trade or investment between the parties. The party to which such request is made shall provide a response containing its comments on the information contained in the request within 20 days from the date of the request's receipt. If the answer is impossible for a specified period, the responding party shall inform the requesting party of the reasons for the delay, and make an estimate of the shortest period within which it will be able to provide its response.[482]

b) Commencement of the procedure

An initiation of the procedure of mediation after sending a detailed request by one party to the other should determine: 1) the specific measure that should be considered 2) an assessment of the possible negative consequences for investment or trade between the parties, and how these consequences are related to the measure. The party to which the request is addressed shall consider it positively or reject it (in writing) within 10 days from its receipt.[483]

After the initiation of the mediation procedure the parties shall agree on a mediator no later than 15days after the receipt of the reply to the request. If the parties cannot agree on the mediator within the established time frame, either of the parties may request the chairperson of the Trade Committee, or the chairperson's delegate, to draw the mediator by lot from the list. If the list is not made at the time of the request, the mediator is chosen by lot from the persons who have been formally proposed by one or by both parties. As a result, the mediator should be selected by the Chairperson of the Committee (or an authorized person) within five working days from the date of the request. The parties may agree that the mediator shall be a citizen of one of the ties[484].The mediator as an arbitrator should be independent and impartial and avoid creating an appearance of impropriety or bias and shall not be influenced by self-interest, outside pressure, political considerations or public clamor.

c) Conduct of mediation

Within 10 days from the appointment of the mediator, the party having invoked the mediation procedure shall present a detailed description of the problem to the mediator and to the other party in writing. Within 20 days from the date of the delivery of this submission, the other party may

---

482 Art. 328 EU-Ukraine AA.
483 Art. 329 EU-Ukraine AA.
484 Art. 330 EU-Ukraine AA.

provide its comments to the description of the problem in writing, and may comment any information that it deems relevant.[485] In its turn, the mediator may decide on the most appropriate way of bringing clarity to the measure concerned and its possible trade-related impact. In particular, the mediator may organize meetings between the parties, consult the parties jointly or individually, seek the assistance of or consult with relevant experts and stakeholders, and provide any additional support requested by the parties.[486] As a result, the mediator can offer an advice and present the solution for the consideration by the parties. The parties may accept or reject a proposed decision or they may agree otherwise. However, the mediator should not give advice or comments on the measure in accordance with the provisions of this Agreement.[487] The parties shall endeavor to reach a mutually agreed solution within 60 days from the appointment of the mediator. Pending a final agreement, the parties may consider possible interim solutions, especially if the measure relates to perishable goods.[488] The procedure of mediation shall take place in the territory of the party to which the request was addressed or by a mutual agreement in any other location or by any other means. The solution may be adopted by means of a decision of the Trade Committee. Either of the parties may make such solution subject to the completion of any necessary internal procedures. Mutually agreed solutions shall be made publicly available.[489] Mediation is terminated with the adoption of a mutually agreed solution to the dispute settlement or after a statement of the mediator that further efforts at mediation would not be promising or in any case by mutual agreement of the parties.

<u>d) Implementation of a mutually agreed solution</u>

In case of an agreed solution among the parties, each party shall take measures necessary for its implementation in the agreed timeframe. The implementing party shall inform the other party in writing of any steps or measures taken to implement the mutually agreed solution. On request of the parties, the mediator issues to the parties a draft factual report, providing a summary. The parties have 15 days to provide comments on the draft of the report, then the mediator submits a final report.[490]

485 Art. 331 para.1 EU-Ukraine AA.
486 Cf. Art. 331 para.2 EU-Ukraine AA.
487 Art. 331 para.3 EU-Ukraine AA.
488 Art. 331 para.5 EU-Ukraine AA.
489 Cf. Art. 331 para.6 EU-Ukraine AA.
490 Art. 332 EU-Ukraine AA.

VI. Evaluation of possible effects of the DSMs (at the example of Ukraine)

Businesses have presumably a great interest in the outcome of disputes relating to trade between AA Parties. Although businesses cannot themselves use the AA/DCFTA DSM, the existence of the DSM might provide an indirect positive effect for the settlement of disputes with local companies, e.g. disputes with companies and –counterparties from EU member states, and disputes with state authorities from EU member states. For the public sector, the effect is probably more direct, as the public sector is a part of the structure of the Contracting Parties, which can use the DSM. Following this, the public sector should receive an effective tool in order to resolve disputes which may arise at the highest level between the associated countries and EU Member States. Already the existence of such a mechanism will make the AAs visible The States could get additional tools of influence to dispute resolution also by way of continued participation in the Committee on Trade. In Ukraine, the establishment of such a dispute resolution procedure which could resolve conflicts concerning the disruption of energy transit through the territory of Ukraine is of particular importance. For example, in 2006 and 2009 the termination of gas transit to the EU there was no clear procedure of resolving the conflict, which arose between Ukraine and Russia. In this case, the authorities had to create a "manual mechanism of dispute settlement", and a lot of time was lost.

VII. Conclusion

Consequently, a new tool for settlement disputes which is foreseen by the every EU – Georgia, Moldova, Ukraine Association Agreement was considered. The Association Agreements provide for a complex system of resolving inter-state trade disputes between the EU and associated States. The mere existence of such mechanisms will establish a clear and understandable procedure of resolving disputes under the AAs. The novelty of the mechanism consists not only in simplified procedures, but also in some provisions of AAs relating to regulatory approximation and to the relationship with the WTO DSM. Whether the AA/DCFTA dispute settlement mechanisms will be effective and often used by Contracting Parties will be visible after the entry into force of the Agreements, also in comparison with the WTO model.

Anastasiia Bessonova

Investment Dispute Settlement between the EU and Ukraine in the Light of the Adoption of the Association Agreement

Foreign direct investment (FDI) plays a crucial role in establishing businesses, creating jobs abroad, as well as in setting up global supply chains. Investment and trade are inter-dependent and complementary. Around half of world trade takes place between affiliates of multinational enterprises that exchange intermediate goods and services. The investor is the key decision maker about where the production of goods and services takes place and their decisions have a direct impact on trade, jobs and capital movements. This is why investment protection is a necessary element of trade policy of every country. Investment policy regulation in the EU has changed dramatically on 1 December 2009 when the Lisbon Treaty came into force. In accordance with this document, the competence to regulate foreign direct investment was taken away from the EU Member States and has become a part of the EU's common commercial policy.[491] In order to understand what this means and of which importance this is regarding investment dispute resolution, it is necessary to look at the situation before the Lisbon Treaty in the sphere of international investment regulation.

Before the entry into force of the Lisbon Treaty, competences on FDI had been mixed; liberalization and protection were divided up between the European Commission (EC) and its Member States. Two layers of rules with regard to FDI co-existed[492]. First, Member States had concluded numerous BITs. These treaties conventionally apply to the protection of established investments against expropriation and discrimination, with enforcement mechanisms through State-to-State and Investor-to-State arbitration, but they do not contain provisions on market access. Second, the trade agreements of the EU with third countries focused on market access and non-discrimination for committed investments, with enforcement mechanisms through a State-to-State dispute settlement mechanism that applied to the whole agreement.[493]

Now the aim of the new EU investment policy is to combine these two layers and replace the old BITs by new Deep and Comprehensive Free Trade Areas (DCFTAs) agreements, which will include provisions on investment protection too. However, the BITs between EU Member States

491 Art. 207 TFEU.

492 European Commission, Issues Paper: Upgrading the EU Investment Policy, 268/06. <http://www.iisd.org/pdf/2006/tas_upgrading_eu.pdf> [cited 15 Dec 2014].

493 Roos Van Os, Pre-Lisbon external investment policy of the EU, EU Investment agreements in the Lisbon Treaty era: A Reader (2014) p.19,http://somo.nl/publications-en/Publication_3558 [cited 15 Dec 2014].

and non-EU countries are still in force ("grandfather") until new DCFTAs between EU and non-EU countries will be concluded.

On 27 June 2014 Georgia, Moldova and Ukraine signed Association Agreements (AAs), including titles on DCFTAs. In accordance with new investment policy of EU this agreements should in principle replace previous BITs between EU member states and Georgia, Moldova and Ukraine. However, these new DCFTAs almost do not contain any provisions regarding investment protection. The main question which arises in this situation is which mechanisms of investment dispute settlement do investors of these countries have now. As all three AAs/DCFTAs are rather similar the choice was to consider in this paper Ukraine as the example. However, all conclusions can be applied to Georgia and Moldova as well. The goal of the present Article is to consider all possible mechanisms of investment dispute settlement on the example of treaties between EU and Ukraine and to understand how these mechanisms work.

I. Investment dispute settlement

Generally speaking, there are two kinds of dispute resolution regarding investment. They are state-to-state dispute settlement (SSDS) and investor-to-state dispute settlement (ISDS).

1. SSDS

There is no uniform classification of the types of State-to-State disputes, as each agreement needs to be considered in the light of its scope, its objectives and purposes, but however it may be useful to distinguish inter-State investment disputes as follows:

a) Diplomatic protection (under traditional international law)

It is the situation in which an investor raises a claim to its home state and the state protects the rights of the investor on behalf its own name. This procedure is very rare and often just prohibited by many investment treaties, because there is no control from the part of the investor. The investor depends on the political discretion of its Government[494] and the Government may refuse to admit the claim or may discontinue diplomatic protection at any time. For states it is not very attractive either as such procedures can seriously disrupt the States' international relations and lead to protracted disputes.

b) Direct disputes between States

Such disputes may arise from the interpretation or application of the investment treaties, as a consequence of a general violation of international law – BITs or WTO agreements. It is also called

[494] Dolzer/Schreuer, Principles of international investment law, 2nd ed. (2012), p. 232.

"abstract interpretation". For example, two States have concluded a BIT which contains the National Treatment standard. Then the Government of the host State passes a law raising some taxes, but only for foreigners. Then, the State of the investor has the right to seek an interpretation of the relevant provisions of the treaty from the arbitral tribunal, without any particular investor of the claimant state.

c) Disputes concerning the relationship (hierarchy?) between different international investment agreements[495]

Such types of cases will probably, on balance, remain exceptional. However, taking into account that international rule-making in the investment sphere is on the rise in various settings, inter-State disputes could arise in relation to this diffusion concerning the hierarchy of different international investment agreements between the same countries that address the same investment issues.

2. ISDS

Through the ISDS the investor gains access to a unique effective international remedy, which empowers the private entity to raise a claim against the host State directly. Investor-State dispute settlement has been described as sharing 'hybrid' or sui generis characteristics. As a system that confers dispute settlement rights on non-state entities, investor-State arbitration is a creation of treaty that yet may involve significant issues of private rights and municipal law. Thus, it embodies elements of both public and private international law.[496] However, host States do not always take advantages from such kind of dispute settlement, because such treaties often limit the rights of the host State to regulate in different social spheres. Now the issue of existence of ISDS is especially acute in the light of the negotiations on TTIP between the EU and the USA. Proponents argue that ISDS strengthens the rule of law and helps to bring investors being reluctant otherwise to capital-hungry jurisdictions. Opponents argue that ISDS weakens the rule of law by bestowing special rights exclusively on foreign investors — typically on multinational corporations — to circumvent domestic legal systems and to win judgments against democratically elected governments, which effectively socialize the risk of international investment. Anyway in the present days ISDS works quite well and is a powerful instrument of investment protection.

495 UNCTAD, Dispute settlement: State-State, IIA Issues Paper Series 2003, p. 4.

496 See generally Douglas, The Hybrid Foundations of Investment Treaty Arbitration, 74 British Y.B. Intl. L. (2003), p.152 et seq.

II. Treaties on investment protection between EU and Ukraine

As already mentioned above, the main aim of this paper is the analysis of the concrete mechanisms of dispute settlement between the EU and Ukraine. For this it is necessary to highlight the treaties, which stipulate provisions on investment protection and in which EU countries and Ukraine participate. There are two large groups of such treaties: trade agreements (including WTO and the AA/DCFTA between the EU and Ukraine) and BITs between EU member States and Ukraine.

1. Deep and Comprehensive Free Trade Area Agreement (AA/DCFTA) and WTO Agreements

The DCFTA is the key part of the EU-Ukraine Association Agreement, encompassing almost all spheres of the economic relationship between the EU and Ukraine. According to the new EU investment policy, DCFTAs should regulate every aspect of trade policy, however for some reasons the EU-Ukraine AA does not include provisions concerning investment protection. As EC officials have said this was connected with the time of negotiations. The point is that the text of the DCFTA was developed before the EC elaborated its new policy relating to investment protection. Actually, the EU-Ukraine DCFTA has only one substantive provision relevant for investment protection - Art.88 on National Treatment and Most Favorable Nation Treatment). In respect of all other provisions, the DCFTA contains a small reference that investment protection, including investor-state dispute settlement procedures, is not covered by the AA. However, according to Article 90 of the DCFTA (other agreements), "nothing shall be taken to limit the rights of investors of the Parties to benefit from any more favorable treatment provided for in any existing or future international agreement relating to investment to which a Member State of the European Union and Ukraine are parties. Arguably, this means that the parties have the right to apply BITs that have been concluded between EU member States and Ukraine independently of the DCFTA. The position could therefore be argued that the State-to-State dispute settlement mechanism in Chapter 14 of the DCFTA can also be applied to investment disputes.

It is important to mention, that the DCFTA between the EU and Ukraine (as other RTAs) is an agreement related to the WTO framework. Provisions relating to investment protection are also contained in such WTO agreements as the General Agreement on Trade in Services (GATS) and the Trade-Related Investment Measures (TRIMs) Agreement. Claims under all these treaties can be brought in WTO dispute settlement body (WTO DSB). The WTO dispute settlement system is widely regarded as one of the most effective and advanced international judicial mechanisms.[497] As codified in the DSU, any WTO Member may initiate dispute settlement proceedings against any other Member because of an alleged violation of the 'covered agreements' (which together comprise the WTO Agreement) before a neutral panel[498]. Claims must arise out of the covered agreements, and not out of sources of law outside the WTO system. This is a pure State-to-State mechanism. Private parties and NGOs cannot bring claims themselves, although they may be able to submit amicus curiae briefs.

2. Bilateral Investment Treaties (BITs) between EU Member States and Ukraine

Ukraine signed BITs with almost every member country of the EU. Such BITs, based on a template developed in the '60s, which in its turn is inspired from XIX century FCN treaties, are highly standardized. Most of the BITs contain basic protection standards and two mechanisms of dispute resolution: SSDS and ISDS. And in the light of Art. 90 of DCFTA all these BITs "grandfather", i.e. they are still in force.

III. SSDS and ISDS between EU and Ukraine

1. SSDS in DCFTAs, the WTO and in BITs

According to the Communication from the European Commission of 2010 relating to the new comprehensive European international investment policy, an effective and expedient state-to-state dispute settlement system in EU FTAs was created. And as it is said in this Communication this dispute settlement system would cover the investment provisions of the EU trade and investment agreements[499] in the future.

However, in the case of the EU-Ukraine relationship there are no such provisions yet. As a result, there are three kinds of SSDS mechanism: BIT DSM, AA/DCFTA DSM and WTO DSM.

The mechanism of dispute settlement in the AA/DCFTA is very detailed and contains a description of consultation procedure (Art. 305), a step-by-step guidance of arbitration procedure; rules of mediation. The text of the AA also includes Rules of arbitration procedure and a Code of con-

497 See, e.g., Palmeter/Mavroidis, Dispute Settlement in the World Trade Organization: Practice and Procedure, 2d ed.(2004), p.305; Allen, The Use of Non-Pecuniary Remedies in WTO Dispute Settlement: Lessons for Arbitral Practitioners, in Schneider/Knoll eds., Performance as a Remedy: Non-Monetary Relief in International Arbitration (2011), p.283.

498 DSU, Dispute Settlement Rules: Understanding on Rules and Procedures Governing the Settlement of Disputes, Annex 2, art 11, accessible at https://www.wto.org.

499 Communication from the Commission to the Council, the European Parliament, the European Economic and Social Committee and the Committee of the Regions - Towards a comprehensive European international investment policy, COM 0343 final (July 2010) [hereinafter Commission Communication].

duct for arbitrators and mediators in Annexes. To compare this with the mechanism of BITs, the Germany-Ukraine BIT may be considered. In the respect of SSDS this BIT has only one Article 10[500] where very short provisions about the choice of arbitrators and about making a ruling and financial costs are provided. In contrast to the DCFTA the BIT does not include provisions on mediation or consultation procedure.

When one analyzes the provisions in these treaties the question arises which mechanism should be chosen in case of an investment dispute. For this situation the DCFTA in contrast to the BIT contains a "fork-in-the-road" clause in Article 324 (relation with WTO obligations) which permits the parties to choose between the WTO and the DCFTA mechanism, but forbids parallel proceedings in these institutions or other fora. However, it is not yet entirely clear which mechanism will be applied in which situation. And since the BIT does not forbid parallel proceedings, there must be a certain confusion in cases of such disputes.

2. ISDS in the Germany-Ukraine BIT (in comparison with CETA)

According to the Commission Communication, future EU agreements including investment protection should include investor-state dispute settlement. However, the Commission also declares that the ISDS system needs some reforms[501]. The EU-Ukraine AA/DCFTA does not cover ISDS, but, according to Article 90 of the AA (other agreements), which was mentioned earlier, it is possible to use other agreements between Ukraine and EU Member States relating to investment protection. Provisions about ISDS are contained only in BITs between Ukraine and EU member states, which mostly were concluded in the 1990s after the dissolution of the Soviet Union. Since that time these countries have obtained valuable experience in the area of investment law and realized the necessity of changes, and the European Commission developed its recommendation in relation to investment policy. One of the latest examples of a high quality investment agreement is Chapter 10 of the Comprehensive Trade and Economic Agreement (CETA)[502] between the EU and Canada. CETA is similar to the AA/DCFTA between EU and Ukraine, but it is more developed and thorough. The main distinction in the sphere of investment dispute resolutions is that CETA provides for investor-to-state dispute settlement. In order to understand which improvements CETA includes it is necessary to compare its ISDS mechanism with another one in a BIT. Having a look again at the Germany-Ukraine BIT, this treaty has only one article on ISDS,

500 Vertrag zwischen der Bundesrepublik Deutschland und der Ukraine über die Förderung und den gegenseitigen Schutz von Kapitalanlagen Art. 10, 1993. <http://investmentpolicyhub.unctad.org/Download/TreatyFile/1442> [17 Dec 2014].

501 Commission Communication, p.9.

502 The Comprehensive Trade and Economic Agreement, 2014, <http://trade.ec.europa.eu/doclib/docs/2014/september/tradoc_152806.pdf> [17 Dec 2014].

where the term on peaceful resolution and the same (as in SSDS) short provisions about arbitration and reference to the ICSID Convention are given. So, what innovations does CETA offer on the procedural field? Firstly, CETA is the first agreement, which includes a binding Code of conduct for arbitrators acting in an ISDS dispute. Secondly, CETA introduces full transparency in ISDS disputes: all documents (submissions by the parties, decisions of the tribunal) will be available publicly on a website financed by the EU. All hearings will be open to the public. Interested parties (NGO's, trade unions) will be able to make submissions. This will be binding and cannot be waived by the tribunal or the parties to a dispute. Thirdly, CETA prohibits parallel proceedings: investors cannot seek remedies in domestic courts (or other international tribunals) and through ISDS at the same time. The next innovation are rules preventing fraudulent or manipulative claims. For example, the making of an investment or business reorganization for the purpose of bringing a case. Also ISDS under CETA cannot lead to the repeal of a measure adopted by Parliaments in the European Union, a EU Member State or Canada; the most that can be required of a country is compensation and this only to the level of the losses actually suffered. Another new element is the introduction of statutory limits (3 years, extended if a domestic court proceeding is pursued) for raising a claim. The treaty also has a fast track system for rejecting unfounded or frivolous claims. The losing party pays the costs. CETA also contains specific provisions on mediation to encourage an amicable solution. It furthermore introduces the possibility of a sole arbitrator when both parties agree and it limits the fees paid to arbitrators. The agreement also provides an objective first mentioned in the Commission's Communication on Investment Policy of 2010 for the possible creation of an Appeal Mechanism. As we can see at the example of CETA, modern investment agreements make the ISDS clearer and more comfortable for both parties, because they take into account some negative practice of the previous years.

IV. Conclusion

In this Article all possible mechanisms of investment dispute settlement between EU and Ukraine were considered and analyzed. According to the treaties that were mentioned above, disputes regarding investment between EU and Ukraine can be settled by the WTO Dispute Settlement Body, the DCFTA Dispute Settlement Mechanism and by arbitration panels constituted under BIT rules. All these mechanisms do now exist because of a transition period in the investment policy of EU and need some reforms. One of the best ways is to include a special chapter on investment into the DCFTA between EU and Ukraine, which would replace old BITs, following the example of CETA. CETA is a sample of a high qualified and balanced agreement, where interests of both parties (investor and host State) are taken into account. Besides, uniform documents would help to avoid all kinds of possible confusions.

Biographical notes

Badalova, Felicia, Master in Law, Law Faculty of the State University of the Republic of Moldova; Consultant, Departament of International Relations and European Integration, Ministry of Justice of the Republic of Moldova

Bessonova, Anastasia, L.L.M. Student (CAU, Germany), PhD student (Urals State Law University, Russia)

Iliushyna, Tetiana, Ph.D. student, Faculty of Economics and Law, I.I. Mechnikov National University, Odesa, Ukraine

Karnaukh, Vadym, PhD student, Faculty of Law, Taras Shevchenko National University of Kyiv, Ukraine

Kavtaradze, Salome, PhD student Faculty of Law, Ivane Javakhishvili Tbilisi State University, Georgia, LL.M, MA

Khomyn, Yuliya, Master in Law, Law Faculty of the Ivan Franko National University (Lviv, Ukraine), PhD candidate, Jagiellonian University (Krakow, Poland)

Menabdishvili, Solomon, PhD, Director of the Center for Competition Law and Consumer Protection

Negritu, Ludmila, PhD, Faculty of Law of the University of Moldova

Otgon, Ala, PhD candidate, Faculty of Law, State University of Moldova

Rogozina, Anastasiia, L.L.M. Student (CAU, Germany), PhD candidate (Urals State Law University, Russia)

Romanchenko, Anastasia, Master in Law, Law Faculty of the Donetsk University (now at Vinnitsa), Ukraine, L.L.M. Student (CAU, Germany)

Serpukhovitina, Olena, National University of Kyiv-Mohyla Academy, Master of Law, work at Kyiv office of Baker&McKenzie

Smeshko, Mykhailo, Ph.D student, Institute of international relations Taras Shevchenko National University of Kyiv, Ukraine

Smyrnova, Kseniya, Dr. jur. sc. (Dr.hab.), Associate Professor, Institute of International Relations of Kyiv National Taras Shevchenko University, Member of the Public Council of the Antimonopoly Committee of Ukraine (Kiev), Ukraine

Shevchuk, Oleksandr, Ph.D student, Institute of international relations Taras Shevchenko National University of Kyiv, Ukraine

Tokhadze, Ana, PhD student, LL.M., LL.B, Faculty of Law, Ivane Javakhihvili Tbilisi State University, Georgia

Trunk, Alexander, Prof. Dr. jur., Director of the Institute of East European Law of Kiel University, Germany

Zakharko, Marta, Master of Law, National University of Kyiv-Mohyla Academy